2001
Free Things
for the
Garden

~2001~
FREE THINGS
for the
GARDEN

Marilyn & Robert Hendrickson

ST. MARTIN'S PRESS
NEW YORK

Design by Mina Greenstein

Hendrickson, Robert, 1933–
    2001 free things for the garden.

        Includes index.
            1. Gardening—United States—Directories.
2. Gardening—Directories.   3. Gardening—Equipment
and supplies—Directories.   4. Gardening—Miscellanea.
5. Free material—Directories.   I. Hendrickson,
Marilyn.   II. Title.   III. Title: Two thousand one free
things for the garden.   IV. Title: Two thousand and one
free things for the garden.
SB450.943.U6H46   1983   635.9′028   82-16893
ISBN 0-312-82746-6
ISBN 0-312-82747-4 (pbk.)

FIRST EDITION

10   9   8   7   6   5   4   3   2   1

To Irene and Bob McShane
Many good times for next to nothing

Contents

Introduction:
How to Use This Book

This extensive directory of free things for the garden contains a total of well over two thousand free or low-cost books, pamphlets, magazine subscriptions, charts, posters, recipes, catalogs, comics, puzzles, building plans and other publications you can write for; seeds, plants and garden equipment that are yours for the asking; gardens, arboretums, conservatories and agricultural laboratories you can visit; no-admission-charge flower shows and fairs you can attend; free things you can make with materials on hand; valuable tips on how to save money in the garden—and much, much more. They represent the choicest free garden offers made by the government, the nursery industry and related businesses.

All of these things are free, but in some cases handling and postage charges of from ten cents to a dollar have been stipulated by the sponsor. In these cases we have carefully examined or considered the offer before including it here, making sure that it is worth many times the handling charge. Very occasionally great values for as much as a dollar have been included; the average handling charge is about thirty cents and over three-quarters of the items in the book are absolutely free, postage included.

The authors have taken every precaution to ensure that the free things listed in this book are currently available and will be for a reasonable period, but it is conceivable that an offer may be withdrawn by the supplier, that supplies may become temporarily exhausted, or that handling charges may be subject to change. Naturally, *every source in these pages reserves the right to discontinue or change his offer.* Thus, though we believe all these offers have been made in good faith, neither the authors nor the publisher can be responsible for a reader receiving any item, and cannot act as your representative or intermediary in the matter, so please do not write us requesting such assistance.

To help ensure that you'll receive the free things you want, act promptly and follow these common-sense rules:

1. Turn to the chapter or chapters that most interest you and choose the free things you really want; *don't order indiscriminately.*

2. Order only one of each item; multiple requests will not be honored by suppliers.

3. Send a postcard for all free items *without* handling charges, unless a stamped, self-addressed return envelope is requested.

4. If a stamped, self-addressed return envelope is requested, make sure you use a large, legal-size 10-inch envelope.

5. Be sure that your name and address is printed legibly or typed on the return envelope or on the correspondence side of the postcard. Always include your zip code.

6. Request the item by name; by name and publication number if it is a government publication.

7. If handling charges are called for, send a check or money order, no matter how small the amount. This is not always required (and some people do tape coins to their letters), but we would not rely on any other way. *Do not send stamps.*

8. Expect a wait of four to eight weeks for your order to be received, processed and returned, though it may take only one to two weeks.

Please note that due to a recent change in government policy traditionally free publications will no longer be offered by any federal agency. Some publications previously distributed free to the public will now be sold by the Superintendent of Documents, which advises us, as we have indicated in listing all such offers we felt might be valuable, that readers must write to obtain a price for the item wanted.

We've tried hard to make this a book that will last a long time by choosing what appear to be long-term offers and by including a great deal of money-saving garden advice that will never grow outdated. We hope you find that *2001 Free Things* is worth a million!

Marilyn Hendrickson
Robert Hendrickson

Sample Postcard for a Free Item

(For the first offer in this book, p. 00.)

FRONT SIDE

John Doe
2419 Main St.
Everytown, N.Y. 11692

Mississippi Cooperative Extension Service
P.O. Box 5404
Mississippi State University
State College, Mississippi 39762

REVERSE SIDE

date

Dear Sir:

Please send me your free booklet "The Garden Tabloid," publication number 1091. Thank you.

John Doe
2419 Main St.
Everytown, N.Y. 11692

You May Want to Photostat or Copy This Form
for Offers with a Handling Charge

Date _____

Dear Sir:

Please send me the following item(s):

_____

_____

Enclosed is my check for _____.

Thank you.

Name _____

Address _____

_____

Print legibly, and be sure to include the title or name of the item and publication number, if any. Enclose a stamped, self-addressed return envelope if requested. Always include your zip code.

2001
Free Things
for the
Garden

1

Free Things for the Vegetable Garden

Read All About that Red Hot Tomato!
A Vegetable Garden Tabloid

This free 32-page publication isn't all that provocative, but *is* printed in the form of a newspaper tabloid and does include a vast amount of information about all aspects of raising vegetables. Request "The Garden Tabloid," publication number 1091, Mississippi Cooperative Extension Service, P.O. Box 5404, Mississippi State University, State College, Mississippi 39762.

Vegetable Garden Tips

Here's a free four-color illustrated booklet loaded with tips on how to care for your vegetable garden, from when and how to plant to when and how to pick. Request "Success with Vegetable Gardens," from Scotts, Marysville, Ohio 43040.

One university garden survey found recently that the average gardener spends $34.50 on his garden annually, but harvests $165 worth of vegetables, or about $4.75 in food for every $1 spent.

Free Vegetable Gardening Newspaper

If you take a trial subscription to *Gurney's Gardening News* (your $4.95 will be refunded if you're not satisfied), you'll receive seven issues instead of six with your subscription—the first issue free. Write *Gurney's Gardening News,* Gurney Seed and Nursery Company, Yankton, South Dakota 57079.

Vegetable Garden Basics

"Gardening for Beginners" is a free booklet aimed at the novice gardener who wants things explained in the simplest terms. Request it from the West Virginia Department of Agriculture, Information Division, State Capitol, Charleston, West Virginia 25305.

Home-Grown Vegetables in One Day: Save $500 and More

Not many years ago a veteran plantsman observed that home gardeners could save little money raising their own vegetables, considering the labor involved, although he admitted that the taste difference between garden and commercially grown vegetables was almost beyond description. No longer is this the case. Home grown vegetables remain vastly superior in taste compared to commercial farm produce, but present market prices, astronomical even in season, prove conclusively that the home gardener can effect great savings growing his own vegetables, especially when much of the labor is eliminated.

Take just tomatoes, for example. Using the plan described below you can grow at least 40 tomato plants, which will yield anywhere from 500 to 800 fruits weighing a total of 250 to 400 pounds. Even at a low in-season price of about 50¢ a pound, that many tomatoes would cost from $125 to $200 at the supermarket. As 40 small plants, mulching material, and fertilizer will cost no more than $10, it is easy to see the resultant savings. Even figuring your labor under this scheme—a maximum of 4 hours work planting and labor throughout the season, at $5 an hour—your profit in growing tomatoes alone will be from $75 to $150. Your savings on this entire vegetable garden should easily total $500.

Actually, just two mornings in late spring is practically all the time needed to plant and care for the entire garden. The secret is to choose easy-to-grow, disease-resistant vegetables, to plant them at the proper time, and then to mulch them. If you are not interested in working your garden, there is no need to worry about early spring planting and early-maturing vegetables such as radishes or peas.

Begin about the last week in May, choosing a sunny day to turn over the ground, rake in fertilizer and plant your seeds. Composted cow manure or 5-10-5 commercial fertilizer is best for most vegetables and should be applied according to the directions on the package. As for the best vegetables, select varieties that tolerate, or, indeed, thrive in hot summer weather. Neither should time and effort be wasted on vegetables that taste almost the same purchased from the store.

For both taste and adaptability, we would recommend tomatoes, sweet corn, bush string beans and cucumbers. All are relatively easy to grow, prolific bearers, and each provides a taste treat that money can't buy. Plant everything but the tomatoes from seed, purchasing your tomato plants at any reliable nursery or garden center. There are numerous excellent varieties to choose from. For tomatoes try either the Burpee Big Boy, Manalucie, Climbing Triple Crop, or a few of each. The sweetest corn is Illinichief Super Sweet, but others such as Golden Bantam and Seneca Chief Hybrid are also delicious. String or bush beans include Tenderpod and Topcrop. Your best bet for cucumbers is a mosaic-resistant seed such as the Burpee E-1 Hybrid or Park's Commanche. Garden catalogs, of course, will provide you with many more excellent choices.

In planting the garden choose a sunny site with good drainage. After fertilizing, plant the beans, then the cucumbers, then the tomato plants and finally the corn—the crops that grow tallest last. The tomatoes and cucumbers will need about 1½ feet between both plants and rows; the beans require a foot between rows and six inches between plants; and the corn can be planted about one foot apart each way. Sow the seeds according to the directions on the packages, but do not thin them farther apart than above, directions notwithstanding. The spacing directions recommended here will be regarded as heresy by some gardening experts, but they *do* work and are well worth a try in your backyard. Gardening will not be as convenient, and immense (and pulpy) prizewinning vegetables will not be grown, but in what better way can the average homeowner with little room to spare raise sufficient produce for the table? With this plan you can plant three rows of each vegetable in a 15 × 20-foot space. Three such 20-foot rows of beans should yield about 240 portions; cucumbers, 240 portions; corn, 60 portions; and tomatoes at least 500 portions.

The plants should be thinned about three weeks to a month later—your second morning of work. Before this it will only be necessary to turn on the sprinkler and weed the young plants occasionally. Immediately after the plants are thinned, in about the last week in June, they should be mulched. In most sections of the country the ground will be warm enough at this time to apply mulch thickly, which will eliminate most of the need for weeding and watering all the rest of the season. Choose any good mulch (see our list of free mulches further on), such as salt hay, straw or wood chips—all can be scavenged somewhere or purchased at most gardening centers. Even last autumn's leaves will do—only, however, if they are first shredded or are partially decomposed (we've used them many times). First, water the ground thoroughly—soak it. Then literally cover the garden with the mulch, right up to the stems of the plants, applying it at a depth of six inches or more. Your second morning of work ends after you set five-foot stakes behind each tomato plant for the vines to grow on, unless you choose to let the tomato plants sprawl unstaked. The cucumbers—although it is also best to erect supports for them to climb on—will do well sprawling over the mulch.

Except for tying the tomatoes as they climb up on the stakes, adding mulch as the plants grow, and watering occasionally with a water-soluble fertilizer if you wish, your only remaining work in the garden will be harvesting the crops. To repeat, the mulch will all but eliminate weeding and watering in the hot summer sun and the disease-resistant varieties of vegetables will make spraying unnecessary.

A Free Postage Stamp Vegetable Garden Book from a Major Publisher

Duane Newcomb's illustrated book on intensive gardening, *The Postage Stamp Garden Book,* has gone through ten printings and is among the best works available on vegetable gardening in a small space. Subtitled "How to turn a pint-sized patch into a bushel-sized vegetable garden—and grow all the food your family can eat," the 212-page paperback is published by Bantam Books at $1.95. But our readers can order a special edition of it from a leading manufacturer of garden equipment at no charge other than $1 a copy to cover mailing and handling. Write to Garden Maid, Inc., P.O. Box 912, Lebanon, Missouri 65536, enclosing check or money order. (First class postage on our copy came to 80¢, and 20¢ is a fair handling charge.)

More Free Guides on Minigardens

Recent studies have shown that a properly tended plot of land 25 × 50 feet can produce all the fresh vegetables a family of five will be likely to eat in a season. Two free guides that offer further help in gardening in a limited space to reduce your food bills are the U.S. Department of Agriculture pamphlets "Minigardens for Vegetables" (Home and Garden Bulletin G163) and "Growing Vegetables in the Home Garden" (Home and Garden Bulletin G202). Write for prices to Superintendent of Documents, Washington, D.C. 20402.

Oddball Ways to Save Space in the Vegetable Garden

Last summer a Georgia gardener grew 230 tomato plants in exactly *one square yard* of garden space. He accomplished this spectacular feat by building a 27-foot tower spiked with planting holes, filling it with rich compost, and fitting it with a long perforated pipe down the center that he could water through. Picking the fruit did prove to be something of a problem, but this was more than compensated for by an "outta space tomato patch" equal to about 800 square feet of conventional garden that yielded hundreds of tomatoes.

If you think that tomato patch way off in Athens, Georgia, is way out, then watch out, for a tomato patch may be coming at you down the highway. One California man actually grows tomatoes atop his Volkswagen, which he drives all over town. The car roof was bashed in with a sledgehammer so that it formed a receptacle for soil, and four tomato plants were set in it. The driver estimates that a ratio of six hours' street use for every one hour of care promotes the best growth, and he never plants on the front hood, as that would obstruct visibility!

Vegetable Gardening Charts, Maps and Tips: A Free Guide to Higher Yields

If you have a tiller or plan to buy one, chances are you'll learn a lot from the booklet "Tilling Your Garden, A Guide to Higher Yields." Although it obviously centers on the use of a rotary tiller in the garden, this excellent publication also describes in detail how to plan a vegetable garden, prepare a seedbed and care for plants. It includes a "best planting time" map of the United States, a garden planning chart, and valuable gardening tips. For a free copy write John Deere, Moline, Illinois 61265.

Free Food That Lasts a Lifetime: Plant a Perennial Vegetable Garden

Here's a way to save money on food your whole lifetime without any backbreaking planting at all after the first year. You can have a perennial vegetable and herb garden with a wholesome delicious harvest every year from just one planting. How much space do you need? If you want to grow four or five different crops, you'll need at least a 25 × 25-foot plot. For easy cultivation, plan a series of straight rows running north-south, if possible, so plants don't shade each other. Herbs fit easily into small spaces and you can even border a flower bed with them.

Since the following perennials don't like to be moved and will occupy their site permanently, a little advance planning on your part will ensure success. Choose a sunny, fertile area that drains well, and try to situate your plot away from trees and large shrubs. Wait until danger of frost is past.

Before planting, clear the area of weeds; then work the soil thoroughly to a depth of 12 to 16 inches. Spade in generous amounts of compost or manure and add about ten pounds of complete fertilizer (5-10-5 or 5-10-10) for every 50-foot row. Because they are heavy feeders, perennial vegetables like soil that is rich and high in organic matter.

It's quicker and more reliable to buy crowns, parts of crowns, roots, or seedlings, rather than try to grow your perennial plants from seeds. Once they're established, you need only watch for weeds. The amount of cultivation needed to keep the planting area weed-free works the soil sufficiently and discourages insect pests as well. Prompt removal of plant refuse also helps control bugs.

In a normal season, watering isn't necessary. In a dry spell, however, give your plants one or two thorough waterings per week, applying the water gently to the soil to avoid runoff.

Asparagus is probably the all-time favorite perennial vegetable. Buy year-old crowns with a root spread of 15 inches or more. The Mary Washington and Paradise varieties are reliably delicious. In early spring, prepare a trench by removing six to ten inches of topsoil. Put your crowns in the trench so that, with roots spread out, they are 18 inches apart. A 50-foot row provides more than enough "grass" for the average family's once-a-week serving. Cover the crowns and roots firmly with an inch or two of soil at first, and add the remaining soil to fill in the trench as the shoots grow during the spring and summer, always taking care that the shoots are never completely covered.

Asparagus is sensitive to soil acidity and grows best at a pH range of 6.0 to 6.8. If you're not sure what the acidity of your soil is, purchase an inexpensive soil test kit and run a simple test. If the soil reaction is below 6.0, apply about 20 pounds of ground limestone per 100-foot row along with your fertilizer.

Don't cut any spears the first year, and do only moderate cutting, if you must, the second season. This long waiting period ensures big, fleshy stalks for many years afterward. When the roots are three years old and seven to ten inches tall, cut the stalks just at ground level so that still-buried shoots are not injured. Never make any cuttings once the fernlike growth of the plant appears (about July first). This top growth, essential for root nourishment, shouldn't be cut down until the first frost, after it has produced bright red berries. Fertilize liberally every fall, and cultivate carefully. The bed shouldn't need renewing for 20 years.

Rhubarb, another early spring crop, grows well near asparagus. Try the Valentine, McDonald, or Victoria varieties. A family-size plot of ten roots set three feet apart makes an excellent border. The culture of rhubarb is the same as for asparagus, except that rhubarb clumps must be divided every seven or eight years so that they will not produce too many slender stems. Remember, rhubarb leaves are poisonous—don't cook the leaves!

Tender globe artichokes may require extra care, but they are well worth the effort. This plant is not related to the Jerusalem artichoke, which is raised as a perennial for its edible tubers. Globe artichokes are cultivated for their immature flower buds. They are a cool-weather crop, best suited for mild climates. The roots will survive as far north as Boston, however, with winter protection. Cut them back to a foot above the ground and cover with bushel baskets. Pile a heavy mulch of straw or corn stalks over the baskets.

Globe artichokes need lots of room, so set plants five feet apart in very rich, moist soil. They want plenty of fertilizer, and a slightly alkaline soil. Use your soil test kit. Like asparagus, artichokes don't bear until the second year.

A number of annual vegetables raised from seed can be treated as perennials. Chard, for example, takes up little room and has pleasantly flavored outer leaves and stalks. Varieties Fordhook Giant, Rhubarb Chard, and Lucullus produce a vigorous top without a large fleshy root. Kale, collards, corn salad, broccoli and even celery are also in this category. These marginal plants for the perennial garden must have winter protection in cold states.

Aromatic herbs will perk up your cooking and are often helpful insect repellents when planted with vegetables or other plants. One good example is the Egyptian or tree onion, which keeps bugs away from rose bushes. If planted early, this little-known herb produces small, succulent onions on top of its stem by July. They're mild and great for salads. Plant four inches apart in a row.

Horseradish, propagated by crowns or root cuttings, needs rich soil and should be planted in early spring. Place the roots, with their tops or thick ends near the surface, about four to five inches apart. You can dig up the large, fleshy roots for grating any time in the fall, on mild winter days, or early the following spring. Leave small side roots to start a new crop without replanting.

Organically Grown Vegetables

For an informative little handbook on how to raise vegetables without commercial fertilizer or pesticides, send 75¢ for "Facts about Organic Gardening," publication number IB-36, New York State Cooperative Extension Office, Mailing Room, Building 7, Research Park, Cornell University, Ithaca, New York 14850.

An Organic Seed Catalog

This free yearly catalog—one of the few of its kind—features untreated vegetable and flower seed raised organically for the organic gardener. Send 35¢ for postage and handling to Natural Development Company, Box 215, Bainbridge, Pennsylvania 17502.

Free Organic Gardening Books

Organic Gardening Magazine, a pioneer in the organic gardening movement, often offers valuable free books or booklets with trial subscriptions. Right now they're offering *Home Power,* a thick booklet featuring excellent tips on how to save money gardening at home. Keep your eyes peeled for ads, or request the latest offer from Organic Gardening, Organic Park, Emmaus, Pennsylvania 18099.

Imported Organic Seeds

The handsome annual catalog of this British nursery features European vegetable, herb and flower seeds raised organically for the organic gardener. Send $1 for postage and handling to Chase Compost Seeds, Ltd., Benhall Green, Benhall, Saxmundham, Suffolk, Great Britain.

Natural Seed

Mother Nature is not fooled in the slightest by this nursery, which will send you a free annual descriptive price list offering only open-pollinated, untreated seed of vegetables, herbs and flowers for organic gardeners. Write Ozark Natural Seed Order, Drury, Missouri 65638.

Organic Medicinal Seed

Untreated seed from medicinal plants grown by organic gardeners is offered in this free annual Canadian catalog. Write Sanctuary Seeds, 1913 Yew Street, Vancouver, B.C. V6K 3G3, Canada.

How About a Few Chickens or Geese?

If it is legal in your area, why not raise a few chickens or geese alongside the garden? These illustrated booklets are aimed at the beginner who wants to raise a small poultry flock for eggs or meat. Write for the price of "Small Poultry Flocks," publication number F-2262, and "Raising Geese" (F-2251) to Superintendent of Documents, Washington, D.C. 20402.

Be a Beekeeper

Many people combine beekeeping with their vegetable gardening hobby and manage to keep themselves stocked with fresh honey or even make money selling it. This illustrated pamphlet tells the neophyte everything he or she needs to know about bees and the equipment needed for beekeeping. Write for price of "Beekeeping for Beginners," publication number G-158, and "Identification and Control of Honey Bee Diseases" (F-2255) to Superintendent of Documents, Washington, D.C. 20402.

Four More Free Bee Books

"Plan for a Ten-Frame Bee Hive," "Guide for Diagnosis of Brood Diseases of the Honeybee," "Controlling the Wax Moth in Honey Comb" and "Swarming of Honey Bees" are free bee pamphlets you can obtain by writing the West Virginia Department of Agriculture, Information Division, State Capitol, Charleston, West Virginia 25305.

$300 for $5—Free

The detailed story of how hundreds of families rented a few acres of farmland at a cost of about $5 each and earned a profit of $295 each in food is available free from the man who inspired the project: Rev. Wilbert Staudenmaier, Sacred Heart Rectory, 222 East Fremont Street, Appleton, Wisconsin 54911.

How to Rent a Vacant Lot Nominally for a Big, Profitable Vegetable Garden

The owner of that vacant lot near your house may be glad to rent it to you for a nominal sum if you want to use it as vegetable garden. Always obtain permission for such land use. In New York and other cities, it works this way:

1. Note all the street names surrounding the lot you choose, and the numbers of adjoining houses.

2. Visit the borough Real Estate Registry (listed in the phone

book) and consult the map that gives block, lot, and index or parcel numbers. From the Deed Index find the name of the deedholder, or contact the owner through the lawyer listed on the deed.

3. If the lot is city-owned, a letter should be written to the Commissioner of the Department of Real Estate. Describe the project planned; give block, lot, and index or parcel numbers.

4. The lease for the lot should be in writing.

5. Before proceeding with any gardening, it is advisable to obtain "third person" liability insurance. With city land this is almost always required.

Thinking About Farming

Some gardeners like raising their own food so much that they think of moving up a step in self-sufficiency to the ownership of a small farm. This free publication will help your thinking on the matter. Request "Definition of the Terms—Agriculture, Farming and Farm" from Agricultural Publications U-35, College of Agriculture and Natural Resources, University of Connecticut, Storrs, Connecticut 06268.

Getting the Most for Your Vegetable Seed Money

According to the National Garden Bureau, tomatoes are the best crop to plant in the home vegetable garden because they produce the most for the gardener's effort in relation to the space required. The space-efficient tomato plant produces $2 per square foot or $12 a vine when staked, based on current market prices. Following are the runners-up in order of their ranking:

2. leaf lettuce
3. summer squash (zucchini, scallop and yellow squash)
4. peas
5. beans

6. beets
7. carrots
8. cucumbers
9. pole beans

The lowest-ranked vegetables were the space hogs: corn, winter squash, melons and watermelons, with pumpkins receiving the lowest rating of all.

Tips on Early Vegetable Seed Care

• Soak vegetable seeds for eight hours at room temperature before planting and you'll prevent chilling injury upon their exposure to the outdoors, ensuring better growth and yield.

• To make straight guidelines for vegetable garden seed rows, either use a garden hose or stretch a rope taut and walk on it. This will leave a slight indentation in the ground.

• Very fine vegetable seed can be mixed with sand and sown from an old saltcellar.

• Stave off light frost damage by lightly watering newly planted vegetable seed every evening; be sure to sprinkle the leaves of each plant.

Asparagus Catalog

Here is a free yearly catalog concerned mainly with asparagus (and strawberry) varieties. Write Brittingham Plant Farms, P.O. Box 2538, Salisbury, Maryland 21801.

Asparagus Culture

You'll find all you need to know about growing the one vegetable everyone should have in the perennial vegetable garden in this booklet. Send 20¢ for "Asparagus," publication number HO-96, Mailing Room, Agriculture Administration Building, Purdue University, West Lafayette, Indiana 47907.

Beans, Peas

This annual catalog offers a very large selection of easy-to-grow bean and pea seed. Write Vermont Bean Seed Company, Garden Lane, Box 308, Bomoseen, Vermont 05732.

Bean Culture

The excellent booklet "Growing Dry Beans" is available for 65¢ from Distribution Center C, 7 Research Park, Cornell University, Ithaca, New York 14850.

Free Green Bean Booklet

"Beans in the Home Garden" tells all you'll need to know about growing green beans to eat fresh, rather than beans to store, and is available free from Agricultural Publications U-35, College of Agriculture and Natural Resources, University of Connecticut, Storrs, Connecticut 06268.

Cut off the tops of bean plants when they begin to yellow; they will bear more beans at the base of the plant.
Pole beans can be planted next to corn in the garden; the beans will use the corn stalks for support as they climb.

Sugar Beet Growing

With sugar as high-priced as it is, you might want to try growing sugar beets to make sugar with. Seed companies selling the seed usually provide recipes and it takes only two or three large beets to make a cup of sugar.

Canadian Cold-Weather Vegetables

This free four-color French language catalog is published annually, and features a large selection of vegetables for cold regions. Write Semences Laval Inc., 3505 Boulevard Street—Martin, West Laval, Quebec H7T 1A2, Canada.

Cauliflower and Broccoli

For this free illustrated booklet giving the basics for cauliflower and broccoli growing, request "Commercial Cauliflower and Broccoli," publication number 81-29, Agricultural Publications U-35, College of Agriculture and Natural Resources, University of Connecticut, Storrs, Connecticut 06268.

Chinese and Oriental Vegetables

Our first free annual catalog in this category offers a large selection of unusual vegetable and flower seed from all over the Orient. Write Sunrise Enterprises, P.O. Box 10058, Elmwood, Connecticut 06110. For another free descriptive price list offering little-known Asian vegetable seed, write Kitazawa Seed Company, 356 West Taylor Street, San Jose, California 95110. Seed for many Chinese vegetables is described in the free annual price list of Tsang and Ma International, 1306 Old Country Road, Belmont, California 94002. Other catalogs featuring Chinese vegetables include those of The Banana Tree, 715 Northhampton Street, Eaton, Pennsylvania 18042 (25¢); Nichols Garden Nursery, 1190 West Pacific Highway, Albany, Oregon 97321; and Park Seed Company, 915 Cokesbury Road, Greenwood, South Carolina 29647.

Corn Kernels of Truth

Chances are that even if you've grown corn in the garden for years, you don't know the thousands of uses to which the 6-billion-bushel annual U.S. corn crop is put. They include everything from aspirin manufacture to the making of yeast. Read all about them in this informative free booklet "Tapping the Treasure in Corn," by sending a 10-inch-long self-addressed stamped envelope to Corner Refiners Association, 1001 Connecticut Avenue N.W., Washington, D.C. 20036.

European Vegetable Seed

This free annual catalog features vegetable and flower seed from Europe and also offers a large selection of sweet pea seed, as well as seed for trees, shrubs and herbs. Write Unwins, P.O. Box 9, Farmingdale, New Jersey 07727.

Giant Vegetables—"The World's Most Unusual Seed Catalog"

Dubbing itself "The World's Most Unusual Seed Catalog," and featuring color photos, U.S. and world records of vegetable giants, and verified stories of two-pound tomatoes, this annual catalog offers seed for huge vegetable and flower varieties that will be the envy of the neighborhood. Send 25¢ for postage and handling to Grace's Gardens, Autumn Lane, Hackettstown, New Jersey 07840.

Ginseng Catalogs

Some gardeners make pin money growing ginseng, which many people believe is a potent aphrodisiac (in fact, the U.S. exports ginseng to several Asian countries, where it is so valued). Ginseng seed and roots of various sizes suitable for planting are described, along with planting directions and growing tips in the free annual catalog of Barney's Ginseng Patch, R24P, Montgomery City, Missouri 63361. A second firm specializing in the reputed aphrodisiac, again both roots and seed, offers a free annual descriptive price list. Write Colling's Ginseng, North Main Street, Viola, Iowa 52350.

Growing Eggplant

The free pamphlets "Growing Eggplant in the Home Garden," publication number 81-27, and "Commercial Eggplant Production" are available from College of Agricultural and Natural Resources, University of Connecticut, Storrs, Connecticut 06268.

Growing Peas

Here's a free pamphlet on raising all kinds of peas in the home garden. Request "Growing Peas," publication number 79-178, from Agricultural Publications U-35, College of Agriculture and Natural Resources, University of Connecticut, Storrs, Connecticut 06268.

Growing and Using Gourds

This illustrated booklet shows you how to grow gourds in the vegetable garden and use them in flower decoration schemes. Send 15¢ for "Culture and Use of Ornamental Gourds," publication number E-1022, New York Cooperative Extension Service, Mailing Room, Building 7, Research Park, Cornell University, Ithaca, New York 14850.

Gourmet Vegetables

Seeds for gourmet vegetables such as endive are the main attraction in this free yearly catalog. Write Epicure Seeds, Avon, New York 14414. For a second epicurean seed catalog send 25¢ for postage and handling to J. A. Demonchaux Company, 827 North Kansas Avenue, Topeka, Kansas 66608.

Gourmet Recipes

Unusual recipes are included among the imported vegetable and herb seeds offered in this free annual catalog. Write Le Jardin du Gourmet, Box 48, West Danville, Vermont 05873.

Helpful Herb Catalogs

Many herb plants and herb seeds, as well as aids for the herb gardener, are described in the free annual price list of Capriland's Herb Farm, Silver Street, Coventry, Connecticut 06238.

Another descriptive annual price list, featuring herb seed (and unusual plants such as the Egyptian or top onion), costs 25¢ for postage and handling from Greene Herb Gardens, Greene, Rhode Island 02827.

For a third annual catalog featuring many herb plants, write Taylor's Herb Garden, 1535 Lone Oak Road, Vista, California 92083.

Herb Gardening

Here are two fine illustrated booklets on herb growing that include plans for herb gardens. Write for 1) "Herbs," publication number B-2019, 20¢ from Wisconsin Cooperative Extension Service, Agricultural Bulletin Building, 1535 Observatory Drive, University of Wisconsin, Madison, Wisconsin 53706; and 2) "Culinary Herbs," publication number B-284, 20¢ from Minnesota Cooperative Extension Service, Bulletin Room, Coffey Hall, University of Minnesota, St. Paul, Minnesota 55101.

Lettuce Culture

The authoritative booklet "Growing Lettuce," publication number NE-44, is available from Agricultural Publications U-35, College of Agriculture and Natural Resources, University of Connecticut, Storrs, Connecticut 06268.

Mushrooms in the Wild

"Wild Mushrooms," a booklet designed to help you collect mushrooms in the wild, is available free from the College of Agriculture and Natural Resources, University of Connecticut, Storrs, Connecticut 06268.

Mushroom Favorites

Whether you're a closet mushroom grower or raise mushrooms in a dark, cool cellar, you'll be interested in a free mushroom "cookbooklet" featuring many mushroom recipes. It is offered by the American Mushroom Institute, P.O. Box 373, Kennett Square, Pennsylvania 19348. Send request and stamped, self-addressed envelope.

Novelty Vegetables

This free four-color catalog, published annually, offers many unusual plants, including novelties like the tree tomato and "pomato." Write Lakeland Nurseries Sales, 340 Poplar Street, Hanover, Pennsylvania 17340.

Oldtime Vegetable Seed

"There's something to be said for those older varieties that goes much deeper than nostalgia," writes Joan Faust, garden editor of *The New York Times*. "Those vegetables are part of the nation's, the world's genetic heritage. When a traditional cultivated variety (cultivar) of a vegetable or flower becomes extinct, genetic diversity in that food crop or flower strain is diminished. Sometimes these older varieties represent valuable genetic material needed for breeding crops. Dr. Jack Harlan, professor of Plant Genetics at the University of Illinois, goes so far as to state that 'these [genetic] resources stand between us and catastrophic starvation on a scale we cannot imagine.'"

Ms. Faust goes on to recommend the directory of the Frank Porter Graham Center, a nonprofit organization that tries to save the genetic heritage of our crops by publishing a descriptive directory listing sources of hard-to-find traditional vegetable, fruit and nut varieties. The directory is available for $1 from the Graham Center, Route 3, Box 95, Wardsboro, North Carolina 28170.

Along these same lines, America's oldest seed company, founded in 1784 and patronized by George Washington and Thomas Jefferson, among other greats, publishes its oldtime vegetable seed catalog annually. Send $1 for postage and handling to D. Landreth Seed Company, 2700 Wilmarco Avenue, Baltimore, Maryland 21223.

For a free descriptive yearly price list featuring many oldtime varieties, including seeds for tomatoes that grandfather grew, send $1 for postage and handling (credited to first order) to Garden of Eden Nurseries, Box 1086, Route 2, Spruce Pine, North Carolina 28777.

Onions, Scallions and Company

To obtain an informative booklet about growing all the members of the onion family, send 20¢ for "Onions and Their Relatives," publication number HO-60-1, Mailing Room, Agricultural Administration Building, Purdue University, West Lafayette, Indiana 47907. The booklet "Storage for Northern-Grown Onions," publication number IB-148, is available for $1 from Distribution Center C, 7 Research Park, Cornell University, Ithaca, New York 14850.

The Great American Garlic Catalog

Here's a free catalog, complete with gardening and kitchen tips, on— of all things—garlic. The illustrated catalog includes unusual offerings like huge elephant garlic and perennial Egyptian onions, which grow atop the plant instead of below the earth as ordinary onions do. Write S & H Organic Acres, P.O. Box 27M, Montgomery Creek, California 96065.

Parsnips sown from seed in August can be covered with a heavy mulch of hay after the first fall freeze and dug all winter long. Carrots, too, can be treated in this way.

Potatoes

Here is a free descriptive price list featuring many varieties of organically grown seed potatoes for organic gardeners. Write Wilson's Organic Potatoes, Box 28, Aspen, Colorado 81611.

Potato Planting

Learn all about unparalleled potato culture from the free booklet "Growing Potatoes in the Home Garden," publication number 78-34, and "Disease Control for Potatoes," publication number 77-52, available from Agricultural Publications U-35, College of Agriculture and Natural Resources, University of Connecticut, Storrs, Connecticut 06268.

Potato-Tomato Space Savers

Here's a novelty we've tried *but can't recommend unless you're willing to take the risk.* Nevertheless, tomatoes and potatoes *can* be grown on the same plant, their roots intertwined. Just raise your tomato seedlings as you normally would and then transplant the seedlings into one-inch holes filled with soil that you have made in whole seed potatoes (sprouting potatoes or potatoes with "eyes" will do). Lay the potatoes in a shallow flat filled with soil and wait until the tomato roots grow through the potatoes and into the soil. When transplanting the tomatoes to the garden, set the plants (potatoes and all) in one-foot deep holes in rich garden soil. This novelty is certainly a space saver, yielding tomatoes on the plant above ground and potatoes below. (The potato plant will also send up vines, of course.) The chief drawback is that potatoes can transmit several diseases to tomatoes, and vice versa, which is the reason potato fields on farms are always widely separated from tomato fields. We had no such trouble though, luckily. If you have an out-of-the-way area available you may want to experiment. Many such experiments have been made with tomato plants. At North Carolina State University, for example, tomatoes were grafted on tobacco plant roots. The result was a tomato with a high nicotine content! One of the earliest experiments with tomatoes, in 1919, produced a tomato-eggplant chimera having characteristics of both parents on the same branch. Lakeland Nurseries (see "Novelty Vegetables") offers a potato-tomato, or "pomato," ready to plant if you don't want to go to the trouble of propagating your own.

Pick a Peck of Peppers

For a free descriptive price list offering an extensive selection of pepper seed, write Horticultural Enterprises, Box 340082, Dallas, Texas 75234.

Raising Soybeans

Everything you need to know about growing soybeans is included in the free pamphlet "Soybeans for the Garden," publication number 75-25, available from Agricultural Publications U-35, College of Agriculture and Natural Resources, University of Connecticut, Storrs, Connecticut 06268.

Raising Squash

This primer on squash culture covers the subject expertly. Request "Growing Squash," publication number NE-51, from Agricultural Publications U-35, College of Agriculture and Natural Resources, University of Connecticut, Storrs, Connecticut 06268.

Rare Vegetables and Herbs

To obtain a free annual catalog chock full of unusual vegetable and herb varieties, both seeds and plants, write Nichols Garden Nursery, 1190 North Pacific Highway, Albany, Oregon 97321.

Short-Season Vegetables

This yearly catalog offers vegetable seed, including several tomato varieties, developed especially for northern areas with short growing seasons. Send 50¢ for postage and handling to Johnny's Selected Seeds, Albion, Maine 04910.

Short-Season Vegetables from Canada

Here's a free yearly catalog from a Canadian firm featuring seeds for vegetable and flower varieties that bear early and well in regions with a short growing season. Write Vesey's Seeds, York, P.E.I. COA 1PO Canada.

Southern Seed and Plants

This free catalog, published twice a year, offers vegetable seed and plants particularly suitable for hot southern areas. Write Wyatt-Quarles Seed Company, P.O. Box 2131, Raleigh, North Carolina 27602.

Sweet Potato Catalogs

Sweet potato plants ready to set in the garden are the chief feature of a free descriptive price list published once a year by the Margrave Plant Company, 117 Church Street, Gleason, Tennessee 38229. The plants are also the specialty featured in the free annual catalog of the Steele Plant Company, Box 191, Gleason, Tennessee 38229.

Tomato Growing

Americans grow more tomatoes than any other fruit or vegetable in the home garden. This excellent free illustrated booklet provides information on their culture, ranging from the best varieties to grow in your region to plant care and control of pests and diseases. Request "Growing Tomatoes," publication number NE-43, from Agricultural Publications U-35, College of Agriculture and Natural Resources, University of Connecticut, Storrs, Connecticut 06268.

Early Tomatoes

This is a descriptive annual price list featuring a large selection of early variety tomatoes for regions with short growing seasons, not to mention the gardener who wants to produce the first garden-ripe tomatoes in town. Send 25¢ for postage and handling to Mountain Seed and Nursery, Route 1, Box 271, Moscow, Idaho 83843.

Square Tomatoes (Yes!), Ruffled Tomatoes and Pepper-shaped Tomatoes

The above are only a few of the many oddities offered in Glecker's free annual catalog of unusual seeds. Write Glecker's Seedsmen, Metamora, Ohio 43540.

British Tomatoes

A *striped* tomato variety (we've grown it and the stripes are pronounced) is one of the many interesting selections featured in this free annual four-color catalog. Write Sutton & Sons Seed Growers, Ltd., Reading, England.

Plant cherry tomato plants right on the patio in hanging baskets. Space can also be saved by growing full-size tomatoes and other vegetables in tubs or against a fence.

Tomato Factories: More for Your Money

Some modern tomato varieties are so prolific that they are virtual "tomato factories." A number of tomato plants actually grow more than *twenty feet* high when trained against a building, and several gardeners claim to have harvested *250* tomatoes from a single rampant vine. There is documentation of a sprawling, unstaked California plant that "covered a space of eight feet *square*" and yielded *170* pounds of fruit before frost killed the vine. Many "supertomatoes" are capable of such heavy fruiting, with proper watering and fertilization, but below are the best plants for gardeners out to break production records:

Boatman Miracle Climber	Ponderosa
Climbing-Trip-L-Crop	Terrific
Giant Tree	Trellis 22
Jung's Giant Climber	Vineripe
Lakeland Climber	Winsall
Oxheart	

Worldwide Vegetable Seed

Vegetable seed from every corner of the world is featured in this big annual catalog. Send 66¢ for postage and handling to De Giorgio Company, 1411 Third Street, Council Bluffs, Iowa 51501.

Worthy Wild Edibles

For the free pamphlet "Edible Wild Plants," write the West Virginia Department of Agriculture, Information Division, State Capitol, Charleston, West Virginia 25305.

The Five Most Entertaining Free Vegetable Catalogs

The following are our choices for the most entertaining and informative free general catalogs specializing in vegetables:

BURPEE SEED COMPANY. An extensive four-color 180-page catalog, published every spring, offering vegetables, shrubs, trees, perennials, annuals, fruits, nuts, houseplants and garden supplies. In autumn a smaller fall catalog is published. Among the finest nursery catalogs, both offer many gardening tips and often feature contests and attractive offers. Write Burpee Seed Company, Warminster, Pennsylvania 18991.

HENRY FIELD. A four-color catalog published once a year that offers a wide range of plants, including vegetable and flower seed, fruit and nut trees, berries, vines, ornamentals, bulbs and houseplants. This entertaining, informative 125-page catalog contains a large section of gardening advice. Write Henry Field Seed and Nursery, 407 Sycamore, Shenandoah, Iowa 51602.

GURNEY SEED. Possibly the most entertaining of all catalogs, this free homespun annual garden book comes to over 75 outsize gaudy color pages and is filled with planting tips, free offers (for example a 1¢ seed packet for kids only), and gardening stories. It features everything from flowers and vegetables to fruit trees and ornamentals, at least 2000 offerings in all. Write Gurney Seed and Nursery Company, Yankton, South Dakota 57079.

J. W. JUNG. A large free four-color catalog that is published annually and informatively describes many varieties of vegetables, flowers, fruits, berries, trees, shrubs and houseplants. Write J. W. Jung Seed Company, 339 South High Street, Randolph, Wisconsin 53956.

R. H. SHUMWAY. A free oversize four-color catalog that is published once a year and is full of planting information. Write R. H. Shumway Seedsman, Inc., 628 Cedar Street, Rockford, Illinois 61101.

A List of More Fine Free Vegetable Catalogs

ABBOTT & COBB, INC., 4744 Frankford Avenue, Philadelphia, Pennsylvania 19124

BRAWLEY SEED COMPANY, 1010 North Main Street, Mooresville, North Carolina 28115

D. V. BURRELL SEED GROWERS COMPANY, P.O. Box 150, Rocky Ford, California 81067

COMSTOCK, FERRE & COMPANY, 263 Main Street, Wethersfield, Connecticut 06109 (One of America's oldest nurseries, dating back to 1820.)

DESSERT SEED COMPANY, INC., P.O. Box 181, El Centro, California 92243 (Only large quantities sold.)

JOSEPH HARRIS COMPANY, Moreton Farm, 3760 Buffalo Road, Rochester, New York 14624

CHARLES C. HART SEED COMPANY, Wethersfield, Connecticut 06109

HERBST BROTHERS SEEDSMEN, 1000 North Main Street, Brewster, New York 10509

R. L. HOLMES SEED COMPANY, 2125 46th Street N.W., Canton, Ohio 44709

EARL MAY SEED & NURSERY COMPANY, 100 North Elm, Shenandoah, Iowa 51603

MELLINGERS, 2310 West South Range Road, North Lima, Ohio 44452

MEYER SEED COMPANY, 600 South Carolina Street, Baltimore, Maryland 21231

MIDWEST SEED GROWERS, 505 Walnut, Kansas City, Missouri 64106

L. L. OLDS SEED COMPANY, P.O. Box 7790, Madison, Wisconsin 53707

REUTER SEED COMPANY, 320 North Carrollton Avenue, New Orleans, Louisiana 70119 (Southern varieties.)

ROSWELL SEED COMPANY, Box 725-115, 117 South Main Street, Roswell, New Mexico 88201

SEEDWAY, INC., Railroad Place, Hall, New York 14463

STOKES SEEDS, INC., Box 548, 737 Main Street, Buffalo, New York 14240

OTIS S. TWILLEY SEED COMPANY, P.O. Box 65, Trevose, Pennsylvania 19047

WETSEL SEED COMPANY, Harrisonburg, Virginia 28801

NOTE: Many of the catalogs listed in other chapters also offer vegetable seeds and plants.

Harvesting Tips

Pick all vegetables when young. Not only will they taste better but the plants will bear more.

Specific harvesting tips: pick corn when silks are brown; cucumbers are best when slender and dark green; parsnips and carrots taste better after a sharp frost, tomatoes when dead ripe. All root crops should be picked in the morning, and all above-ground crops in the afternoon or early evening.

Gathering and Saving Free Seed from the Vegetable Garden

When saving old family varieties, or any seed gathered from the vegetable garden, select fruit or vegetables from the healthiest plants you have. Pick the vegetable when it's dead ripe (but not overripe) and scrape the seeds out with a knife. Next soak the seeds for three days in a pot of water at room temperature to allow them to "ferment." Stir the mixture several times a day and finally pour off whatever pulp and dead seeds are floating on top. (The seeds with life in them will have settled to the bottom.) Then rub the seeds until the remainder of the pulp comes off—this is important, for seeds with flesh on them are apt to rot. After the flesh has been removed, wash the seeds in cold water and dry them on sheets of paper in a dry, warm, well-ventilated room, taking care to turn them over periodically to prevent formation of mold on their undersides.

Once the seed is dry, treat it to help prevent losses due to soil microorganisms, insects, or seed-borne diseases. This procedure can be combined with cleansing the seed, but is given separately here because it is a good idea to process commercial seed, too, if it hasn't been treated. (Examine all commercial seed packets to see if the seed has been treated.) To treat, simply immerse the seeds in a pot of water at 112°F., stir with a paddle, and let the seed soak for at least 25 minutes before drying it. Do the same with seed saved from the garden. This heat treatment will kill bacteria and fungi responsible for many diseases, but won't kill the seed.

As an added disease precaution, you can lightly coat vegetable seeds with thiram, a chemical dust that provides good protection against seed-rotting fungi in the soil. Do this after the seed is dry by dipping the tip of a knife in the dust, flicking it into the seed packet, and shaking it. Only a very light coating is necessary. Store the thiram and the treated seed in a safe place beyond the reach of children and pets.

Ideally, seed from the garden (or from partially used seed packets, for that matter) should be stored where the temperature is 40°F. to 50°F. and there is a low relative humidity of 45 percent or less. However, some seed will last up to five years or more in a cool dry place out of direct sunlight. If the seed is in partially used commercial seed packets, reseal the packets with a tape or staple them closed after folding over the top edge several times. Seed gathered from the garden can be kept in sealed envelopes, coffee cans with plastic airtight lids, empty baby food jars, or in homemade paper packets taped or stapled closed at the top. Some gardeners store their seed in the refrigerator in a fruit jar, along with a little bag of desiccant to absorb moisture. Where vermin are a problem, put any paper packets in a metal box as an added precaution. Be sure that the seed containers are adequately marked with the variety name and the date of storage.

Before you plant the stored seed you will want to test it for germination. Try the "rag doll" germination test before planting. Just place ten or so seeds a half-inch apart on a moist cloth about a foot long and a foot wide. Roll up the cloth, covering the seeds, tie the ends of this "rag doll" with string or rubber bands, and place it in a plastic bag (pinholed for ventilation) to prevent it from drying out. After five to seven days, untie the "doll" and count the number of sprouted seeds. Divide these by the number of seeds in the rag doll, then multiply by one hundred, and you will have the percentage of germination: e.g., eight seeds sprouted divided by ten seeds in the doll equals .80 × 100, or 80 percent germination.

The same formula applies if seed is tested in a damp paper towel kept moist between two plates, in pasteurized soil, or in any other sterile planting medium. If more than 70 percent of the seeds germinate, it is safe to assume that the seeds are quite viable or good to use. If less than 50 percent sprout, you may want to try sowing them thickly when planting, but don't bother saving the seeds for the following year.

How Long You Can Save Vegetable Seed

You can save money by storing vegetable seed for years to come if you're careful (see preceding article), but how long can you save it and still expect it to sprout? The following seed viability table tells all. The first figure is the average period of viability, the figure after the dash is the record of extreme longevity that has been reported for that vegetable:

Angelica	1–3 years	Bean	3–8
Basil	8–10 +	Beet	6–10 +

Borage	8–10+	Leek	3–9
Broccoli	5–10+	Lettuce	5–13
Cabbage	5–10	Mustard	4–9
Caraway	3–4	Okra	5–10+
Cardoon	7–9	Onion	2–7
Carrot	4–10+	Parsley	3–9
Cauliflower	5–10	Pea	3–8
Celery	8–10	Pepper	4–13
Chicory	2–6	Pumpkin	4–9
Coriander	6–8	Radish	5–10+
Corn	2–4	Rhubarb	3–8
Cucumber	10–10+	Sage	3–7
Eggplant	6–10	Spinach	5–7
Endive	10–10+	Squash	6–10+
Fennel	4–7	Thyme	3–7
Gourds	6–10+	Tomato	4–13
Kohlrabi	5–10	Turnip	5–10+

2

Fruit and Nut Nuggets

A Fruit and Nut Primer

Everything you'll need to know about starting a small orchard is covered in this free booklet. Request "Beginning a Backyard Orchard" from West Virginia Department of Agriculture, Information Division, State Capitol, Charleston, West Virginia 25305.

Fruit Selection

This complete booklet tells you the best fruits and fruit varieties to grow in the home garden. Send 40¢ for "Choosing Fruits for Home Growing," publication number 78-31, to Agricultural Publications U-35, College of Agriculture and Natural Resources, University of Connecticut, Storrs, Connecticut 06268.

All About Dwarf Fruit Trees

Even the smallest home grounds can boast a dwarf fruit tree that bears bushels of fruit. This free authoritative illustrated booklet describes different varieties of fruits available in dwarf form that produce the best fruit, advising how to plant and care for them. Request "Dwarf Fruit Trees," publication number L-407, U.S. Department of Agriculture, Publications Division, Washington, D.C. 20250.

Average Bearing Age of Fruit Plants

When figuring how much you'll save on fruit by buying fruit plants for the garden, always take into account the average bearing age of the fruit tree or bush you plant:

Apple	5–20 years	Orange	3–6 years
Blackberry	1	Peach	2
Cranberry	3	Pear	4–7
Currant	3	Persimmon	1–3
Gooseberry	1–2	Plum	3–5
Grape	4	Quince	2–3
Grapefruit	3–6	Raspberry	1–2
Lemon	3–6	Strawberry	1–2

Fruit Tree Pruning

How to prune and properly train a fruit tree at the same time is the theme of this illustrated pamphlet. Send 20¢ for "Pruning and Training Fruit Trees, publication number NR.538, Ohio Cooperative Extension Service, Ohio State University, 2120 Fyffe Road, Columbus, Ohio 43210.

Grafting Fruit Trees

Here is a brief course in grafting for the beginner in an informative illustrated booklet. Send 50¢ for "Top-Working and Bridge-Grafting Fruit Trees," publication number IB-75, New York State Cooperative Extension Office, Mailing Room, Building 7, Research Park, Cornell University, Ithaca, New York 14850.

Pin Money from Berries

If you have considered making pin money growing strawberries, figure it this way. Commercial growers in California, using all the latest methods, harvest 50,000 quarts of berries from an acre. Do the same in a 33 × 66-foot home strawberry patch, which is exactly one-twentieth of an acre, and you can harvest 2,500 quarts. Sell these at an average seventy cents a pint (home berries should be worth even more) and you've made $3,400. Not bad for a little plot of land and no more than a few days' work, even if you cut these figures in half. And you'd do even better with perishable gourmet berries like raspberries, which few commercial growers handle.

An Apple Fence

For a free illustrated pamphlet showing you how to train dwarf apple trees on wire to make a living, fruitful fence anywhere in the yard, request Extension Circular 1000 from Agricultural Extension Service, Virginia Polytechnic Institute, Blackburg, Virginia 24060.

Apple Tree Catalogs

Write for the free four-color annual catalog of an old fruit nursery once associated with Luther Burbank that specializes in Golden and Red Delicious apples: Stark Brother Nurseries and Orchards, Louisiana, Missouri 63353.

For a free annual descriptive price list devoted to old and new varieties of apple trees write Converse Nursery, Amherst, New Hampshire 03031.

A tin can nailed to the end of a broomstick or larger pole, open side up, makes an excellent device to reach apples or other fruit high up on a tree.

Banana "Trees" and Other Tropical Fruit Plants

Cashew and cocoa seed and seed for many tropical fruit and nut trees are among the exotic items in this twice-a-year catalog. Send 25¢ for postage and handling to The Banana Tree, 715 Northampton Street, Easton, Pennsylvania 18042.

Growing Blackberries, Currants and Gooseberries

Well illustrated with photographs, this pamphlet gives the basics of growing blackberries, currants and gooseberries, providing information on good varieties as well. Send 30¢ for "Blackberries, Currants and Gooseberries," publication number IB-97, New York Cooperative Extension Service, Mailing Room, Building 7, Research Park, Cornell University, Ithaca, New York 14850.

Thornless Blackberry Catalog

For a free descriptive price list published annually and featuring thornless blackberries and raspberries, write Faubus Berry Nursery, Star Route 4, Elkins, Arkansas 72727.

Blueberry Growing

From these two excellent pamphlets on home garden blueberry culture choose the one issued nearest your home. Write for: 1) "Highbush Blueberry Culture," publication number IB-151, 75¢ from New York Cooperative Extension Service, Mailing Room, Building 7, Research Park, Cornell University, Ithaca, New York 14850; or 2) "Growing Blueberries in Wisconsin," publication number A-2194, 25¢ from Wisconsin Cooperative Extension Service, Agricultural Bulletin Building, 1535 Observatory Drive, University of Wisconsin, Madison, Wisconsin 53706.

A Fruiting Blueberry Fence

Try growing attractive fruit-bearing blueberry bushes instead of privet as hedges in your yard. A flowering, fruiting blueberry hedge is made quite simply by planting blueberry bushes three feet apart instead of the usual six feet. Depending on the variety, a fruiting fence can range from three to six feet high. Recommended varieties (and use several of these for good fruiting) are Earliblue, Blueray, Berkeley, Herbert, Coville, and Jersey. Set and care for the plants as you would any blueberry bush.

A Blueberry Catalog

The founder of Alexander's Nurseries, who died recently, in our opinion knew more about blueberries than any nurseryman in the world. Mr. Alexander, who devoted a long life to the bush fruit, developed several excellent varieties and was in the habit of writing long informative letters to anyone who had a question about blueberry growing (he once wrote us a five-page single-spaced missive). The nursery carries on using his strictly organic methods and its descriptive price lists, published twice a year, offer one the very latest in blueberry bushes (and lilacs as well). Write Alexander's Nurseries, 1225 Wareham Street, Middleboro, Massachusetts 02346.

Southern "Rabbiteye" Blueberries

Varieties of the rabbiteye, a very tall plant and the only blueberry that does well in the South, are featured in this free descriptive price list. Write Finch's Rabbiteye Blueberry Nursery, Bailey, North Carolina 27807.

Chestnuts

This free annual descriptive price list offers Chinese chestnut trees, which are immune to the blight that destroys native American chestnuts. Write Jersey Chestnut Farms, 58 Van Duyne Avenue, Wayne, New Jersey 07470.

Espalier Fruit Trees

This prestigious free little booklet is published yearly and centers mainly on espalier-trained fruit of many types and sizes, with some dwarf trees, berries and grapes. Write Henry Leuthardt Nurseries, Inc., Montauk Highway, East Moriches, New York 11940.

Grape Knowhow

You'll learn a lot from this illustrated guide, which clarifies the sometimes difficult cultivation of grapes. Send 35¢ for "Grape Growing," publication number NR-509, Ohio Cooperative Extension Service, Ohio State University, 2120 Fyffe Road, Columbus, Ohio 43210.

The herb hyssop planted under a grapevine will increase its yield.

Juniper: The Bathtub Gin Berry

The common juniper berry (*Juniper communis*) has been used for centuries to flavor gin and game dishes like wild boar. Following is an old bootlegger's recipe for bathtub gin made from juniper berries. We have not tested it, do not recommend it, and offer it merely as a historical curiosity. You must take full responsibility if you make it or drink too much of it.

BATHTUB GIN

2 parts alcohol
3 parts water
1 teaspoon juniper berry juice
1 tablespoon glycerin (to smooth)

It cost bootleggers about two cents an ounce to make this concoction, which supposedly was ready to drink upon mixing.

Melon Seed

Seed for many varieties of melons, including muskmelons and water-melons, is featured in this free annual four-color catalog. Write Willhite Melon Seed Farms, P.O. Box 23, Poolville, Texas 76076.

New Fruits

A free annual catalog describing the most recent developments in fruit tree, berry and grape varieties is available from the New York State Fruit Testing Cooperative Association, Geneva, New York 14456.

Recently developed strawberry varieties and other new small fruits are featured in the free annual catalog of the New Jersey Small Fruits Council, P.O. Box 185, Hammonton, New Jersey 08037.

Nut Growing

Everything about growing nuts from filberts to walnuts is covered in this informative booklet. Send $1 for "Nut Growing in the North-east," publication number IB-71, New York Cooperative Extension Service, Mailing Room, Building 7, Research Park, Cornell University, Ithaca, New York 14850.

A Catalog of Nuts

For a free annual catalog featuring grafted nut trees write Dave Wilson Nursery, 4306 Santa Fe Avenue, Hughson, California 95326.

Oldtime Fruit Trees

The first of our free descriptive price lists here offers delicious difficult-to-find oldtime fruit varieties, including at least 250 varieties of apples and many varieties of peaches, nectarines, plums, pears, apricots, cherries, grapes, quince, currants, gooseberries, and conservation plants for wildlife. Write Southmeadow Fruit Gardens,

2363 Tilbury Place, Birmingham, Michigan 48009. (The extensive Southmeadow *catalog* is $6, and, some say, well worth it.)

Another free descriptive price list offering many varieties of fruit trees that were oldtime favorites but are rarely available today can be ordered from Lawson's Nursery, Route 1, Box 294, Ballground, Georgia 30107.

Our third descriptive price list featuring old fruit tree favorites is available from Baum's Nursery, RD2, New Fairfield, Connecticut 06810.

Persimmon Trees

For a free annual price list featuring persimmon (and grafted nut) trees, write Louis Gerardi Nursery, RR1, O'Fallon, Illinois 62269.

Peach Culture

Peaches are the fruit trees quickest to bear (in one or two years) and this excellent free illustrated booklet tells you how to get the best and most fruit from them. Request "Home Peach and Nectarine Culture," publication number NE-52, from College of Agriculture and Natural Resources, University of Connecticut, Storrs, Connecticut 06268.

Raspberry Growing

Fresh raspberries are considered too delicate to handle by all but posh greengrocers, and have to be grown at home unless one is willing to pay exorbitant prices for them. All you need to know about growing red raspberries, the most delicate of fruits, and preventing raspberry diseases, can be found in this free booklet. Write for "Growing Raspberries," publication number NE-45, from College of Agriculture and Natural Resources, University of Connecticut, Storrs, Connecticut 06268.

Raspberry Catalogs

Delicious raspberries of many varieties are featured in the free yearly catalogs offered by 1) Ahrens Nursery, RR1, Huntingburg, Indiana 47542, and 2) Makielski Berry Farm, 7130 Platt Road, Ypsilanti, Michigan 48197.

A Soapmaking Berry to Cleanse Your Hands of Garden Grime

The scientific name for the tree it grows on explains this berry's use— *Sapindus* is a combination of the Latin for soap and "Indus" (Indian), in reference to American Indians using the berries for soap. Soap-berries, the pulp of which contains saponin, lather up easily and were valued for shampooing, although the soap made from them does damage some materials. Two species are of horticultural importance. *Sapindus marginatus* is a deciduous tree that grows up to 30 feet tall with yellow, egg-shaped fruit about one inch long; it is found only from the southern part of zone 7 southward. *Sapindus Saponaria,* an evergreen, also grows up to 30 feet, but is only hardy outside in zone 9, that is, southernmost Florida. Both trees can be propagated by seed and do best in dry, sandy soil. The lather-producing agent saponin in soapberries can be poisonous if taken internally; in fact, some American Indians caught fish by stupefying them with bits of the fruit thrown into pools.

Southern Berries

This free twice-a-year price list describes hot-weather berry varieties appropriate for the south. Write Boston Mountain Nurseries, Route 2, Highway 71, Winslow, Arizona 72959.

Strawberry Growing

Here's an illustrated booklet that will give you a good start in straw-berry growing, from selecting varieties and preparing the bed to picking. Write for "Strawberries," publication number RB-987, 50¢ from Ohio Cooperative Extension Service, Ohio State University, 2120 Fyffe Road, Columbus, Ohio 43210.

A dozen strawberry plants can be grown in a plain 2 × 2-foot box placed on the patio. Fill the box with a rich potting soil and place in the corner a decorative stone that you can run the hose against when watering the plants.

A Free Strawberry Tree

The "tree" is simply half-cylinder wire nailed to a 12-inch board and lined with sphagnum moss to hold your soil mix. The strawberries are planted all over it or can be interspersed with flowering plants for a very attractive display.

Strawberry Suppliers with Free Colorful Catalogs

All kinds of berries are grown by these folks down on Strawberry Lane. For their informative free catalog write W. F. Allen Company, 2179 Strawberry Lane, Salisbury, Maryland 21801.

An annual catalog featuring many varieties of strawberries is yours free from Bountiful Ridge Nurseries, Box 250, Princess Anne, Maryland 21853.

Over 40 varieties of strawberries are offered in this free annual four-color catalog, most of the berries pictured full size. Write Buntings Nurseries, Inc., Selbyville, Delaware 19975.

A free annual catalog from another strawberry specialist features many varieties of strawberries. Write Nourse Farms, Inc., New England Strawberry Nursery, Box 485, RFD, South Deerfield, Massachusetts 01373.

NOTE: Many of the other nurseries listed in this book, especially in this chapter, also offer strawberries.

Wild Strawberries

The epicure's famous French wild strawberry, *fraise des bois,* a sweet little berry rarely an inch long that can be grown in the home garden, is featured in this free brochure. Write the Guilde of Strawberry Bank, Inc., 93 State Street, Portsmouth, New Hampshire 03801.

French Strawberries

For a free annual four-color catalog, written in French, featuring the many delicious cultivated strawberries of France, write to Vilmorin, 4 Quai de la Megisserie, 75001 Paris, France.

Making a New Prolific Strawberry Bed from an Old Tired One

If you don't want the expense and effort of starting a new bed when production begins to fall off in the old strawberry patch, there is an alternative that works at least passably—although you should remember that commercial growers almost always plow under a bed after two years and usually do so after the first year's crop is picked. Nevertheless, up to one-half production from an old bed (and sometimes more) can be maintained for two to three years or longer if the following method is used. Begin the renewal at the end of the harvest season in early summer. Don't wait two or three weeks but get to work as soon as the berries have been picked. At this time run your hand or powermower, set on high (two to three inches), through the strawberry patch, cutting off the tops of the plants (a scythe or hoe will do just as well). The plants will then put all their strength into producing new leaves and fruit buds for the next year (the more new leaves a plant has, the more berries it will produce). Help them along by weeding the patch thoroughly and fertilizing the remaining plants. Also turn under every other row in the patch, including all plants and any mulch that may be present. Runners from the alternate rows will soon fill up these now empty rows and you will get fruit from both the topped plants and their runners the following season—more from the topped ones. If the plants don't send out many runners, encourage them to so by digging in a little cottonseed meal around each plant.

This method works best where very productive varieties like Pocahontas have been planted. When you use the hill system or spaced row system, no thinning of plants is necessary. With the matted row system, thin plants (that is, pull out excess ones) when weeding until the plants are six to eight inches apart. Sprinkling an inch or so of compost through the bed after renewing is also a good idea. Within two to three weeks new foliage will appear on the plants, which will look so bad at first that you'll think you made a mistake following this advice, but in another three or four weeks the plants will be thriving.

Free Informative Color Catalogs Featuring Many Kinds of Fruit

AUBIN NURSERIES, LTD., Box 268, Carmon, Manitoba ROG OJO, Canada

BILL BOATMAN AND COMPANY, NURSERY STOCK, Bainbridge, Ohio 45612

BONAVISTA, Box 813, Laramie, Wyoming 82070

DEAN FOSTER NURSERIES, Route 2, Hartford, Michigan 49057

KELLY BROTHERS NURSERIES, 23 Maple Drive, Dansville, New York 14437

J. E. MILLER NURSERIES, INC., Canandaigua, New York 14424

TENNESSEE NURSERY COMPANY, INC., Cleveland, Tennessee 37311

VAN WELL NURSERY, INC., P.O. Box 1339, 1000 North Muller Street, Wenatchee, Washington 98801

ZILKE BROTHERS NURSERY, Baroda, Michigan 49101

NOTE: Many of the catalogs listed in other chapters also offer fruit plants, especially the vegetable catalogs listed at the end of chapter 1.

3

Flower Garden Freebies

Flowers from Scratch

Get off to a good beginning with this excellent little pamphlet instructing you how to grow flowers from seed and including some valuable tips. Send 35¢ for "Flowers from Seed," publication number IB-20, Mailing Room, Building 7, Research Park, Cornell University, Ithaca, New York 14850.

Very tiny flower seeds can be mixed with sand and sown from a salt shaker.

Flowering Perennials

Perennial flowers, which often last a lifetime once planted, are thoroughly covered in the booklet "Growing Flowering Perennials," publication number G-114, available from Superintendent of Documents, Washington, D.C. 20402. Write requesting price.

Vest Pocket Gardens

Planning and designs for small flower gardens that could be made of the many vacant lots in American cities is described in the free booklet "A Little about Lots" available from the Park Association of New York City, Lots Book, Box 600, New York, N.Y. 10010. Another similar aid is the free leaflet series "Nature Enjoyment Areas," Environmental Impact Office, University of Utah, Salt Lake City, Utah 84112.

When designing a flower garden bed with a curve, use the garden hose, arranged in the pattern you want.

Seeds for Minigardens

The Pine Tree Seed Company, which offers an informative free catalog, specializes in supplying seeds to people who have small flower and vegetable gardens. You can save money here by buying their extensive collection of smaller, lower-priced packets of seed. Write Pine Tree Seed Company, P.O. Box 1399, Portland, Maine 04104.

Encourage flowers to bloom a second time by fertilizing them with a strong solution of liquid manure after their first flowering.

Free Flower Charts

This free four-color catalog is published quarterly, and besides listing an extensive selection of flower seed, as well as plants and bulbs, contains a large section of very precise charts indicating when flowers should be planted, how much sun they require, and so on. Write George W. Park Seed Company, Box 31, Greenwood, South Carolina 29647.

Seaside Gardens

Just the booklet you've been looking for if you have a place by the seashore, this informative work covers everything one needs to know about gardening by the sea, from trees to use as windbreaks to the best flowers to grow. Send 25¢ for "Plants for the Seashore," College of Agriculture and Natural Resources, Agricultural Publications Division, Storrs, Connecticut 06268.

Growing Flowers on the Beach

To grow flowers in pure beach sand—say in dune areas near a summer cottage—strip off the sand to a depth of about a foot. Then lay plastic over the bottom of the ditch and spread several inches of shredded leaves or other organic matter over the plastic. Refill the trench with the removed sand, adding potash and phosphorus to it at the rate suggested on the bags. Before the plastic rots out it will serve as a water barrier, preventing water and nutrients from leaching away. By the time the plastic does disintegrate, rotting roots and other vegetation will have formed a true soil in the treated area. Plants grown in such soil, even the first year, won't have to be fertilized any more than plants grown in heavier soils. The only other way to grow flowers in sand is by constant daily watering with a weak fertilizer solution, which won't yield results nearly as good.

A Weed Primer

A weed, Emerson said, is only a flower that hasn't been cultivated, but gardeners generally feel more negatively about them. This authoritative illustrated booklet covers all the weeds likely to bother the home gardener and then some. Send 25¢ for "Weeds," publication number IB-72, Distribution Center C, Building 7, Research Park, Ithaca, New York 14850.

Pick flowers only in early morning or late afternoon when the sun is not strong. They'll last much longer.

Money to Beautify Your Town

Money to restore and improve the environment will be supplied to garden clubs and other organizations, on approval, by the nonprofit

America the Beautiful Fund, 806 15th Street, N.W., Washington, D.C. 20005, if the local organization matches the Fund grant. Write for details.

Empty medicine vials, thoroughly washed out, make convenient moisture-free flower seed storage containers. By punching a few holes in the top of the vial you have a handy seed dispenser.

Growing Alpines

Many kinds of alpine flowers and ferns are featured in this annual catalog, along with cultivation directions. Send 50¢ for postage and handling to Siskiyou Rare Plant Nursery, 522 Franquette St., Medford, Oregon 97501.

An Alyssum Source

The free annual catalog of this seed company features alyssum, among other flower species. Write Butchart Gardens, Ltd., P.O. Box 150, Rocky Ford, California 81067.

Amaryllis

For a free annual catalog featuring amaryllis planting tips and a large selection of amaryllis, write Wyndham Hayward, Lakemont Gardens, 915 S. Lakemont Avenue, Winter Park, Florida 32789.

Aquatic Plants

Aquatic plants and supplies for aquatic gardens are featured in the free annual catalog of Lilyponds Water Gardens, 16108 Hort Road, Brookshire, Texas 77423.

An illustrated 32-page booklet entitled "Tricker's Water Lilies," featuring all kinds of plants and pumps for the home water garden, is also yours free. Write William Tricker, Inc., Saddle River, New Jersey 07458.

Aquatic and Bog Plants

For an informative annual catalog featuring aquatic and bog plants, as well as wildflowers, send $1 for postage and handling to Gardens of the Blue Ridge, Box 10, Pineola, North Carolina 28662.

English Aquatic Gardens

Three English firms offer free catalogs featuring delightful water gardens. Their addresses are: Perry's Hardy Plant Farm, Enfield, Middlesex, England; L. Haig & Company Ltd., The Aquatic Nurseries, Newdigate, Surrey, England; and Taylor's Nursery, Bracknell, Berkshire, England.

Australian Flowers

This annual catalog features Australian-grown flowers, especially daffodils and tulip varieties. Send 40¢ for postage and handling to J.N. Hancock & Co., Jackson's Hill Road, Menzies Creek, Victoria 3159, Australia.

Take cuttings of garden annuals like begonias, impatiens, marigolds, fuchsia and coleus before the first frost and grow them inside for the winter.

Begonia Catalogs

Few nurseries offer more begonia varieties (over 400) than are described in this annual price list. Send 50¢ for postage and handling to Begonia Paradise Gardens, 9471 Dana Road, Cutler Ridge, Florida 33157.

Another free descriptive begonia price list, also featuring a very large selection, is available from Rainbow Begonia Gardens, Box 991, Westminster, California 92683.

The long taproots of blue cornflowers, which grow wild in many

*areas, make an excellent substitute coffee when scrubbed clean, roasted
until hard and ground or chopped up very fine.*

Bulbs for Summer Gardens

Contrary to popular belief, there are many colorful bulbs, such as the
tuberose and achimenes, that can be planted in the summer garden.
Here is an excellent booklet that provides instructions for the cultiva-
tion of a score of them. Request the price of "Summer Flowering
Bulbs," publication number G-151, Superintendent of Documents,
Washington, D.C. 20402.

Bulb Booklet

Here is a free bulb booklet from Canada that tells you everything you
need to know about starting and growing flower bulbs and tubers, the
information provided in an easy-to-follow, condensed and well-illustrated form. Write for "May Garden Bulb Tips" to McFayden Seed
Company, Ltd., P.O. Box 1800, 30-9th Street, Brandon, Manitoba
R7A6N4.

Bulb Catalogs

A free 56-page color catalog, complete with planting tips and featuring many kinds of bulbs, is available from John Scheepers, Inc., 63
Wall Street, New York, N.Y. 10005.

Other excellent general sources offering free catalogs for both
spring and summer bulbs include: Burnett Brothers, Inc., 92 Cham-
bers Street, New York, New York 10007; Brecks, 6523 North
Galena Road, Peoria, Illinois 61632; De Jager Bulbs, 188 Asbury
Street, South Hamilton, Massachusetts 01982; and Dutch Bulb Company, Cherry Lane Road, Tannersville, Pennsylvania 18372.

Discount Bulbs

For a free annual brochure describing low-priced discount bulbs write Michigan Bulb Company, 1950 Waldorf Street, Grand Rapids, Michigan 49550.

Rare Bulbs

This is an annual catalog listing a wide assortment of rare bulbs grown in England. Send 50¢ for postage and handling to J. A. Mars of Haslemere, % Black and Thompson, 124 North 181st Street, Seattle, Washington 98133.

Dutch Bulbs

This free yearly catalog from a Dutch bulb grower features an extensive variety of bulbs grown in Holland. Write Dutch Gardens, Inc., P.O. Box 338, Montvale, New Jersey 07645.

Bulbs of All Nations

An extensive selection of bulbs imported from all over the world is offered in the free annual catalog of French's Bulb Importer, Route 100, Pittsfield, Vermont 05762.

Snowdrop Bulbs

Here is an English nursery that sells nothing but snowdrop bulbs, their catalog presenting scores of these little flowers, which are one of the first flowers of spring (or last of winter). Write The Giant Snowdrop Company, Hyde, Chalford, Gloucestershire, England.

Caladiums

For a free annual brochure describing a large selection of caladium varieties, write Pickens Caladium Bulb Farm, Route 3, Box 1655, Bartow, Florida 33830.

Canadian Cold-Climate Flowers

This free 75-page four-color catalog, published twice a year, is packed with a vast selection of flower seeds and bulbs, plus an unusually large number of discount coupons, bonus offers and gardening tips. Write McFayden Seed Company Ltd., P.O. Box 1800, 30-9th St., Brandon, Manitoba R7A6N4. An American nursery featuring hardy flower seed in its free four-color catalog is Farmer Seed and Nursery Company, 818 Northwest 4th Street, Faribault, Minnesota 55021.

Growing "Mums"

Chrysanthemums bloom late and hold up very well as cut flowers, two reasons this big colorful flower is so popular in the home garden. This free illustrated booklet tells how to plant and care for them. Request "Growing Chrysanthemums in the Home Garden," publication number 74-83, from College of Agriculture and Natural Resources, University of Connecticut, Storrs, Connecticut 06268.

Chrysanthemum Catalog

An extensive selection of mums is depicted in this free annual 30-page color catalog, and it gives abundant planting information as well. Write Sunnyslope Gardens, 8638 Huntington Drive, San Gabriel, California 91788.

Extra Hardy Mums

Here is a free annual catalog offering over 100 varieties of extra hardy chrysanthemum plants. Write The Lehman Gardens, 420 Tenth Street S.W., Faribault, Minnesota 55012.

A City Garden Catalog

For a free annual catalog offering plants and products catering to the needs of the city gardener, write The City Gardens, 437 Third Avenue, New York, New York 10016.

English Clematis

This British nursery offers a large selection of clematis in its free catalog, including the largest clematis yet developed, the lavender variety William Kennett. Write Fisk's Clematis Nursery, Westleton, Saxmundham, Suffolk, England.

Daffodils from Ireland

And sure the unusual daffodils described in this free annual catalog from Ireland make it well worth the trouble of obtaining. Why, you'll write just for the pleasure of adding to your collection a name like the Ballydorn Bulb Farm, Killinchy, Newtownards, County Down, Northern Ireland.

Another Irish nursery specializing in daffodils, their catalog free and published once a year, is Cancairn Daffodils, Ltd., Broughshane, Ballymena, County Antrim, Northern Ireland.

Dahlia Catalogs

Dahlias of all kinds are depicted and described, along with planting directions, in these large free catalogs, which are published annually. Write S & K Gardens, 401 Quick Road, Castle Rock, Washington 98611, and Antonelli Brothers, 2545 Capitola Road, Santa Cruz, California 95060.

Daylilies with a Difference

If you believe the daylily looks the same as it did in your grandmother's time, coming only in one shade of orange, you'll be in for a surprise on opening this free once-a-year catalog. Write Amaryllis, Inc., P.O. Box 318, Baton Rouge, Louisiana 70821.

Ferns

For a free price list describing many hardy and exotic ferns, write Bolducs Greenhill Nursery, 2131 Vallejo Street, Saint Helena, California 94574.

Geraniums

Well over 400 varieties of geraniums are offered in this yearly catalog. Send 35¢ for postage and handling to Carobil Farms, Church Road, RD 1, Brunswick, Maine 04011.

> *Save your geraniums by lifting them out in the fall and shaking almost all of the soil from their roots. Hang them upside down in a cool place until May, when they should be cut back to about six inches and planted outside.*

Growing Gladioli

All you need to know to grow beautiful "glads" can be found in the illustrated booklet "Gladioli in the Home Garden," publication number IB-102, available for 30¢ from Distribution Center C, 7 Research Park, Cornell University, Ithaca, New York 14850.

Gladioli Catalog

This free annual catalog offers an extensive collection of gladiolus varieties, including past and present champions. Write Noweta Gardens, 900 Whitewater Avenue, Saint Charles, Minnesota 55972.

Worldwide Gladioli

A large selection of gladiolus varieties from around the world is featured in this free yearly catalog. Write Summerville's Gladiolus World Wide, RD1, Box 449, Glassboro, New Jersey 08028.

Wild Gladiolus

The little wild gladiolus is a rarity far different from the giant conventional gladiolus varieties available everywhere. This free British catalog specializes in the wild flower, featuring many varieties. Write

C. Newberry, Esq., Bulbs Green Nursery, Knebworth, Herts, England.

Growing Unusual Decorative Grasses

Over 40 ornamental grasses are covered in this unusual illustrated booklet, which not only describes the cultivation of these little-grown plants but shows how the grasses are used in dried flower arrangements. Send 30¢ for "Ornamental Grasses for the Home and Garden," publication number IB-64, New York Cooperative Extension Service, Mailing Room, Building 7, Research Park, Cornell University, Ithaca, New York 14850.

Groundcover Catalog

A large selection of groundcovers that can take the place of grass is listed in this descriptive annual price list. Send 25¢ for postage and handling to Prentis Court Groundcovers, P.O. Box 8662, Greenville, South Carolina 29604.

Hawaiian Plants

Native Hawaiian plants and novelties are featured in this free annual descriptive brochure. Write Hana Gardenland, Honokalani Farm, Box 177YP, Hani, Maui, Hawaii 96713.

Heathers

This free catalog from England offers many unusual and little-grown heathers. Write Maxwell & Beale Ltd., Broadstone, Dorset, England.

Hostas

Here's a free descriptive annual price list featuring many varieties of hosta, or plantain lily. Write Savoy's Greenhouses, 5300 Whiting Avenue, Edina, Minnesota 55435.

Three Iris Sources

An excellent selection of iris plants is the main attraction of the free annual 42-page catalog offered by Riverdale Iris Gardens, 7124 Riverdale Road, Minneapolis, Minnesota 55430.

A free annual 55-page catalog offering a large selection of iris plants from here and abroad can be ordered from Cooley's Garden, Silverton, Oregon 97381.

To obtain a free 72-page four-color catalog chock full of planting tips and featuring an outstanding iris collection, write Schreiner's Gardens, Inc., 3625 Quimaby Road, N.E., Salem, Oregon 97303.

Free Iris Perfume

Dried iris rhizomes tossed into a fire in the fireplace produce a delicate scent that permeates the whole house. They also are excellent to place in chests or closets where linen is stored. Simply take them up at a dividing time, cut the leaves off flush and scrub and pare them as you would a potato. When they become thoroughly dry, the perfume becomes evident and often lasts for years.

Ivies

For a free annual descriptive price list offering many rare ivy varieties write The Garden Spot, 4032 Rosewood Drive, Columbus, South Carolina 29205.

You can ensure better germination of morning glory seeds by scratching the seed coat with a knife and soaking the seeds in warm water for two days before planting.

New Flowers and Vegetables

Goldsmith Seeds is a research firm that develops and produces hybrid flower and vegetable seeds, which are eventually sold by major seed companies throughout the world. Though they do not sell retail or direct to growers, we have arranged to have them send free copies of their beautiful annual color catalog, featuring the latest new varieties, to the first 500 readers who request it. Write Goldsmith Seeds, Inc., P.O. Box 1349, Gilroy, California 95020.

A Pansy Catalog

To obtain this free catalog offering a large selection of pansies, from the traditional type to giant Swiss varieties, write Ward's Pansy Gardens, 6028 Houston Road, Macon, Georgia 31206.

Peonies Galore

For a free annual 20-page catalog devoted mainly to many varieties of peonies write Mission Gardens, Techny, Illinois 60082.

To get giant blooms on flowers like peonies and chrysanthemums, remove small side buds, leaving only the larger central buds.

Perennials

This free yearly catalog features a large selection of perennial plants for the garden, including many delphinium and chrysanthemum varieties. Write Bluestone Perennials, 7211 Middleridge Road, Madison, Ohio 44057.

Soft yarn is an excellent material for tying perennial plants. It won't bruise them.

Poison Plant Primers

Each year many children and adults are killed or become seriously ill eating poisonous plants. These three illustrated booklets familiarize the gardener with common poisonous plants that can cause a lot of trouble. Write for "Poisonous Plants in the Garden," publication number AXT-22, 25¢ from California Coop-Extension Service, Public Service, University Hall, University of California, Berkeley, California 94720; and "Common Poisonous Plants in Home and Grounds," publication number 466-A, 25¢ from Colorado Cooperative Extension Service, Bulletin Room, Colorado State University, Fort Collins, Colorado 80521.

The classic work in the field, "Common Poisonous Plants," publication number IB-104, by Professor John Kingsbury, costs $1 and is available from Distribution Center C, 7 Research Park, Cornell University, Ithaca, New York 14850.

Poison Ivy Protection

Here is a very useful, well-illustrated free booklet on how to identify, take precautions against and eradicate poison ivy and similar plants in the garden. Request "Poison Ivy, Poison Oak and Its Control" from West Virginia Department of Agriculture, Information Division, Charleston, West Virginia 25305.

Rock Gardens

To obtain this illustrated booklet explaining how to make a rock garden and care for it, send 25¢ for "The Rock Garden," publication number E-403, New York Cooperative Extension Service, Mailing Room, Building 7, Research Park, Cornell University, Ithaca, New York 14850.

Rock Garden Plants

This is a free annual 52-page catalog featuring plants for the rock garden, with much advice on how to care for them. Write Lamb Nurseries, 101 E. Sharp Avenue, Spokane, Washington 99202.

Silver Plants

In this unusual free British catalog are a great number of silver-colored plants, including a real rarity, the silver-leaved *Senecio cineraria maritima,* a variety of dusty miller that has been called "the most brilliant example of silver in nature." Write Ramparts Nurseries, Braiswick, Colchester, Essex, England.

Southern Flower Gardens

This free annual four-color catalog with several pages of planting tips, offers a large selection of flowers especially suited for southern gardens. Write H. G. Hastings, Company, P.O. Box 42-74, Atlanta, Georgia 30302.

Southeastern Flowers

Varieties of daylilies and other plants that do well in the southeast are the main attraction in this free annual catalog. Write Thomasville Nurseries, P.O. Box 7, 1842 Smith Avenue, Thomasville, Georgia 31792.

Tropical Seed

This free annual catalog features only seed for plants that will grow in tropical climates, including flowers and grasses. Write Kilgore Seed Company, 1400 West First Street, Sanford, Florida 32771.

Violets

Here is a free annual catalog offering a large selection of violets for the home garden. Write Capitola Violet Gardens, 3645 Gross Road, Santa Cruz, California 95060.

Unusual Plants

For a free yearly catalog listing odd flower, vegetable and tree seeds from around the world, write J. L. Hudson Seedsman, World Seed Service, Box 1058, Redwood City, California 94964.

A free descriptive price list published annually that features such rarities as Fo-ti-teng plants and Gotu-kola plants is available from Jack Gouverneur, Grand Avenue Road, Carthage, Missouri 64836.

Wild Animal Food Plants

There is no catalog quite like this annual publication, which offers a large selection of plants that can be grown to provide food and shelter for birds and other animals. Send $1 for postage and handling to Kester's Wild Game Food Nurseries, P.O. Box V, Omro, Wisconsin 54963.

Wildflower Folklore

This interesting catalog featuring wildflower seed is filled with tidbits about wildflower folklore, fact and culture. Send 25¢ for postage and handling to Midwest Wildflowers, P.O. Box 64B, Rockton, Illinois 61072.

New England Wildflowers

For a free four-color annual catalog featuring wildflowers, ferns and a good selection of perennials, write Putney Nursery, Inc., Putney, Vermont 05346.

North Carolina Wildflowers

Native wildflowers are the specialty of this plantsman, whose free catalog is published annually. Write Griffey's Nursery, Route 3, Box 27, Marshall, North Carolina 28753.

Colorado Wildflowers

This company specializes in herbs and teas as well as wildflower seeds, not to mention seeds for sprouting (an extremely nutritious food) and vegetables for containers. The yearly free catalog is from the Apple-wood Seed Company, 833 Parfet Street, Lakewood, Colorado 80215.

West Coast Wildflowers

Here is a free annual price list for west coast gardeners featuring only wildflower seed native to California. Write Theodore Payne Foundation for Wildflowers and Native Plants, Inc., 10459 Tuxedo Street, Sun Valley, California 91352.

Free Wildflowers

It costs nothing to plant more wildflowers in the area around you to beautify the country. Simply gather seed from any wildflowers in the area after the seeds turn black or dark green, let the seeds dry thoroughly and sow them.

Zinnias, marigolds and other flowers can make good insect repellents when planted next to vegetables; try a few combinations this year to see how effective they are in your garden.

Two Hundred Free Flower Catalogs

In addition to the many free flower catalogs considered unusual or valuable enough to rate a separate entry in these pages, here is a long list of some 200 additional free catalogs you might want to send for. These might be particularly useful because the nurserymen are in your vicinity, or because you want a large catalog collection, or simply because a nursery specializes in one of your favorite plants. A large collection of catalogs should be part of every gardener's library. Not only do they describe the newest varieties available and keep you up-to-date on the latest cultural methods for many species, collectively they also provide you with a color picture file of plants that would be hard, if not impossible, to match in any garden reference book. The better catalogs do not exaggerate a plant's blessings, which the gaudier ones do, but it doesn't take a Luther Burbank to distinguish between them.

ACKMAN'S DAHLIA GARDENS, 9114 Oakview, Plymouth, Michigan 48170

ARTHUR ARENIUS, 123 Western Drive, Longmeadow, Massachusetts 01106

ARMSTRONG ROSES, Box 473, Ontario, California 91761

ATHA GARDENS, West Liberty, Ohio 43357

AVALON MOUNTAIN GARDENS, Dana, North Carolina 28723

BARNES NURSERY, Box 250, McMinnville, Tennessee 37110

BARNHAVEN PRIMROSES, Far North Gardens, 15621 Auburndale Avenue, Livonia, Michigan 48154

BAY VIEW GARDENS, 1201 Bay Street, Santa Cruz, California 95060

BLACKBIRN'S OLINDA GARDENS, Route 4, Box 329 C, Rocky Mount, North Carolina 27801

BRAND PEONY FARMS, Faribault, Minnesota 55021

BROWN'S IRIS GARDEN, 12624 84th Ave. N.E., Kirkland, Washington 89033

BURGE'S IRIS GARDEN, 1414 Amhurst, Denton, Texas 76201

BUSHEY'S GARDENS, 6731 Akrich St., Redding, California 96001

CANADA BULB & PLANT BREEDERS, Box 346, Kelowna, B.C., Canada

CAROBIL FARMS, Church Road, RD1, Brunswick, Maine 04011

CARROLL GARDENS, P.O. Box 310, Westminster, Maryland 21157

CHAMPLAIN VIEW GARDENS, Div. of P. DeJager, South Hamilton, Massachusetts 01982

CHARJOY GARDENS, P.O. Box 511, 117 Acacia Drive, Lafayette, Louisiana 70501

FRANK CHILDS NURSERY, Jenkinsburg, Georgia 30234

CLARKE NURSERY, Long Beach, Washington 98631

COBLE'S NUT TREE NURSERY, Box 171, Route 1, Aspers, Pennsylvania 17304

COMERFORD'S, P.O. Box 534, Augusta, Arkansas 72006

COUNTRY GARDEN ROSES, 555 Irwin Lane, Santa Rosa, California 95401

CRANGUYMA FARMS, Long Beach, Washington 98631

CROOKED CREEK GARDENS, Star Route, Marquand, Missouri 63655

RYLAND CROSHAR, Columbus, New Jersey 08022

DAHLIADEL IN THE MOUNTAINS, Box 990, Waynesville, North Carolina 28786

DARST BULB FARMS, Box 81, Mount Vernon, Washington 98273

DAVIDSON GARDENS, 1215 Church Street, Decatur, Georgia 30030
DAVIS CACTUS GARDEN, 1522 Jefferson Street, Kerrville, Texas 78028
BILL DODD NURSERIES, P.O. Box 235, Semmes, Alabama 36575
DOOLEY GARDENS, Route 1, Hutchinson, Minnesota 55350
DOUGLAS DAHLIAS, Myrtle Creek, Oregon 97457
DUTCH MOUNTAIN NURSERY, Augusta, Michigan 49012
EDDIE'S NURSERIES, 4100 S.W. Marine Drive, Vancouver 13, B.C., Canada
FRED EDMUNDS, Box 68, Wilsonville, Oregon 97970
ELLESMERE ROSES, Brooklin, Ontario, Canada
ENGLERTH GARDENS, Route 2, Hopkins, Michigan 49328
MURRAY W. EVANS, Route 1, Box 525, Corbett, Oregon 97019
FLEUR DE LIS, Chet Tompkins, P.O. Box 670, Canby, Oregon 97013
FLOWERLAND, 816 English Street, Racine, Wisconsin 53402
J. HOWARD FRENCH, Box 37, Lima, Pennsylvania 19060
N. FREUDENBURG IRIS GARDENS, 310 East Maple Street, Norfolk, Nebraska 68701
GABLE IRIS GARDENS, 2543 38th Avenue S., Minneapolis, Minnesota 55406
GABLE'S NURSERY, Haralson, Georgia 30229
THE GARDEN PLACE, 6780 Heisley Road, Mentor, Ohio 44060
THE GARDEN SPOT, 4032 Rosewood Drive, Columbia, South Carolina 29205
GARDENS OF THE BLUE RIDGE, Ashford, McDowell County, North Carolina 28603
GOODWILL GARDEN, Route 1, Scarborough, Maine 04074
GOSSLER FARMS NURSERY, 1200 Weaver Road, Springfield, Oregon 97477
GREER GARDENS, 1280 Goodpasture Island Road, Eugene, Oregon 97401
GRIGSBY CACTUS GARDENS, 2354 Bella Vista, Vista, California 92083
GRUBER'S GLAD GARDEN, 2910 West Locust Street, Davenport, Iowa 52804
HHH HORTICULTURAL, 68 Brooktree Road, Hightstown, New Jersey 08520
THE HANCOCK GARDENS, 210 2nd Avenue S.W., Box 52, Steele, North Dakota 58482
HARDY'S NURSERY, Mount Olive, Alabama 35117
HATFIELD GARDENS, Route 1, Stoutsville, Ohio 43154
A. H. HAZZARD, 510 Grand Prix Avenue, Kalamazoo, Michigan 49007
HEART'S-EASE FARM, Ed Howell, Califon, New Jersey 07830

THE HEATHS' DAFFODIL MART, Gloucester, Virginia 23061

THOMAS HENNY NURSERY, 7811 Stratford Drive, N.E., Brooks, Oregon 97305

HILDENBRANDT'S IRIS GARDEN, Star Route, Box 4, Lexington, Nebraska 68850

THE HOUSE OF SPIC AND SPAN, P.O. Box 63, Newfield, New Jersey 08344

HOWELL GARDENS, 2587 Letitia Street, Baton Rouge, Louisiana 70808

HUFF'S GARDENS, Box 241, Burlington, Kansas 66839

HUGHES GARDEN, Highway 287, Route 1, Box 127-C, Mansfield, Texas 76063

IRON GATE GARDENS, Route 3, Box 101, Kings Mountain, North Carolina 28086

JOSEPH J. KERN ROSE NURSERY, Box 33, Mentor, Ohio 44060

KING'S MUMS, 3723 East Castro Valley Boulevard, Hayward, California 94546

CHARLES KLEHM & SON, 2 E. Algonquin Road, Arlington Heights, Illinois 60005

EDGAR L. KLINE, 17495 S.W. Bryant Road, Lake Grove, Oregon 97034

KRIDER NURSERIES, INC., Middlebury, Indiana 46540

LABARS' RHODODENDRON NURSERY, Stroudsburg, Pennsylvania 18360

CONRAD LAGERQUIST, Skeens Lane, Toronto 14, Canada

LAKE ANGELUS GARDENS, 270 Waddington Road, Birmingham, Michigan 48009

LAMB NURSERIES, 101 E. Sharp Avenue, Spokane, Washington 99202

EDNA LANKART, Route 4, Cherokee Trail, Tyler, Texas 75701

H. L. LARSON, 3656 Bridgeport Way, Tacoma, Washington 98466

LAURIE'S GARDEN, 17225 McKenzie Highway, Route 2, Springfield, Oregon 97477

LEGG DAHLIA GARDENS, RD 2, Hastings Road, Geneva, New York 14456

LENINGTON GARDENS, 7007 Manchester Avenue, Kansas City, Missouri 64133

LESLIE'S WILDFLOWER NURSERY, 30 Summer Street, Methuen, Massachusetts 01844

LETHARMAN'S, 1203 East Tuscaranas, Canton, Ohio 44701

LIENAU PEONY GARDENS, 9135 Beech Daly Road, Detroit, Michigan 48239

THE LINN COUNTRY NURSERIES, Center Point, Iowa 52213

LOUISIANA NURSERY, Route 1, Box 43, Opelousas, Louisiana 70570

MATHEWS IRIS GARDENS, 201 Sunny Drive, College Place, Washington 99324

MAXWELL'S GARDEN, Route 1, Box 155, Olla, Louisiana 71465

McCORMICK LILIES, P.O. Box 700, Canby, Oregon 97013

GEORGE MELK & SONS, Plainfield, Wisconsin 54966

JAMES F. MILES, Box 1041, Clemson, South Carolina 29631

E. RAY MILLER'S DAHLIA GARDENS, 167 North East 12th Avenue, Hillsboro, Oregon 97123

THE MINIATURE PLANT KINGDOM, 4488 Stoetz Lane, Sebastopol, California 95472

MINKS GARDENS, 114 The Gairway, Albert Leam, Minnesota 56007

MISSION GARDENS, Techny, Illinois 60082

GRANT E. MITSCH, Daffodil Haven, Canby, Oregon 97013

MRS. RUTH MOONEY, Hi-Mountain Farm, Route 1, Box 24, Seligman, Missouri 65745

WALTER K. MORSS & SON, RFD 3, Bradford, Massachusetts 01830

MOUNT-CLARE IRIS GARDENS, 3036 N. Narragansett Avenue, Chicago, Illinois 60634

MOUNTAIN VIEW NURSERY, Route 5, Box 231, Arlington, Washington 98223

CHARLES H. MUELLER, River Road, New Hope, Pennsylvania 18938

OAKHILL GARDENS, Route 3, Box 87, Dallas, Oregon 97338

PALETTE GARDENS, 26 W. Zion Hill Road, Quakertown, Pennsylvania 18951

PARRY NURSERIES, Signal Mountain, Tennessee 37377

PEEKSKILL NURSERIES, Shrub Oak, New York 10588

PELLETT GARDENS, Atlantic, Iowa 50022

PENNYPACK NURSERY, Cheltenham, Pennsylvania 19012

PERRY'S HARDY PLANT FARM, Enfield, Middlesex, England

PIKE'S PEAK NURSERIES, Box 670, Indiana, Pennsylvania 15701

PILLEY'S GARDENS, Valley Center, California 92082

PINE HILLS HERB FARM, Box 307, Roswell, Georgia 30075

PLEASANT VALLEY GLADS, 163 Senator Avenue, Agawam, Massachusetts 01001

PRIMROSE ACRES, 14015 84th Avenue, N.E., Bothell, Washington 98011

RAINIER MT. ALPINE GARDENS, 2007 South 126th, Seattle, Washington 98168

DAVID L. REATH, Box 251, Vulcan, Michigan 49892

RIVERBANK GARDENS, 2931 Tyburn Street, Los Angeles, California 90039
RIVERDALE IRIS GARDENS, 7124 Riverdale Road, Minneapolis, Minnesota 55430
ROAD RUNNER RANCH, 2458 Catalina Avenue, Vista, California 92083
MARGE & EARL ROBERTS, 5809 Rahke Road, Indianapolis, Indiana 46217
ROBINSON NURSERY, 56 North Georgia Avenue, Mobile, Alabama 36604
ROCKY RIVER DAHLIA GARDENS, 13089 E. River Road, Columbia Station, Ohio 44028
RUSCHMOHR DAHLIA GARDENS, Box 236, Rockville Center, New York 11571
SAVAGE FARMS NURSERY, Box 125, McMinnville, Tennessee 37110
SAVORY'S GREENHOUSES, 5300 Whiting Avenue, Edina, Minnesota 55435
SCHOONOVER GARDENS, 404 South Fifth Street, P.O. Box 7, Humboldt, Kansas 66748
SEQUOIA NURSERY, Moore Miniature Roses, Visalia, California 93277
SHERIDAN NURSERIES, 100 Sherway Drive, Etobicoke, Ontario, Canada
SHOP IN THE SIERRA, Box 1, Midpines, California 95345
SILVER FALLS NURSERY, Star Route, Box 55, Silverton, Oregon 97381
C. G. SIMON NURSERY, INC., Box 2873, Lafayette, Louisiana 70501
FRANCIS M. SINCLAIR, RFD 1, Newmarket Road, Exeter, New Hampshire 03833
SKY HOOK FARM, Johnson, Vermont 05656
SOUTHERN MEADOWS GARDEN, Box 230, Centralia, Illinois 62801
SPAFFORD GREENHOUSES, 1721 Pallister Avenue, Barker, New York 14012
SPRING HILL FARM, Box 42, Gig Harbor, Washington 98335
STARMONT DAYLILIES, 16415 Shady Grove Road, Gaithersburg, Maryland 20760
RAYMOND F. STEIDL, RR 1, Paris, Illinois 61944
STRIBLING'S NURSERIES, INC., 1620 W. 16th St., P.O. Box 793, Merced, California 95340
SUMMERLONG IRIS GARDENS, R.D. 2, Box 163, Perrysville, Ohio 44864
ALEX J. SUMMERS, 141 U. Willets Road West, Roslyn, New York 11576
SUNNYSLOPE GARDENS, 8638 Huntington Drive, San Gabriel, California 91778
SUTER NURSERY, 3220 Silverado Trail North, St. Helena, California 94574
SYLVAN NURSERY, 1028 Horseneck Road, S. Westport, Massachusetts 02790
TALBOTT NURSERY, Rte. 3, Linton, Indiana 47441

TANNER'S GARDEN, P.O. Box 385, Cheneyville, Louisiana 71325

P.O. TATE NURSERY, Route 3, Tyler, Texas 75701

TAYLOR'S GARDEN, 2649 Stingle Avenue, Rosemead, California 91770

THOMASVILLE NURSERIES, INC., Box 7, Thomasville, Georgia 31792

THE THREE LAURELS, Marshall, Madison County, North Carolina 28753

TINGLE NURSERY, Pittsville, Maryland 21850

TOP O' THE RIDGE, 100 N.E. 81st Street, Kansas City, Missouri 64118

TRANQUIL LAKE NURSERY, River Street, Rehoboth, Massachusetts 02769

WILLIAM TRICKER, INC., 74 Allendale Avenue, Saddle River, New Jersey 07458

MRS. C. W. VALLETTE, Declo, Idaho 83323

VANS PINES, INC., West Olive, Michigan 49460

D. STEVE VARNER, N. State Road, Monticello, Illinois 61856

VICK'S WILDGARDENS, INC., Box 115, Gladwyne, Pennsylvania 19035

VISTA VIOLET FARM, 1211 Monte Vista Drive, Vista, California 92083

GERALD D. WALTZ, Box 977, Salem, Virginia 24153

WAYNESBORO NURSERIES, Waynesboro, Vermont 22980

WESTERN MAINE FOREST NURSERY, Fryeburg, Maine 04037

WHEELER'S DAYLILY FARM, 10024 Shady Lane, Houston, Texas 77016

WHISPERWOOD GARDENS, P.O. Box 357, Canton, Texas 75103

WHITE DAHLIA GARDENS, 2480 S. E. Creighton Avenue, Milwaukee, Oregon 97222

MRS. J. A. WITT, 16516 25th N.E., Seattle, Washington 98155

WOODLAND ACRES NURSERY, Crivitz, Wisconsin 54114

ZOLLING RHODODENDRON NURSERY, 6750 S. W. Oleson Boulevard, Portland, Oregon 97223

125 Bargain Garden Catalogs

The following 125 garden catalogs are not free but a bargain at the price, which ranges in these cases from 10¢ to $6. The lower-priced catalogs are sometimes, but not usually, descriptive price lists of the farms' offerings. The higher-priced ones (especially White Flower Farm, Jones & Scully, and Logee's Greenhouses) have been much praised for their many beautiful color photos, as well as for their excellent plant descriptions and cultivation information. All are worth far more than their cost:

ABBEY GARDEN, 176 Toro Canyon Road, Carpinteria, California 93013 $1

ABC HERB NURSERY, Route 1, Lecoma, Missouri 65540   25¢

ABUNDANT LIFE SEED FOUNDATION, P.O. Box 374, Gardiner, Washington 98334 $1

ACRES OF ORCHIDS, 1450 El Camino Real, South San Francisco, California 94080   25¢

ALBERTS & MERKEL BROS., INC., 2210 South Federal Highway, Boynton Beach, Florida 33435 $1.50

ARTHUR EAMES ALLGROVE, 281 Woburn Street, Wilmington, Massachusetts 01887 $1

ALPENGLOW GARDENS, 13328 King George Highway, Surrey, British Columbia V3T2T6, Canada $1

ALPINE GARDENS, 280 Southeast Fir-Villa Road, Dallas, Oregon 97338 25¢

ALTMAN SPECIALTY PLANTS, 26963 Sea Vista Drive, Malibu, California 90265 $1

BALDSIEFEN NURSERY, P.O. Box 88, Bellvale, New York 10912 $2.50

BEGONIA PARADISE GARDENS, 9471 Dana Road, Cutler Ridge, Florida 33157   50¢

BLACKTHORNE GARDENS, 48 Quincy Street, Holbrook, Massachusetts 02343 $2

BROADLEIGH GARDENS, Barr House, Bishop's Hull, Taunton, Somerset VKTA41AE, England $1

JOHN BRUDY'S RARE PLANT HOUSE, Box 1348, Cocoa Beach, Florida 32931 $1

BUELL'S GREENHOUSES, INC., P.O. Box 218GCO, Weeks Road, Eastford, Connecticut 06242   25¢

CASA YERBA, Star Route 2, Box 21, Days Creek, Oregon 97429 $1

CATNIP ACRES FARM, P.O. Box 142-FA, Seymour, Connecticut 06483 $1

CONLEY'S GARDEN CENTER, 145 Townsend Avenue, Boothbay Harbor, Maine 04538   35¢

COUNTRY HILLS GREENHOUSE, Route 1, Corning, Ohio 43730 $1.50

C. A. CRUICKSHANK, LTD., 1015 Mount Pleasant Road, Toronto, Ontario M4P 2M1, Canada $1

THE CUMMINS GARDEN, 22 Robertsville Road, Marlboro, New Jersey 07746   50¢

DAFFODIL MART, Box 208FA, Route 3, Gloucester, Virginia 23061 $1

DESERT DAN'S CACTUS, Summer Avenue, Minotola, New Jersey 08341 $1

DESERT PLANT CO., P.O. Box 880, Marfa, Texas 79843   50¢

DESROCHES' PERENNIALS, 16 Albert Street, Adams, Maine 01220   25¢

EDEN ROAD IRIS GARDEN, P.O. Box 117, Wenatchee, Washington 98801   50¢

EDGEWATER CALADIUMS, 2144 Northeast Lakeview Drive, Sebring, Florida 33870   25¢

EXOTICA SEED CO., 1742 Laurel Canyon Boulevard, Los Angeles, California 90046 $1

FAR NORTH GARDENS, 15621YP Auburndale Avenue, Livonia, Michigan 48154 $1

FERNWOOD PLANTS, P.O. Box 268, Topanga, California 90290   50¢

FISCHER GREENHOUSES, Oak Avenue, Linwood, New Jersey 08221   50¢

JIM FOBEL, 598-Y Kipuka Place, Kailua, Hawaii 96734 $1

FOX ORCHIDS, 6615 West Markham, Little Rock, Arkansas 72205   30¢

FUKU-BONSAI, Box 178, Homestead Road, Kurtistown, Hawaii 96760   50¢

GLADSIDE GARDENS, 61 Main Street, Northfield, Massachusetts 01360   50¢

GLECKLERS SEEDMEN, Metamora, Ohio 43540 $1

LINDA GOODMAN'S SUN PLANTS, P.O. Box 20014A, Riverside, California 92516   75¢

GOSSLER FARMS NURSERY, 1200 Weaver Road, Springfield, Oregon 97477   50¢

GREAT PLAINS CACTUS CO., Box 218, Calhan, Colorado 80808   25¢

THE GREEN HOUSE, 9515 Flower Street, Bellflower, California 90706   25¢

GREER GARDENS, 1280 Goodpasture Island Road, Eugene, Oregon 97401 $1.50

GRIFFEY'S NURSERY, Route 3, Box 27, Marshall, North Carolina 28753

GRIGSBY CACTUS GARDENS, 2354 Bella Vista Drive, Vista, California 92083 $1

BEN HAINES CO., Box 1111, Lawrence, Kansas 66044 $1.10

ROBERT B. HAMM, 2951 Elliott Street, Wichita Falls, Texas 76308 $1

J. N. HANCOCK AND CO., Jackson't Hill Road, Menzies Creek, Victoria 3159 Australia   40¢

HARBORCREST NURSERIES, 4634 West Saanich Road, Victoria, B.C. V8Z 3G8, Canada   50¢

HARDY AND FOUQUETTE ORCHIDS, 9443 East Heany Circle, Santee, California 92071   25¢

HEATHERBLOOM FARM, Route 1, Box 230A, Lakeville, Connecticut 06039 $1

HEAVENLY VIOLETS, 9 Turny Place, Trumbull, Connecticut 06611   25¢

HEMLOCK HILL HERB FARM, Hemlock Hill Road, Litchfield, Connecticut 06759   50¢

HERB SHIP, Box 362Y, Fairfield, Connecticut 06430   50¢

HICKORY HOLLOW, Route 1, Box 52, Peterstown, West Virginia 23963 25¢

HILLTOP HERB FARM, P.O. Box 1734, Cleveland, Texas 77327 $2

HOWE HILL HERBS, Camden, Maine 04843   50¢

INTERNATIONAL GROWERS EXCHANGE, Box 397, Farmington, Michigan 48024 $2

JACK'S CACTUS GARDEN, 1707 West Robindale Sreet, West Covina, California 91790   25¢

JAMIESON VALLEY GARDENS, Box 646, Route 3, Spokane, Washington 99203 $1

JONES & SCULLY, INC., 220 Northwest 33rd Avenue, Miami, Florida 33142 $4

K & L CACTUS NURSERY, 12712 Stockton Boulevard, Galt, California 95632 $1

KARTUZ GREENHOUSES, 1408 Sunset Drive, Vista, California 92083 $1

KING'S CHRYSANTHEMUMS, 3723 East Castro Valley Boulevard, Castro Valley, California 94546 $1

KIRKPATRICK'S, 27785 De Anza Street, Barstow, California 92311   35¢

LAURAY OF SALISBURY, Under Mountain Road, Salisbury, Connecticut 06068   85¢

LOEHMAN'S CACTUS PATCH, 8014 Howe Street, Box 871, Paramount, California 90723   50¢

LOGEE'S GREENHOUSES, 55 North Street, Danielson, Connecticut 06239 $2

LOYCE'S FLOWERS, Route 2, Box 11, Granbury, Texas 76048   50¢

ANN MANN'S ORCHIDS, Box 202, Route 3, Orlando, Florida 32811 $1

MAPLE HILL HERB FARM, Route 1, Anna, Illinois 62906   50¢

MEADOWBROOK HERBS AND THINGS, Whispering Pines, Rhode Island 02898   50¢

MELROSE GARDENS, 309 Best Road South, Stockton, California 95205 $1

MINIATURE PLANT KINGDOM, 4125 Harrison Grade Road, Sebastopol, California 95472 $1

MINI-ROSES, P.O. Box 873, Gueloh, Ontario N1H 6M6, Canada   25¢

MOBILE GARDENS, Salisbury Turnpike, RR1, Box 250, Rhinebeck, New York 12572 75¢

PAT MORRISON/JEFF HEFFNER, 5305 Southwest Hamilton Street, Portland, Oregon 97221 35¢

MOUNTAIN SEED AND NURSERY, Route 1, Box 271, Moscow, Idaho 83843 25¢

NATURE'S GARDEN NURSERY, Route 1, Box 488, Beaverton, Oregon 97007 50¢

NEW ENGLAND ROOTSTOCK ASSOCIATION, Christian Hill, Great Barrington, Maine 01230 $1

ORCHID GARDENS, 6700 Splithand Road, Grand Rapids, Minnesota 55744 50¢

ORCHIDS BY HAUSERMANN, INC., P.O. Box 363, Elmhurst, Illinois 60126 $1.25

ORINDA NURSERY, Box 217, Bridgeville, Detroit, Michigan 19933 50¢

PALETTE GARDENS, 26 West Zion Hill Road, Quakertown, Pennsylvania 18951 50¢

PETER PAULS NURSERIES, Canandaigua, New York 14424 25¢

PIXIE TREASURES MINIATURE ROSES, 4121 Prospect Avenue, Yorba Linda, California 92686 50¢

THE PLANT ROOM, 6373 Trafalgar Road, Hornby, Ontario LOP 1EO, Canada $1

THE PLANT SHOP'S BOTANICAL GARDENS, 18007 Topham Street, Reseda, California 91335 $1

RAINBOW FOREST, Box 1047, Fremont, California 94538 25¢

RAINMAN SUCCULENT NURSERY, 20101 Hanson Road, Fort Bragg, California 95437 25¢

RAKESTRAW'S PERENNIAL GARDENS, 3094 South Term Street, Burton, Michigan 48529 50¢

REDWOOD CITY SEED CO., P.O. Box 361, Redwood City, California 94064 50¢

REX BULB FARM, Box 774, 2468 Washington, Port Townsend, Washington 98368 10¢

OTTO RICHTER AND SONS, LTD., Box 26, Goodwood, Ontario LOC 1AO, Canada 75¢

CLYDE ROBIN SEED CO., Box 2855, Castro Valley, California 94546 $1

THE ROCK GARDEN, RFD 2, Litchfield, Maine 04350 50¢

THE ROSEMARY HOUSE, 120 South Market Street, Mechanicsburg, Pennsylvania 17055 50¢

ROSEWAY NURSERIES, INC., 8766 Northeast Sandy Boulevard, Portland, Oregon 97220 $1

ROUTH'S GREENHOUSES, Route 1, Highway 65, Louisburg, Missouri 65685   25¢

RUTLAND OF KENTUCKY, Route 1, Box 17, Maysville, Kentucky 41056 $2

SCOTTS VALLEY CACTUS, 5311 Scotts Valley Drive, P.O. Box 66302, Scotts Valley, California 95066   50¢

SEABORN DEL DIOS NURSERY, Route 3, Box 455, Escondido, California 92025 $1

S & G EXOTIC PLANT CO., 22 Goldsmith Avenue, Beverly, Massachusetts 01915 $1

SHADY HILL GARDENS, 791 Walnut Street, Batavia, Illinois 60510   50¢

SHAFFER'S TROPICAL GARDENS, 1220 41st Avenue, Capitola, California 95010 $1

SINGER'S GROWING THINGS, 17806 Plummer Street, Northridge, California 91325 $1

SLOCUM WATER GARDENS, 1101 Cypress Gardens Road, Winter Haven, Florida 33880 $1

LOUIS SMIRNOW AND SONS, 85 Linden Lane, Brookville, New York 11545 $1

SOUTHMEADOW FRUIT GARDENS, 2363 Tilbury Place, Birmingham, Michigan 48009 $6

JOEL W. SPINGARN, 1535 Forest Avenue, Baldwin, New York 11510 $1

ED STORMS, INC., P.O. Box 775, Azle, Texas 76020 $1

SUNNYBROOK FARMS NURSERY, 9448 Mayfield Road, Chesterland, Ohio 44026 $1

SUNRISE PLANTS, Box 481, Robbingsville, New Jersey 08691   25¢

MILLIE THOMPSON, Drawer PP, 310 Hill Street, Southampton, New York 11968 $1

TINARI GREENHOUSES, 2325 Valley Road, Box 190, Huntingdon Valley, Pennsylvania 19006   25¢

TROPIFLORA, 5439 Third Street, East Bradenton, Florida 33507   50¢

VAN NESS WATER GARDENS, 2460 North Euclid Avenue, Upland, California 91786 $1

MARY MATTISON VAN SCHAIL, Box 181, Route 1, Cavendish, Vermont 05142   50¢

VAN TUBERGEN, Willowbank Wharf, Ranelagh Gardens, London SW6 3JY, England   50¢

JOHN H. VAN ZONNEVELD CO., Box 454, 810 Cassel Road, Collegeville, Pennsylvania 19426 50¢

VOLKMANN BROTHERS GREENHOUSE, 2714 Minert Street, Dallas, Texas 75219 20¢

WALTHER'S EXOTIC HOUSE PLANTS, RFD 3, Box 30-OF, Catskill, New York 12414 $1

WASHINGTON EVERGREEN NURSERY, Box 125, South Salem, New York 10590 $1

WAYSIDE GARDENS, Hodges, South Carolina 29695 $1

WELL-SWEEP HERB FARM, 317 Mount Bethel Road, Port Murray, New Jersey 07865 35¢

WESTERN ARBORETUM, Box 2827, Pasadena, California 91105 $1

WHITE FLOWER FARM, Litchfield, Connecticut 06759 $5

THE WILD GARDEN, Box 487, Bothell, Washington 98011 $1.50

GILBERT H. WILD AND SON, INC., Box 338, Sarcoxie, Missouri 64862 $1

WIMBERLYWAY GARDENS, 7024 Northwest 18th Avenue, Gainesville, Florida 32605 25¢

WONDERLY'S EXOTICA, 531 Knott Street, Bakersfield, California 93305 $1

WOOD'S AFRICAN VIOLETS, Proton Station, Ontario, NOC 1LO, Canada 30¢

WOODSTREAM NURSERY, Box 510K, Jackson, New Jersey 08527 15¢

DICK AND RUTH WRIGHT, Route 6, Box 21, Deluz Road, Fallbrook, California 92028 50¢

YANKEE PEDDLER HERB FARM, Dept. Y, Highway 36, North Brenham, Texas 77833 $1

ZEPHYR GARDENS, 9138 San Pedro Avenue, San Antonio, Texas 78212 25¢

Free Catalogs from Afar

You may make some exciting plant discoveries in these free catalogs from these great nurseries little-known in the United States, and they'll certainly enhance your catalog collection:

Argentina
J. A. DIHARCE & CO., Buenos Aires

Australia

Norgates' Plant Farm, Trentham, Victoria 3458
Pacific Seeds, Biloela, Queensland
Thomson Mount View Nursery, Summertown, South Australia 5141

Denmark

A. L. Andersen, Planteskole, Nyborgvej 284, 5700 Svendborg
Th. Buhl, Planteskole, Harridslev, 8900 Randers
H. Christensen, Virum Staudegartneri, Bakkevej 43, 2830 Virum
Norgaards Stauder, Hovedvej 10, Lilballe, 6000 Kolding
J. E. Ohlsens Enke, Dk 2630, Tasstrup
Paul V. Petersen, "Bakkely," Vasby, 2640 Hedehusene
Ole Vergmann, Planteskole, Skovvangsvej Sosum, 3670 Vekso

East Africa

Pop Vriend, Ltd., Arusha, Tanzania

Finland

Keskusosuusliiki Hankkila, Helsinki

France

Croux et Fils, Le Val d'Aulnay, 92290 Chatenay-Malabry
Francois Delaunay, 100 Route des Ponts-de-Ce., 49000 Angers
Tezier Freres, 471 Avenue Victor Hugo, BP 223, Valence-sur-Rhone

Germany

Georg Arends, Staudenkulturen, 56 Wuppertal-21, Ronsdorf
H. Hagemann, Staudenkulturen, 2001 Krahenwinkel, bei Hannover
Kayser & Seibert, Odenwalder Pflanzenkulturen, 6101 Rossdorf, bei
    Darmstadt
L. C. Nungesser, 61 Darmstadt

Holland

Abbing Blookwerkerij, Zeist
Enkhauser Zaadhandel, C. Weishit, The Hague, Holland Royal Sluis,
    Box 22, Engnuizen
Koninklijke Bloembollen en Zaadhandel, van Tubergen BV, Koning
    innewee 86, Haarlem

India
NAMDEO UMAJII & CO., Bombay

Japan
FUJII & SONS, LTD., Osaka

Mexico
GORDON ROSS, Chiapas, Tapachula

New Zealand
PETER B. DOW & CO., Box 696, Gisborne
DUNCAN & DAVIES, Christchurch
HARRISON & CO., LTD., P.O. Box 1, Palmerston
D. J. LIDDLE, LTD., Ngarara Road, Waikanae
F. M. WINSTONE, LTD., Remuera 5, Auckland

Pakistan
SHERIFF FARMS, Karachi, West Pakistan

South Africa
STRAATHOF'S SEED CO., Johannesburg

Spain
SEMILLAS PACIFICO, Sevilla

Sweden
GENERAL SWEDISH SEED CO., Svalov

Switzerland
HAUBENSAK-SCHOLLENBRECKER SEEDS, LTD., Bottmingen

United Kingdom
BLACKMORE & LANGDON, The Nurseries, Bath, Somerset, England
WALTER BLOM & SON, LTD., Leavesden, Watford, Herts, England
BLOOM'S NURSERIES, LTD., Bressingham, Diss, Norfolk, England
T. CARLILE, Loddon Nurseries, Twyford, Berkshire, England
BETH CHATTO, Whitebarn Farm, Elmstead Market, Colchester, Essex,
   England

DAISY HILL NURSERIES, Newry, County Down, Northern Ireland

GREAT DIXTER NURSERIES, Northam, Sussex, England

HILLIER & SONS, West Hill Nurseries, Winchester, Hampshire, England

C. G. HOLLETT, Greenbank Nurseries, Sedburgh, Cumbria, England

TH. W. E. INGWERSEN, LTD., Birch Farm Nursery, Gravetye, East Grinstead, Sussex, England

GEORGE JACKMAN, LTD., Woking Nurseries, Woking, Surrey, England

REGINALD KAYE, LTD., Waithman Nurseries, Silverdale, Carnforth, Lancastershire, England

KELWAY & SON, LTD., Langport, Somerset, England

MRS. M. LAWLEY, 2 Dovecote, Wallington, Cambo, Morpeth, Northumberland, England

SIDNEY LINNEGAN, 5 New Road, Ruscombe, Twyford, Reading, Berkshire, England

NOTCUTT, LTD., The Nurseries, Woodbridge, Suffolk, England

OLD COURT NURSERIES, LTD., Colwall, Malvern, Worcestershire, England

ORPINGTON NURSERIES, CO., LTD., Rocky Lane, Gatton Park, Surrey, England

PERRY'S HARDY PLANT FARM, Enfield, Middlesex, England

THE PLANTSMEN, BUCKSHAW GARDENS, Holwell, Sherborne, Dorset, England

J. R. PONTON, Kirknewton, Midlothian, Scotland

ROBINSON'S HARDY PLANTS, Greencourt Nurseries, Crockenhill, Swanley, Kent, England

L. R. RUSSELL, LTD., Richmond Nurseries, Merriott, Somerset, England

SOUTH DOWN NURSERIES, Southgate Street, Redruth, Cornwall, England

SUNNINGDALE NURSERIES, LTD., Windlesham, Surrey, England

SUTTON SEEDS, LTD., London Road, Earley Reading, Berkshire, England RG6 1AB

THOMPSON & MORGAN, LTD., Ipswich, Suffolk, England

TOYNEBEE'S NURSERIES, LTD., Barnham, Sussex, England

TRESEDER'S NURSERIES, LTD., Truro, Cornwall, England

MRS. DESMOND UNDERWOOD, Ramparts Nursery, Colchester, Essex, England

WALLACE & BARR, LTD., Marden, Kent, England

WILLIAMSON WYEVALE NURSERIES, King's Acre, Hereford, England

Free Plant Detectives

There are several ways to track down the source of a rare plant or seeds that you can't find listed in any of the many garden catalogs previously listed. *The Plant Buyer's Guide,* published by the Massachusetts Horticultural Society, is a good source, and can be consulted free in most large libraries. You can also consult the most comprehensive collection of garden catalogs in the world, which is fully indexed, by writing the L. H. Bailey Hortorium, Cornell University, Ithaca, New York 14850, for details. Several organizations charge a fee to find rare plant sources. Among the least expensive is Plantsearch, 1328 Motor Circle, Dallas, Texas, 75207, which will supply the source for any plant for a fee of $1 per item and refunds your money if they can't locate the plant you desire.

Experts at the National Arboretum will *identify* any plant for you if you can't obtain help locally. Try to include flowers and/or fruit as well as foliage, dry the plant first and mail between cardboards with a letter or label telling all you know about the plant, its habitat, growing conditions, and so on. Mail to Herbarium, U.S. National Arboretum, Washington, D.C. 20250.

4

Lawn and Landscaping Lagniappes

Getting Down to Grass Tacks

This illustrated lawn care primer provides all the information needed to make a poor lawn a good one, from watering to fertilizing and mowing tips. Send 50¢ for "Lawn Problems," publication number 81-6, College of Agriculture and Natural Resources, University of Connecticut, Storrs, Connecticut 06268.

Contrary to popular belief, the best time to plant grass seed is from August 15 to September 20—not in autumn—in most areas. Later planting results in a loss of new grass.

A Free Two-Year Magazine Subscription

Lawn Care, a little magazine for homeowners who tend their own lawns, will give you a free two-year subscription upon request. Write Scott's Lawn Care Subscription, Marysville, Ohio 43041.

Save by Seeding on Time

A good time to reseed a patchy lawn is toward the end of winter when the snow is melting. The seed will sink into the ground and germinate when the temperature is right. Keep a dry mixture of half topsoil and half seed on hand for reseeding lawns; level bare spots with the turf and fill with the mixture.

Buying Lawn Seed

Shady lawns require different grass seed than lawns in the sun and there are many grass seeds suited for other special conditions. This helpful free pamphlet discusses all the varieties available and tells you how to read the labels on grass seed boxes so that you know what you're buying. Send 55¢ for "Lawn Seeds," publication number 70-79, College of Agriculture and Natural Resources, University of Connecticut, Storrs, Connecticut 06268.

Saving on Grass Seed

A simple way to figure the relative efficiency of grass seed brands is to multiply the percentage of germination by the percentage of pure seed marked on each label; the package yielding the highest figure will produce the most new grass.

Avoid annual species when buying grass seed. A pound of smaller, more expensive perennial seed will sow an area larger than eight pounds of large cheap seed can cover, saving you money and making a higher quality lawn. The smaller the seed the bigger the bargain.

Lawn and Garden Guide

A pamphlet on lawn and garden fertilizing that sells for 49¢ is yours free from Vertogreen, a fertilizer manufacturer. Most of the tips involve using Vertogreen products. Request "Guide for Lawns and Gardens," U.S. Agri-Chemicals, P.O. Box 1685, Atlanta, Georgia 30301.

No grass can live where there is less than 35 percent daily sunlight. For most shady areas you can use a special mixture containing fescue species. In really dense shade, only groundcovers will grow.

Free for the Real Lawn Buff

This outsize 20-page booklet in full color consists of articles and drawings from various authoritative scientific magazines on the effects of fertilization and will be of special value to the devoted lawn buff who wants to know a little more than his neighbor about growing grass. Request "Turfgrass Performance Guide," Estech Chemicals Corporation, Professional Products Division, P.O. Box 1996, Winter Haven, Florida 33880.

Newly planted lawns should be watered daily—carefully with a fine spray. Established grass needs about an inch of water a week to thrive. For example, irrigate a lawn of 1000 square feet with a 50-foot hose and sprinkle for three and a half hours, or until there's an inch of water in three coffee cans placed near the sprinkler.

Lawn Pests

For an illustrated booklet showing how to identify and control the chief insect enemies of lawns, send 50¢ for "Insects and Related Pests Attacking Lawns," publication number B-1078, Texas Cooperative Extension Service, Department of Agricultural Communications, Texas A & M University, College Station, Texas 77843.

Mow new grass as soon as the leaves reach your mower blades, set no lower than two inches. The higher the cut, the healthier your lawn will be: tall grass shades its own roots and deprives weeds of sunlight.

A lawn can be mowed to death by overcutting, as grass lives primarily on food manufactured by its leaves.

Mowing Magic

Want to cut grass on a hillside, terrace or ditch where erosion could become a problem? Then cut it at a three-inch height (as opposed to the usual one-and-a-half- to two-inch cut), which will encourage more and faster root growth. This and an acre of free information on lawn care is available to anyone contacting Jari, The Goin' Mowers' Machine, Box 2075, Mankato, Minnesota 56001.

Mow your lawn in different patterns to avoid setting the grass in one direction and causing stripes.

Save Money by Renting a Sheep for a Lawn Mower

Seriously, if you have a big lawn, Louis R. Valente of Cornwallville, New York (phone 518-239-4839) will rent you a sheep from his flock of 128 to mow your lawn all summer for $35. This might well soon prove cheaper than gas, and certainly saves a lot in time and labor. The sheep costs nothing to keep. "During the summer, as long as you have enough grass, that's all the food they need," Mr. Valente says. "You just give them a little water and some shade and use a dog collar and rope to keep them on one part of the lawn. And you have to move them every couple of days so they don't eat the grass too short."

Long matted grass clippings should be removed after cutting or they will smother the lawn. But if you mow often enough, the resulting shorter clippings will decay—there's no need to rake them up— and feed the lawn at the same time.

Double Your Yield by Using the Front Lawn
for a Vegetable Garden

"We live in a grass country; we live in a grass world," a New Rochelle, New York gardener lamented not long ago, pointing an accusing finger at a lush lawn across the street. "Do you ever see anyone walking on lawns like that or sitting on them? Of course not—all that green, inedible stuff is totally useless!"

Many Americans are beginning to think like the New Rochellian and have, like him, planted their front lawns in vegetables. One Texas man actually planted wheat on his front lawn, enough to make one hundred loaves of bread—and persevered even though his neighbors complained to City Hall! In most communities, there's no law against using your front lawn to plant any crop, and if there is, you might be able to have it changed. The plush front lawn that yields harvests of bills, worry, and backaches is strictly a modern invention and one that often makes little sense.

Gardens planted on the front lawn not only save money and reward one with healthy, tasty food, but can be attractive as well. Use a little imagination, and a big garden or a small tomato patch will blend in nicely with other plantings. As for the work involved, it can be minimal. If you don't want to turn over the front lawn, take a short cut and mow the grass close, spreading about three inches of decayed leaves over the portion of the lawn to be used. After this compost has settled down, simply make planting holes for the vegetables and set them in, two feet apart each way. Try to use attractive mulches such as stones or gravel. Plant marigolds to combat the meadow nematode and care for plants, just as you would in the backyard. The turf grass, smothered, will soon become compost and yield bushels of free food.

An easy-to-remember proverb reminds us that the best times to fertilize lawns are four holidays—St. Patrick's Day, Memorial Day, the Fourth of July and Labor Day.

Weeds in Place of a Lawn?

"No one feels himself easy in a garden which does not look like the open country," Goethe argues, which is at least a good rationalization for letting the lawn go to seed. There are other good reasons, too, for letting weeds take over in the yard; they are not only "uncultivated flowers;" many are good to eat as well. To name just a few weeds that make excellent salads: chicory, lambs quarters, violet leaves, dandelion, and mustard greens. Excellent books to consult on the subject are Sturtivant's *Edible Plants of the World* and Euell Gibbons's *Stalking The Wild Asparagus.*

Lawn Mushrooms

Before you eat the fungi on the front lawn read this authoritative illustrated booklet—it could save you trouble, even your life. Send 20¢ for "Some Mushrooms: Edible and Poisonous," publication number E-386, New York Cooperative Extension Service, Mailing Room, Building 7, Research Park, Cornell University, Ithaca, New York 14850.

Landscaping Your Home

For a free illustrated pamphlet containing many tips on how to improve the appearance and ambience of your home grounds write for "Home Beautification," from the West Virginia Department of Agriculture, Charleston, West Virginia 25305. Enclose a stamped, self-addressed envelope.

> *Experts say that full-grown trees on a residential property increase the value of the property by five to ten percent. Trees and shrubs lost in storms, fire or accidents and not covered by insurance are tax deductible.*

Selecting Plants for Landscaping

This free four-color booklet tells you how to plan a landscape and select plants for it. Write Stark Brothers, Louisiana, Missouri 63353.

Use only pressure-treated railroad ties in landscaping garden beds. They're more expensive but last 15 years or so, whereas dip-treated ties last only up to five years and quickly become an unsightly mess.

Three More Home Landscaping Booklets

If you live in one of the states below, write for either: 1) "Home Landscaping," publication number B-980, 25¢ from Texas Cooperative Extension Service, Department of Agricultural Communications, Texas A & M University, College Station, Texas 77843; 2) "A Guide for Home Landscaping," publication number A-1923, 20¢ from Wisconsin Cooperative Extension Service, Agricultural Bulletin Building, 1535 Observatory Drive, University of Wisconsin, Madison, Wisconsin 53706; or 3) "Beautiful Home Grounds," publication number E-425, 50¢ from Michigan Cooperative Extension Service, MSU Bulletin Office, Box 231, Michigan State University, East Lansing, Michigan 48823.

If unsightly moss is spoiling the appearance of your walks or walls, tidy up the place like this: Scrub the affected areas with 10 percent muriatic acid (wearing rubber gloves and protective glasses). Then wash off with water and the brick or stone will be shining through again.

Landscape Planning Kit

Here's a very helpful practical kit complete with instructions to help you plan your landscape, and including stencils of plants and drafting paper. Send $1 for "Homescaping Kit," Agricultural Extension Service, University of Wyoming, Box 3354, University Station, Laramie, Wyoming 82070.

Planting in Problem Areas

The London plane tree, grown widely on city streets, is a well-known example of plants that grow well in difficult places. But there are many more such plants available to the home gardener who has to live with an overabundance of shade, poor drainage or poor soil. Should you have such problems send 25¢ for "Plants for Difficult Situations," College of Agriculture and Natural Resources, Agricultural Publication, Storrs, Connecticut 06268.

Growing Outdoor Plants in Containers

To obtain basic know-how and many tips on successful outdoor container growing, send 15¢ for "Container Culture of Ornamental Plants for the Home Grounds," publication number E-1152, New York Cooperative Extension Service, Mailing Room, Building 7, Research Park, Cornell University, Ithaca, New York 14850.

Transplanting Tips

• An excellent free transplanting spade that cuts easily through tree roots can be made by cutting a wide V notch into a regular spade blade and then sharpening the edges of the V.

• You'll give shrubs a better chance to recover from transplanting shock if you drive a spade around plant roots a few days before moving.

• Always take as large a ball of soil as possible when transplanting a plant from the wild into your garden. And choose a site for it as similar as possible to the site where it originally grew.

• When tying or bunching branches together before moving shrubs from one place to another, you'll find that an old belt works better than rope or wire.

Landscaping with Stones

Here's a free 22-page booklet filled with hints and plans for using stone in your landscaping scheme. Write Featherock, Inc., 6331 Hollywood Boulevard, Los Angeles, California 90028.

Garden Fountains

This free illustrated booklet covers many types of fountains and tells how they can be used in landscaping. Write Rain Jet Corporation, 301 S. Flower Street, Burbank, California 91503.

Lighting the Outdoor Garden

For an illustrated 32-page free booklet containing many tips for outdoor lighting around the home, request "Landscape Lighting," from General Electric Company, Large Lamp Department, Nela Park, Cleveland, Ohio 44122.

Ice or snow which accumulates on shrubs and trees for more than a day should be removed with a broom or shovel before it permanently distorts or breaks branches. Use sand, not salt, on icy sidewalks near shrubs. Salt can kill plantings, as can many commercial melting agents.

Cartoons on Ecology

Adults, too, will enjoy this 16-page cartoon booklet for kids about plants and ecology. Send 25¢ for "Plants—How They Improve Our Environment," to Men's Garden Clubs of America, 5560 N.W. Merle Hay Road, Des Moines, Iowa 50301.

Azalea and Rhododendron Varieties

For a free annual price list describing the native American azalea and rhododendron varieties that this company specializes in, write S.D. Coleman Nurseries, Box 412, Fort Gaines, Georgia 31752.

Rare Azaleas

Another free yearly catalog with a good selection of unusual rare azalea varieties is offered by Nuccio's Nurseries, 3555 Chaney Trail, Altadena, California 91001.

Barberry Bush Candy

The barberry bush is a very commonly planted ornamental in America, but little use is ever made of its attractive red berries. In case you want to make use of those barberry bushes outside, here is an unusual (untested) recipe for "Candied Barberries" that we came across in a nineteenth-century cookbook:

"Take some large barberries very ripe and of a fine red colour. Leave them in clusters. For 2 pounds of berries cook 2½ pounds of sugar to 'the large feather' [232°F]. Put in the barberries and boil very hastily to produce 10 to 12 bubbles. Take off the stove. When the fruit is beginning to cool, put it in a hot cupboard leaving it to drain on a cloth until next day. Put it on sheets of paper to drain further. Dust the clusters of berries with fine sugar rubbed through a drum sieve [a very fine sieve]. Put them to dry in a hot cupboard."

Evergreen Culture

To obtain an informative booklet about the culture of ornamental evergreens on the home grounds, send 20¢ for "Ornamental Evergreens," publication number E-426, Michigan Cooperative Extension Service, MSU Bulletin Office, Box 231, Michigan State University, East Lansing, Michigan 48823.

An Evergreen Catalog

For a free annual brochure describing an extensive selection of evergreen trees, write Western Maine Forest Nursery Company, Fryeburg, Maine 04037.

Rare Evergreens

This free annual catalog offers a large selection of rare and dwarf evergreens, as well as tree seeds. Write Girard Nurseries, P.O. Box 428, Geneva, Ohio 44041.

Eucalyptus Trees

As unlikely as it seems, here is an English nursery specializing in eucalyptus trees, as their free catalog indicates. Write G. Reuthe, Ltd., Keston, Kent, England.

Growing Festive Hollies

For an illustrated booklet that tells all about growing the beautiful hollies that play such an important part in the Christmas season, request "Growing Hollies," publication number 66-33, College of Agriculture and Natural Resources, University of Connecticut, Storrs, Connecticut 06268.

Palm Trees

For a free annual price list offering various palm trees and anthurium plants write Kuaola Farms, P.O. Box 4038, Hilo, Hawaii 96720.

Renowned Rhododendrons

This British firm, renowned world-wide for its rhododendron hybrids, offers an annual catalog featuring a very large stock of plants. Write Knapp Hill Nursery, Ltd., Woking, Surrey, England.

1000 Roses

Over 1000 cultivars are expertly described and rated in the "Handbook for Selecting Roses," an invaluable booklet for rose growers. Send 10¢ for handling and a stamped, self-addressed return envelope to the American Rose Society, Shreveport, Louisiana 71130.

Irish Roses

The free annual catalog of this Irish nursery features many varieties of roses. Write Dickson Nurseries, Ltd., Newtonards, County Down BT23 4SS, Northern Ireland.

Miniature Roses

For a free descriptive price list with a large selection of miniature roses of all types, write McDaniels Miniature Roses, 7523 Zemco Street, Lemon Grove, California 92045.

Northeastern Miniature Roses

This free yearly catalog features miniature roses of many types and colors. Write Nor'East Miniature Roses, Inc., 58 Hammond Street, Rowley, Massachusetts 01969.

Climbing and Hanging Basket Miniature Roses

A free catalog of miniature roses featuring new introductions and old reliables, including hard to find climbing miniature roses, is free from Mini-Roses, P.O. Box 4225 Station A, Dallas, Texas 75208. A recent catalog instructs how to grow miniature roses in hanging baskets, a new trend, and suggests the appropriate varieties.

An Encyclopedia of Old-fashioned English Roses

You'll enjoy reading this free catalog which has been described as "a miniature encyclopedia" of old-fashioned English shrub roses that were grown in Victorian times and long before. The old varieties are still available in one or two British nurseries. Write T. Hilling & Co., Ltd., Cobham, Surrey, England.

Free Rose Seed

To get free rose seed let the orange rose hips ripen on the plant until they begin to split. The seed inside is then ready to sow. Be warned, however, that the seed won't grow true to type but will revert back to characteristics of its ancestors.

Rare Roses of Yesterday and Today

Rare roses of the past and unusual new developments are featured in this annual color catalog. Send $1 for postage and handling to Roses of Yesterday and Today, 802-G Brown's Valley Road, Watsonville, California 95076.

Canadian Rare Roses

Here is a free catalog offering a large selection of rare roses not often seen on the market. Write Clark Pallek and Sun Nurseries, P.O. Box 137, Virgil, Ontario LOS 110, Canada.

Rose hips, 60 times richer in vitamin C than oranges, can be eaten ripe (when they begin to split) right off the bush.

Scottish Roses

Scotland is famous for its roses and this free once-a-year catalog shows why. Write P. and J. Anderson, Ltd., Friarsfield Road, Cults, Aberdeen, 48881, Scotland.

Scottish Scented and Tiger-striped Roses

This valuable free color catalog depicts 149 varieties of beautiful scented roses which are mostly priced at a low $1.40 to $1.65 a bush and include every color imaginable, even a tiger-striped variety. Write Anderson's Rose Nurseries, Cults, Aberdeen, Scotland.

Rose petals dipped in eggwhite and then sugar and then dried on a rock are an easy-to-make delicious candy that serves well as a decoration on cakes.

Jackson & Perkins Roses

For a free four-color annual catalog of America's foremost grower of roses, write Jackson & Perkins Company, 307 Rose Lane, Medford, Oregon 97501.

More Free Rose Catalogs

ARMSTRONG NURSERIES, P.O. Box 4060, Ontario, California 91761

INTER-STATE NURSERIES, INC., 504 E. Street, Hamburg, Iowa 51640

RICE NURSERIES, INC., Box 333, Lyons, New York 14489

ROSES BY FRED EDMUNDS, 6235 Southwest Kahle Road, Wilsonville, Oregon 97070

STOCKING ROSE NURSERY, 785 North Capitol Avenue, San Jose, California 95133

WYANT ROSES, Johnny Cake Ridge, Rt. 84, Mentor, Ohio 44060

NOTE: Roses are also offered in many of the free catalogs cited in chapter 3.

Prune flowering shrubs only after their blooming period. Non-flowering shrubs should be pruned in early spring.

Shade Trees

This free booklet tells which trees to grow for shade in which regions of the country, how tall they will ultimately grow and how to plant and care for them. Request "Shade Tree Care" from West Virginia Department of Agriculture, Information Division, State Capitol, Charleston, West Virginia 25305.

After pruning, always coat any cut larger than a quarter with a commercial wound dressing.

Selecting Trees for Better Living

For a free illustrated booklet that discusses in detail how to select trees to enhance the environment, request "Trees for a More Livable Environment," Public Affairs Department, Chevron Chemical Company, San Francisco, California 94119.

Cut back wisteria shoots in late July to encourage flowering for next year. Root pruning also helps nonflowering wisterias.

Free Tree and Shrub Catalogs

For a free 48-page four-color catalog published yearly and offering many varieties of trees and shrubs, including planting directions, write Earl Ferris Nursery, 376 Bridge Street, Hampton, Iowa 50441.

The unusual Franklin tree (it has never been located growing in the wild since it was cultivated) is one of the ornamental offerings in the free annual catalog of Tingle Nursery Company, Pittsville, Maryland 21850.

A free 52-page four-color catalog that features many varieties of trees and shrubs for the home grounds, along with cultivation tips, is available from Burnet Brothers, Inc., P.O. Box 218, Galesburg, Michigan.

Trees and shrubs are also offered in many of the free catalogs listed in chapters 1, 2 and 3.

Tree Seed

If you want to start trees from seed, a very large selection of hard-to-come-by tree seed is featured in this free yearly catalog. Write F. W.

Schumacher Company, 36 Spring Hill Road, Sandwich, Massachusetts 02563.

Those beautiful trees so close to the house may be a fire menace if they grow too near the chimney. Cut back any overhanging branches that may be set afire by sparks.

A Free Home Firewood Rating Chart

This handy large-postcard-size chart rates the heating, burning, smoking, sparking and splitting quality of over 30 hardwood and softwood trees. Also provided free are interesting pamphlets on chain saw safety and the use of chain saws. Write: Omark Industries, Oregon Chain Saw Division, 9701 S.E. McLoughlin Blvd., Portland, Oregon 97222.

The Best Wood to Gather for the Fireplace

Wood	Starting Ease	Heating Rank
Ash	Fair	2
Beech	Poor	1
Birch	Good	2
Cedar	Superior	3
Elm	Fair	2
Hemlock	Good	3
Hickory	Fair	1
Locust	Poor	1
Maple	Poor	1
Oak	Poor	1
Pine	Superior	3

Heating with Wood

This up-to-date free booklet deals with the types of fireplaces, stoves and furnaces available; buying, installing and using wood stoves; buying and burning wood efficiently and safely. Request "Heating with Wood," publication number F-S7, enclosing 50¢ for postage and handling, to College of Agriculture and Natural Resources, University of Connecticut, Storrs, Connecticut 06268.

5

Houseplant Handouts

Indoor Gardening Illustrated

Learn the basics of indoor gardening from this amply illustrated 48-page booklet that rivals many a paperback book on the subject. It covers everything from plant selection to artificial lighting. Request price for "Indoor Gardening," publication number G-220, from Superintendent of Documents, Washington, D.C. 20402.

A Houseplant Tabloid

This free publication in tabloid newspaper form contains all the basic information you need to know about houseplants, and then some. Request "Care and Selection of Houseplants," publication number 1012, Mississippi Cooperative Extension Service, P.O. Box 5404, Mississippi State University, State College, Mississippi 39762.

Houseplant Lighting

Light is the most important factor in growing houseplants: Without proper lighting no indoor plant can thrive. Inexpensive lighting systems for indoor gardening are now available. If you don't have bright, sunny windows, such artificial light is a must. Heating is next in importance. Generally, house plants do best at 60-70 degrees in the daytime and 5-15 degrees lower at night.

Indoor Plant Light Sources

The following companies will send you free literature about indoor plant growth lighting on request: Westinghouse Electric Corporation, Lamp Division, Bloomfield, New Jersey 07003; General Electric Company, Lamp Division, Nela Park, Cleveland, Ohio 44112; Duro-Test Corporation, North Bergen, New Jersey 07047; and Sylvania Lighting Products Division, 100 Endicott Street, Danvers, Massachusetts 01923.

Houseplants will not grow spindly if you give them less warmth and more light and humidity. "Leggy" plants are usually plants reaching for light.

Free Fluorescent Lamps for Garden Clubs

The much acclaimed Tru Verilux Bloom fluorescent lamps are among the best fluorescent lamps for lighting indoor plants. If your garden club sponsors a flower show the company may provide you with a free lamp for any award or door prize. Write Verilux, Inc., 35 Mason Street, Greenwich, Connecticut 06830 for details.

Experts say that you can stimulate a houseplant's growth by rotating it counterclockwise a little each day; but you will inhibit its growth by rotating it clockwise.

Long Bloomers

More than a dozen plants that bloom for several months in the winter or all year are described in the booklet "Miracle Plants under Lights," yours for 35¢ from Mrs. A. D. Morrison, Corresponding Secretary,

Indoor Light Gardening Society of America, 5305 S.W. Hamilton Street, Portland, Oregon 97221.

Saving Those Gift Plants

Gift plants, which often wind up in the trash can after they finish blooming, can be saved and become a permanent part of the indoor garden, as this unique 56-page booklet shows. Send 20¢ for "Flowering Gift Plants: Their Care and How to Rebloom Them," publication number C-801, Illinois Cooperative Extension Service, Agricultural Publication Office, 123 Mumford Hall, University of Illinois, Urbana, Illinois 61801.

A discarded car radio antenna makes a good stake for tall, leaning houseplants.

Bigger Yields by Pampering Your Houseplants

It's said that W. C. Fields cussed out his plants occasionally, but recent evidence suggests that you'd be better off treating yours with tender loving care; speak gently and carry a big watering can might be the motto. It isn't our intention to go into plant sensitivity theories here; there are many books available on that subject. But the fact is that many gardeners claim excellent results from treating their plants like people. It may well be that these gardeners are simply more aware of and responsive to their plants' needs as they talk and sing to them, and are rewarded accordingly. Or plants may indeed be more like people than is generally thought. Anyway, here are some of the specific stratagems that have been suggested:

• Some gardeners play music to their plants, claiming that this stimulates growth. Scientists say that sonic stimulation may be a valid horticultural technique, and various experiments seem to have indicated this, though they are far from conclusive. Classical music, it's said, works better than rock. All of Bach, "Rhapsody in Blue," "Nights in the Gardens of Spain," and Ravi Shankar's classical Indian sitar music have been highly recommended. So if you hang a transistor radio near a plant, don't leave it on an acid-rock station; if you do, the plants will "cringe, lean sharply away from the sound, and die in a few weeks," advised one professor.

• Plants are also responsive to the human voice, say other experimenters. Don't be a W. C. Fields, they warn. Never scold plants; speak gently at all times. Content, too, is quite important here. Don't even try to curse a plant gently! It will surely know. Encourage your plants, spur them on, tell them things will get better when it's too cold, wet, when the insects are coming, and so on! At least one scientist sings "Happy Days Are Here Again" to her green friends.

• Handle plants very gently as well, we are advised. They respond to petting and tender care. A noted psychiatrist claims that a person with a "true green thumb" can heal wounds in plants by simply touching them. Another university researcher has reported that even "water that a green thumb touches will make plants grow at express speed." How do you get a "true green thumb," though, unless you're born with one? "Brown thumbs" only make matters worse.

• Don't dare think bad thoughts when close by plants if you subscribe to the plant sensitivity theory. Several polygraph researchers have written that plants registered violent reactions on their machines when people even thought about harming them.

• When students studying sensitivity in plants talked about sex, the plants they tended showed signs of sudden excitation on their polygraphs. This led the students to believe that ancient fertility rites, in which humans made love in freshly seeded fields, may have been authentic stimulants to plant growth.

• A professor of natural science at Blake College in California found in a two-year research program into the "emotional lives" of various plant species that most are "susceptible to kindness and flattery." So, if you do talk to plants at all, lay it on with a garden trowel.

• Finally, two Scottish gardeners have created a veritable vest pocket Eden on a half-acre of soil that is mostly sand and gravel. They have accomplished this, they say, solely by "communion with the living plants" and "happiness and joy" in what they are doing.

African Violet Growing

To obtain a valuable little pamphlet on African violet growing in the home, send 20¢ for "How to Grow African Violets," publication number A-1483, Wisconsin Cooperative Extension Service, Agricultural Bulletin, 1535 Observatory Drive, University of Wisconsin, Madison, Wisconsin 53706.

Tips on Growing African Violets

Your African violets will thrive if you utilize the tips given in this booklet offered by Fisher Greenhouses, which specializes in African violets and offers some 169 varieties. The tips are free with every request for the Fisher catalog. Send 25¢ for postage and handling to Fisher Greenhouses, Oak Avenue near Central Avenue, Linwood, New Jersey 08221.

Another Great African Violet Source

This annual descriptive price list featuring a large selection of African violets and supplies for growers is free from the San Francisco Plant Company, 139 Main Street, Half Moon Bay, California 94019.

Anthuriums

For a free descriptive price list offering anthuriums, gingers, dracenas and orchids, write Lehua Anthurium Nursery, 80 Kokea Street, Hilo, Hawaii 96720.

Houseplants should be repotted to the next larger sized container when the present pot is "web-full" of roots.

A Bonsai Sampler

An introduction to the ancient art of bonsai comes free to you in Circular 338 from the Florida Agricultural Extension Service, University of Florida, Gainesville, Florida 32601.

A Bonsai Catalog

For an annual catalog offering plants, shrubs and trees suitable for shaping into bonsai, along with equipment for bonsai gardening, send 25¢ for postage and handling to Hortica Gardens, 6309 Green Valley Road, P.O. Box 308, Placerville, California 95667.

When transplanting young houseplants, avoid transplanting shock by watering with a mild solution of water-soluble plant food. Carefully follow the directions on the package.

Bromeliads

Here is a free price list describing many varieties of bromeliads. Write Blossom World Bromeliads, Route 2, Box 479-N, Sanford, Florida 32771.

5000 Cacti

More than 5000 different species of cacti are described in this free annual price list, including plants even the most devoted cactus lover doesn't have. Write Cactus Gem Nursery, P.O. Box 327, Aromas, California 95004.

Bargain Collectors' Cactus Seeds

A special for our readers, this super roundup of free cactus seeds from American deserts, Mexico and South America offers a gardener's delight of about 20 varieties of cacti. Plant these special seeds according to the detailed directions and then be patient, for it takes from one to three years before you have a good-sized plant. To obtain this cactus seed packet, a $1.25 value, send 50¢ for postage and handling to Henrietta's Nursery, 1345 N. Brawley, Dept. DW, Fresno, California 93711.

The Latest Cactus News

Recent developments in the world of cacti are featured in this free descriptive price list, which offers a wide variety of plants. Write New Mexico Cactus Research, P.O. Box 787, Belen, New Mexico 87002.

Cacti and Succulents

This annual price list features everything, including supplies, for the grower of cacti and succulents. Send 30¢ for postage and handling to Barnett Cactus Garden, 1104 Meadowview Drive, Bossier City, Louisiana 71111.

An old kitchen fork is an excellent cultivating tool for small house plants.

Carnivorous Plants

For a descriptive price list featuring many carnivorous plants and products used in growing them, send 25¢ for postage and handling to Plant Oddities, P.O. Box 94, Kennebunk, Maine 04043.

Low-Cost Venus Fly Trap Seeds

The Venus fly trap, which actually lures, captures and digests insects, is among the most unusual plants in the world. Seeds for it are offered by Peter Paul's Nurseries for a $1 postage and handling fee. Peter Paul's specializes in carnivorous plants, stocking over 75 species, and also offers its catalog free if you enclose a large stamped self-addressed envelope. Write Peter Paul's Nurseries, Route 4, Canandaigua, New York 14424.

More Meat-eating Plants

A great number of carnivorous plants are offered by this nursery. Its $1 catalog is published once a year and the $1 is deducted from the cost of any order. Write Carnivorous Gardens, P.O. Box 331, Smith Road, Hamilton, New York 13346.

When putting houseplants outside in the summer, place each plant—pot and all—into the soil. They will not dry out as quickly underground, and there will be no transplanting shock when they are brought inside again.

Epiphylla

To obtain a free annual 33-page catalog devoted to epiphyllum species, write Beahm Gardens, 2688 Paloma Street, Pasadena, California 91107.

Your geraniums will bloom indoors all winter long if you pick off all flower buds as they appear during the preceding summer. Of course they must have a bright, sunny window.

Four Free Orchid Offers!

Not only do you receive a free 48-page color catalog when you order from the Fennel Orchid Company, which has been specializing in orchid growing since 1927, but Fennel will also give our readers a dollar off on all first orders and a free bonus plant with every order. In addition customers may visit the company's magnificent Orchid Jungle Garden (where admission is charged to all others) completely free of charge. And here's a fifth saving: If you grow orchids at present, the firm's information sheet on making corsages is well worth its

25¢ price. Write Fennel Orchid Company, Inc., The Orchid Jungle, 26715 S.W. 157th Avenue, Homestead, Florida 33032.

Orchid Kits

This free catalog published twice a year features extensive orchid varieties and kits for orchid growing. Write Jungle-Gems, Inc., 210 East Ring Factory Road, Bel Air, Maryland 21024.

Free Orchid Catalogs

For a free annual color catalog of 40 pages crammed with an excellent selection of orchid species, write Hauserman Orchids, P.O. Box 363, Elmhurst, Illinois 60218.

A monthly catalog describing many varieties of orchids is available from the Beall Company, 91st Avenue S.W. and Southwest 186th Street, P.O. Box 467, Vashon, Washington 98070.

To receive a free yearly catalog featuring many varieties of orchids and supplies for the orchid grower, write Black River Orchids, P.O. Box 110, 77th Street, South Haven, Michigan.

Nepalese Orchids

Orchids, ferns and flowering bulbs from Nepal, of all places, are featured in this descriptive free price list, published quarterly. Write J. N. Enterprises, Acres of Orchids, Box 1642, Basbari Nursery Lane, Katmandu, Nepal.

Cold-Climate Orchids

This free yearly catalog features a large selection of orchids, especially varieties that do well in cool climates. Write Santa Barbara Orchid Estate, 1250 Orchid Drive, Santa Barbara, California 93111.

Build Your Own Terrarium

Step-by-step directions for building several kinds of terrariums are included in this booklet, along with terrarium plant lists and illustrations. Send 50¢ for "Terrariums," publication number C-1086, Illinois Cooperative Extension Service, Agricultural Publications, 123 Mumford Hall, University of Illinois, Urbana, Illinois 61801.

"How to Make a Terrarium," publication number E-1029, is available for 15¢ (free to New York residents) from Distribution Center C, 7 Research Park, Cornell University, Ithaca, New York 14850.

Make a Free Miniterrarium

A miniature terrarium for a single small plant can be made by filling a large plastic glass with soil, planting the cutting or plant and fitting the mouth of a smaller plastic glass into the larger one. Prick holes in the bottom of the small glass for ventilation.

Terrarium Plants

Here's an illustrated annual catalog featuring many varieties of terrarium plants and ferns. Send 35¢ for postage and handling to McComb's Greenhouses, New Straitsville, Ohio 43766.

Low-Cost Tropical Plant Seeds

Tropical plants and seeds, including such exotics as seeds for passion fruit, guava fruit, dwarf bananas, coffee plants, and many orchids, are the specialty of Hana Gardenland, P.O. Box 248, Hana, Hawaii 96713. Their catalog, which costs 50¢ for postage and handling, also features a sprouted coconut ready to grow in a saucer of water, lava bonsai planters, and white and black sand from Hawaii. The seeds (only 40¢ each) are attached to full color postcards of the plants they will become if they are grown according to the directions on the cards. Free with the catalog is an authoritative guide for growing tropical plants. Hana Gardenland invites all visitors to Hawaii to visit their tropical display garden in one of the world's most scenic regions.

Tropical Seeds

For a free annual price list featuring exotic tropical seed, write R. S. Drum's Tropical Seeds, 2957 Hemlock Drive, Norristown, Pennsylvania 19401.

Tropical Plant Products

This free 10-page descriptive price list features hard-to-get supplies for tropical plant growers, including treefern boards, slabs and totems, and orchid potting media. Write Tropical Plant Products, 1715 Silver Star Road, P.O. Box 7754, Orlando, Florida 32804.

Five Free Nonspecialized Houseplant Color Catalogs

AMERICAN HORTICULTURAL SOCIETY, River Farm, Mount Vernon, Virginia 22121

BURGESS SEED AND PLANT CO., 67 East Battle Creek Street, P.O. Box 5000, Galesburg, Michigan 49053

GROUP NURSERY SALES, 380 Madison Avenue, New York, New York 10017

JULIUS ROEHRS, Rt. 33, Farmingdale, New Jersey 07727

WILSON BROTHERS FLORAL CO., Roachdale, Indiana 46172

NOTE: Many of the catalogs listed in chapter 3 also feature houseplants.

Ten Houseplants You Can Make for Nothing

• Amuse the children with a carrot "fern." Scoop out a large carrot, fill it with water, and hang it in a sunny window. Feathery foliage will soon hide the carrot itself. Or cut off the top half-inch or so and set it in a flat bowl with about a quarter of an inch of standing water.

• The top of a pineapple, planted in a pint jar of water, will sprout and root, soon making an exotic and most attractive palmlike plant.

• A novelty hanging vine can be grown from a sweet potato (with as many "eyes" as possible) by planting it in a hanging basket or pot of sand (or sandy loam), then watering occasionally. The leaves are dark green and resemble ivy.

• Onions will sprout beautiful leaves in a few days when placed in shallow dishes of water. White potatoes, beets and turnip plants can be grown in pots of soil. Pits from oranges, lemons and other fruits can be planted in soil "pan forests."

6

Fertilizing and Watering Giveaways

Two Soil-testing Offers

One of the country's top soil-testing laboratories offers a 24-page booklet called *The Good Earth,* which explains the composition of soil and soil testing. Also available is the excellent brochure *Acid Alkali Preference,* which contains the pH ranges for over 300 plants. Send 25¢ for postage and handling to Sudbury Laboratory Inc., P.O. Box 1218, Sudbury, Massachusetts 01776.

Building an Organic Soil

Here is a handy little pamphlet explaining how to condition your garden soil organically and evaluating various organic soil conditioners you can use. Send 20¢ for "Organic Soil Conditioners," publication number A-2305, Wisconsin Cooperative Extension Service, Agricultural Bulletin Building, 1535 Observatory Drive, University of Wisconsin, Madison, Wisconsin 53706.

Using Free Organic Fertilizers

In the long run organic fertilizers such as animal manures and leaves—many of which you can often obtain free—will improve soil in the garden (the results can often be seen in as little as a year), whereas commercial fertilizers can actually harm soil by overuse over a period of time. Long-term overfeeding with commercial fertilizer leads to an accumulation of soluble salts in the soil that will cause the locking up of certain nutrients. Another disadvantage is that weeds thrive on inorganic fertilizers and, finally, organic matter in the soil is rapidly depleted by overfeeding with inorganics. One should always be careful to follow directions when applying commercial fertilizers. "Use half as much twice as often," is, in fact, a good time-honored rule to follow if you're ever in doubt.

The value of organic matter in the soil is unquestioned. It improves soil tilth, increases the water-holding capacity of soils, and through its decay, releases nitrogen and other nutrients for plant use. Carbon dioxide from decaying materials helps bring minerals into solution, making them available to plants. Organic matter also stimulates root production, maintains the mycorrhizal fungi that aid plants in the absorption of nutrients, and even reduces insects like nematodes by encouraging the growth of parasitic fungi. That is why farmers have plowed manure and cover crops into their fields for generations.

Organic fertilizers do have certain drawbacks, though. Their chief disadvantage is their slow action. Organic fertilizers do not feed at all in cold early spring weather—plants cannot absorb organic matter until it has decayed in warm soil and broken down into simple chemical forms. On the other hand, organics are long-lasting, feeding plants over the entire growing season, while inorganics may run out by fall.

All and all, organic fertilizers are of much more value to the gardener and they certainly benefit the ecology far more than the inorganics. Try to use them whenever possible. Dig them into the soil in autumn, or incorporate them into planting holes when setting out plants. They also save money because they will never burn plants or leach away during a heavy rain as inorganics will. You'll find through experience that little additional fertilizing will be necessary other than, perhaps, a commercial starter solution in the spring, and an organic fish emulsion can even be used as a starter. Many books are devoted to organic fertilizers, government pamphlets abound on the subject and at least one magazine *(Organic Gardening)* is dedicated to their use. Make it a point to learn more about this important subject. In the meantime, to give you an idea of the value of just a few of the many common organic fertilizers—often free for the taking or saving—their percentages of nitrogen, phosphorus, and potassium (or potash) are listed below as compared to inorganic fertilizer:

Fertilizer	*Nitrogen*	*Phosphorous*	*Potassium*
Inorganic 5-10-5	5.0 percent	10.0 percent	5.0 percent
Bone meal	0.0	20-25	0.0
Blood, dried	8.12	2.5	0.5
Coffee grounds	2.0	0.4	0.7
Cottonseed meal	6.0	7.3	1-2
Cow manure (composted)	0.6	0.15	1.5
Eggshells	1.2	0.4	0.15
Fish scraps	6.10	7.0	0.8
Horse manure (composted)	0.7	0.25	0.55
Leaves (oak)	0.8	0.4	0.2
Pine needles	0.5	0.1	0.03
Poultry manure (fresh)	4.5	1.5	1.5
Rock phosphate	0.0	25-30	0.0
Seaweed	0.6	0.10	1.3
Sewage sludge	5-10	3-13	0.0
Sheep manure (fresh)	2.5	1.5	1.5
Tea grounds	4.0	0.6	0.40
Wood ashes	0.0	1-2	3-7

Organic Soil Management

For an interesting free packet of information about soil management and how organic fertilizers can improve the soil write Canton Mills, Inc., Shur-Gro Natural Base Fertilizer, P.O. Box 465, Minnesota City, Minnesota 55959.

Make Your Own Compost

To obtain explicit advice on how to build a backyard compost pile for free fertilizer that will benefit the soil as well as your plants, send 20¢ for "The Compost Pile," publication number IB-96, New York Co-operative Extension Service, Mailing Room, Building 7, Research Park, Cornell University, Ithaca, New York 14850.

Community Composting

This free brochure on composting is useful to both the individual gardener and community groups. Write for "A Citizen's Guide to Proper Disposal of Leaves and Other Organic Material," Ohio Environmental Protection Agency, Box 1049, 450 East Town Street, Columbus, Ohio 43216.

Two-Week Composting

Rich, nutrient-loaded, organic compost can be made in as little as 14 days with a Revolving Drum Composter, according to this interesting free packet of information that thoroughly explains the device and tells exactly how to make quick rich compost with it. Write Gardening Naturally, Revolving Drum Composter, Stockbridge Industrial Park, Route 102, Stockbridge, Massachusetts 01262.

Flaubert's Compost Pit

"Bouvard . . . became infatuated with fertilizer. Into his compost pits he piled boughs, blood, entrails, feathers—anything he could find. He used Belgian liquor [cesspool matter], liquid manure, lye, smoked herring, seaweed and old rags. In the midst of this stench, Bouvard smiled. To those who seemed disgusted he cried, 'But it's gold! But it's gold!'"

Gustave Flaubert
Bouvard and Pecuchet (1881)

How to Make Free Fertilizer:
A Quick Course in Composting

Composting is simply the disintegration process in which organic materials are broken down by the action of bacteria and fungi. When these materials are broken down in a compost pile, they decay more quickly than they would in the soil, yielding the dark, rich, crumbly compost that has so many uses in the garden. Compost can be mixed in planting holes when plants are set out, dug into the garden, or used as a side dressing for plants throughout the season. It can't burn plants like commercial fertilizer and benefits the soil in the same ways that organic materials do, only faster. A well-made compost has a fertilizer value of about 2-3-5.

There is really no mystery about composting. Almost any plant material can be used to make compost—leaves, grass clippings, vegetable matter, spoiled hay, even weeds can be used. Inexpensive compostmaking kits complete with safe chemicals to speed up decomposition are available at garden outlets. Many elaborate composting techniques exist (and you should consult a composting manual as you get deeper into the subject), but compost can easily be made in about two weeks by following the informal method described here. Do this throughout the gardening season and you'll have enough free compost to cover over 6000 square feet:

1. Set aside an 8 × 4-foot area in the spring and start the compost pile by filling the area with a four-foot high heap of leaves and grass clippings (or whatever other organic material you have on hand). If the pile is low in nitrogen (grass clippings, green plant matter, etc.) add manure to it.

2. Mix up the materials in the pile and shred it all into small pieces with a rotary mower or shredder. This will speed up disintegration by exposing more surfaces to attack by bacteria and fungi.

3. Make four-to-six inch layers with the shredded material, covering each layer with about one inch of rich soil. Water each layer down and add another layer until the heap is four feet high.

4. By the third day the heap will have begun to heat up. Check it with a thermometer and add more nitrogen if it hasn't. Keep the heap moist and turn it with a pitchfork or shovel on the fourth, seventh, tenth and fourteenth day. By the end of two weeks the compost will be ready to use, although it will take on a richer, more crumbly look if you let it decay a while longer.

Covering a compost pile securely with black polyethylene plastic not only eliminates odors and unsightly heaps but speeds up decomposition. Other often free organic materials you can use in the heap include cornstalks, corncobs, vines, sawdust, wood chips, slaughterhouse residues, pine needles, nutshells, bark, coffee grounds, and cocoa bean hulls. Some of these (like wood chips) will take longer to break down than others and need more nitrogen. If you use an acid organic material, such as oak leaves, sprinkle a little lime over them before shredding. It's estimated that the leaves from one large oak tree will make $15 worth of compost.

Free Garden Shredder Literature

Shredders speed up composting and make instant mulches out of many materials. These firms will send you free literature, ranging from colorful brochures to thick booklets, on their equipment and the many ways shredders are useful in the garden:

AMERIND-MACKISSIC, Box 111, Parker Ford, Pennsylvania 19457

ATLAS TOOL AND MFG. CO., 5151 Natural Bridge Avenue, St. Louis, Missouri 63115

AUTO-HOE, South Third Street, De Pere, Wisconsin 54115

COLUMBIA, Box 2741, Cleveland, Ohio 44111

FMC CORPORATION, Outdoor Power Equipment Division, Box 249, Port Washington, Wisconsin 53074

FORMWAY COMPANY, 224 Ahwanee, Sunnyvale, California 94086

GILSON BROTHERS, Box 152, Plymouth, Wisconsin 54073

INTERNATIONAL HARVESTER CO., 401 N. Michigan Avenue, Chicago, Illinois 60611

JACOBSEN MFG. CO., 1721 Packard Avenue, Racine, Wisconsin 53403

KEES MANUFACTURING CO., Box 8, Beatrice, Nebraska 68310

KEMP SHREDDER CO., Box 6275, Erie, Pennsylvania 16512

LINDIG MFG. CORP., 1875 W. Country Road, St. Paul, Minnesota 55113

MAGNA AMERICAN CORP., Box 90, Raymond, Mississippi 39154

M-B COMPANY, 1609-23 Wisconsin Avenue, New Holstein, Wisconsin

McDONOUGH POWER EQUIPMENT, McDonough, Georgia 30253

MITTS & MERRILL, 109 McCoskry Street, Saginaw, Michigan 48601

OSBORNE MFG. CO., Box 29, Osborne, Kansas 67473

RED CROSS MFG., Box 317, Bluffton, Indiana 45714

ROPER SALES CORP., 1905 W. Court Street, Kankakee, Illinois 60901

ROTO-HOE CO., Box 10, Newbury, Ohio 44065

ROYER FOUNDRY & MACHINE CO., 158 Pringle Street, Kingston, Pennsylvania 18704

SOLO MOTORS, INC., Box 5030, Newport News, Virginia 23605

TORO COMPANY, 8111 Lyndale Avenue, S. Bloomington, Minnesota 55420

VANDERMOLEN CORP., 119 Dorsa Avenue, Livingston, New Jersey 07039

WINONA ATTRITION MILL, 1009 W. 54th Street, Winona, Minnesota 55987

W-W GRINDER CORP., 2957 N. Market, Wichita, Kansas 67219

A Rotary Tiller Comparison Chart

If you are considering the purchase of a rear-tine rotary tiller for the garden, you'll want to check this free comparison chart, which helps you to evaluate the quality, versatility, ease of operation, safety features and other aspects of several leading models. Write Central States Mainline, P.O. Box 348, London, Ohio 43140.

Two Free Green Manure Offers

Green manure crops—crops such as rye grass or clover grown on the site and then dug into the soil—and how to use them are the subject of two excellent free booklets you'll want to have. Write for "How to Do Wonders with Green Manure Crops" and "Chart of Green Manures Information," from Garden Way Manufacturing Co., 102nd Street and Ninth Avenue, Troy, New York 12182.

A Who's Who of Worms

For a free descriptive price list from a worm ranch that will sell you live worms of many types and worm casings to enrich the soil of your garden—a practice highly recommended by organic gardeners—write the Three Oaks Worm Ranch, P.O. Box 26, Dresden, Tennessee 38225.

Free Houseplant Fertilizer

Buy any Plant Manager product, ranging from a gardening book to a Plant Care Meter, a useful gadget which measures the light and moisture requirement for over 200 common household plants, and you will receive a free full-size bottle of All Purpose Food for House Plants (7-14-7). Write: Plant Manager, P.O. Box 14, Wayzata, Minnesota 55391.

Fish Fertilizer

Atlas Fish Emulsion Fertilizer, an organic liquid concentrate made from whole fish (*200 pounds* of raw fish are used to make one gallon of the concentrate), will send anyone who requests them free colorful minipamphlets chock full of growing information on trees, chrysanthemums, camellias, rhododendrons, azaleas and other plants. Write Atlas Fish Fertilizer, Inc., 865 Lind Avenue S.W., P.O. Box 757, Renton, Washington 98055.

Prod flowering plants into early bloom by using one of the new hormone products, such as 2-3-5 tridobenzoic acid. Many will flower weeks ahead of schedule.

Fertilizing Tips That Will Save You Money

• A fertilizer marked 1-1-1 on the bag (this indicating the ratio of the primary nutrients—nitrogen, phosphorus and potassium) contains one-tenth of the nutrients in a bag of 10-10-10. The gardener who buys ten one-dollar bags of 1-1-1 on "sale" would get twice his money's worth buying two regularly-priced five-dollar bags of 10-10-10.

• Coffee grounds and used tea bags make excellent humus when applied to the soil in the outdoor garden.

• Save fireplace and barbecue ashes for fertilizer; they are an excellent source of potash and are especially useful sprinkled around the garden during the growing season.

• The best wood ashes to sprinkle around plants—those woods with the highest potash content, that is—are grapevines, elm, willow, oak, ash and spruce. Mature wood ashes have less potash than twig ashes.

• Vegetable peelings spread around garden plants will act as both water-conserving mulch and fertilizer, eventually breaking down into the soil.

• If you have dried dog food around the house that you want to get rid of, don't throw it out. Dried dog food is an excellent organic fertilizer that compares favorably to bone meal and blood meal, and can be worked into the soil around your plants.

• Chicken bones, which decompose quickly with bone meal, make an excellent fertilizer.

• Eggshells cracked neatly in half make nice little planters for seedlings. Poke a hole in the half-shell for drainage, fill it with soil and plant the seed, storing the planted half-shell in the egg carton with 11 more like it. When ready to plant outdoors, crack the shell in your hand and put it into the planting hole. As with peat pots, there will be no transplanting shock and the eggshell will provide fertilizer for the plant.

• If you can obtain hair sweepings from the local barbershop, they make an excellent fertilizer when dug into the soil. Six pounds of human hair contain a pound of nitrogen.

Save Money Making Your Own Soilless Mixes

This handy illustrated booklet gives the formulas and methods for making soilless mixes for potted plants far cheaper than their cost in garden stores. Send 60¢ for "Cornell Peat-Lite Mixes for Commercial Growers," New York Cooperative Extension Service, Mailing Room, Building 7, Research Park, Cornell University, Ithaca, New York 14850.

All About Mulching

For a free illustrated pamphlet advising how mulches can be used in many ways in the garden request "All about Mulching," from Hershey Estates, Department Q, Hershey, Pennsylvania 17033.

The Biggest Moneysavers in the Vegetable Garden: Fifty Free Mulches

You'll be able to obtain at least several of these mulches free or at low cost, depending on where you live, and they'll save you much time and money. Mulches are probably the biggest moneysavers in the vegetable garden. By covering the soil around vegetables with a mulch (a layer of leaves, straw or most any organic or inorganic material) you will not only increase their yield but reap many other benefits. Mulches reduce the need for watering and weeding by as much as 95 percent, protect roots of plants against temperature extremes and sudden changes, and improve the soil and feed plants if organic mulches are used. They also protect the soil against compaction by traffic, prevent soil erosion on hills, encourage feeder roots in the rich upper layers of soil, prevent plants from being splashed with disease spores in heavy rains, reduce pollution caused by soil-applied pesticides, produce carbon dioxide as they decay, and can even stimulate growth in plants by reflecting light to them. Add to this long list of benefits earlier maturity of vegetables, larger vegetables, cleaner, less damaged vegetables and easier harvesting, and it's hard to resist mulching plants in the vegetable garden.

Mulching has been nature's way of protecting and providing for plants since time immemorial, the moist, rich, spongy carpet of the forest floor being a perfect example of mulching. The word mulch itself is an ancient one. In Anglo-Saxon *melsc* was "mellow," and in an old German dialcet *molsch* meant "rotten;" these words led to the English word mulch, which was first used in the mid-seventeenth century. Today mulches are divided into organic materials like leaves and hay, or inorganic ones like black plastic or aluminum foil. The organic mulches are preferred because they add nutrients to the soil, whereas the inorganic ones control weeds better.

Mulches have several minor disadvantages. They do contribute to the holding of excessive soil moisture on poorly drained soils in wet seasons, which harms tomato root systems. They can also attract slugs and mice and conceal mole burrows. But these are usually problems that can easily be solved. Most bad results from mulching are due to improper applications. Mulch properly once and you'll never garden any other way.

‣ To begin with, *don't* mulch early in the spring. Application of organic mulch at this time will slow up the natural warming of the soil. As an insulating blanket, organic mulches reduce solar radiation into the soil and, as a result, frost hazards are greater. So wait until the soil has thoroughly warmed up before you apply mulch. If you keep a mulched garden from year to year, just push aside the mulch and plant seed or plants, pulling the mulch back in place when summer weather arrives.

Before mulching vegetables when the ground is warm, clean out all weeds, cultivate the ground an inch deep, and water it thoroughly. Then pile organic or inorganic materials that are insect-, disease-, and weed-free around the plants to a depth of about four inches. Do not place the mulch closer than a few inches from the plant stems. As for the materials that can be used for mulches, these number in the hundreds. Fifty or so are listed below along with their advantages, drawbacks, and any special ways to apply them. *Apply all of these four inches deep except where noted:*

Aluminum Foil—repels some insects, and reflected light from it often increases yields. Weight down with stones around plants or cover with a heavier, more attractive mulch.

Asphalt Paper—forms a long-lasting barrier against weeds, and can be covered with a more attractive organic mulch.

Bagasse (Chopped Sugar Cane)—long-lasting, clean, light-colored, and holds water well. Apply two inches deep. Sometimes sold as chicken litter.

Bark, shredded—lasts a long time, is aesthetically pleasing, adds much humus to the soil, retains moisture, and will not blow away. Apply two inches thick.

Black Plastic—see Plastic Film.

Buckwheat Hulls—dark, attractive, long-lasting, and do not mat—but blow away when dry. Apply three inches thick.

Cloth—burlap, old rags, old rugs, etc., can be laid between tomato rows if appearance is not important.

Cocoa-bean Hulls—tend to pack and mold; have a chocolate odor for a few weeks. Best mixed with other mulches. Apply two inches thick.

Coconut Fiber—hard to get, but long-lasting and attractive.

Coffee Grounds—excellent soil conditioner with attractive color, but slightly acid. Sprinkle a little lime on the grounds.

Compost—use when only half rotted; cover with other mulches.

Corncobs, Ground—need a little nitrogenous fertilizer sprinkled over them; may attract vermin. Apply two inches thick.

Corn Stalks—can either be shredded or used whole covered with more attractive mulches.

Cottonseed Hulls—good, but hard to obtain.

Dust Mulch—this simply means shallow cultivation of the soil to create a layer of dust that prevents upward movement of water and thus reduces evaporation. Some experts say all it really does is kill weeds by the act of cultivating.

Excelsior—a good mulch, long-lasting, nonpacking, and weed free, but highly flammable. Apply two inches thick.

Fiberglass Matting—repels insects, is permeable to air and water. A brand called Weed Chek is widely available.

Glass Wool—good but tends to blow away unless covered with chicken wire or other mulch. Apply two inches thick.

Grass Clippings—tests show this is one of the best mulches to repel nematodes on tomato roots and increase tomato yield; however, grass clippings will mat, ferment, and smell if used fresh, and can harbor insects. Use dry grass clippings three inches thick or mixed with other mulches; if you use the dry clippings alone, try adding a half cup of blood meal per bushel.

Gravel, Marble, and Quartz Chips—good on their own or for holding down other mulches, and protect well against mice. Experiments at the Colorado Agricultural Experiment Station showed that tomatoes mulched with black gravel yielded 10.27 tons per acre, while white-gravel-mulched tomatoes yielded 8.8 tons, and unmulched plants yielded 2.86 tons. Black-gravel-grown plants were also freer of blossom-end rot. The black gravel mulch was applied one and a half inches deep.

Green Manures—cover crops, usually legumes, grown in place and cut for mulch.

Hay—excellent but may need fastening down. Don't use hay going to seed. Apply six inches thick.

Leaf Mold—rotted leaves, especially nutritious for soil.

Leaves—oak leaves are the best; avoid types like maple that tend to pack unless they are shredded first. You can dust oak leaves with a little lime if you like, but tests show their acidity doesn't affect the pH of the soil when used as a mulch. Wet down and apply one to two inches thick.

Licorice Root—attractive, nonpacking and long lasting, but flammable and hard to obtain.

Mushroom Soil, Spent—has good color, benefits garden soil.

Newspapers—the newsprint repels insects and the wood pulp fertilizes plants, but newspapers can be unattractive and can form a tight mat so that air doesn't reach plant roots. Use four to six thicknesses around plants and cover with a more decorative organic mulch that will also help break the paper down. Newspaper ashes can be used as a mulch, too.

Peanut Hulls—excellent, but can blow away and may attract vermin.

Peat Moss—dries out and crusts too easily. Must be kept wet or it won't permit water to reach plants and will even suck water from the soil below to meet its own needs. Peat moss is best incorporated into the soil, but if it is used as a mulch, choose chunky types and keep them stirred up and wet. Not recommended for areas receiving little rainfall if rain is the only source of water.

Pecan Hulls—good mulch but hard to obtain.

Perlite—blows away too easily; must be weighted down with another mulch. Yields no nutrients.

Pine Needles—attractive and useful, but flammable.

Plastic Film (Polyethylene)—unattractive but very effective. Black (or green) plastic is preferred because it doesn't permit weed growth like clear plastic. Black plastic also absorbs the sun's heat during the day more than organic mulches do and radiates the heat back faster at night; thus plants mulched with it are less liable to frost injury than those mulched with organic materials. Tomato plants, especially, yield more when mulched with black plastic; its chief disadvantage is that it doesn't improve the soil. Transplant tomatoes into holes cut through the plastic *after* it is put down as a mulch. The procedure is simple. On a windless day soak the ground thoroughly. Mark off the area to be covered by the plastic, dig furrows four inches deep along the edges of this space, unroll the plastic, and anchor it in the furrows with soil.

Then make holes in the plastic and set in your transplants. Perforate the plastic for aeration. Remove the sheet at the end of the growing season and use it again next year if it's in good condition. Black or green plastic is best in an .0015 thickness and is available from most garden supply stores.

Salt Marsh Hay—one of the most effective mulches because it contains no weed seed, doesn't mat down, and is light and airy. Can be used for many years, as it doesn't break down quickly.

Sawdust and Wood Shavings—sawdust is a good mulch that is not toxic to plants as is often written; however, it does consume a lot of nitrogen in decomposing, depriving plants of this nutrient. Apply three inches thick and add either a half cup of blood meal or a cupful of nitrate soda per bushel. Wood shavings should be treated the same way.

Seaweed—if you live along the coast, this is a superb, mineral-rich, growth-promoting mulch. Can be placed directly around plants or composted first.

Straws—particularly good are wheat and oat straws, which are coarser than hay but more durable. Straws, however, are more flammable than hay and contain weed seed. Apply four inches thick.

Rocks and Stone—attractive, warm up the soil, and add trace elements to the soil as they imperceptibly wear away. Ring each plant with them a half inch from the stalk and five inches outward, piling the rocks three inches high. Round, flat rocks weighing a few pounds are the easiest to work with, but many rocks and stones can be used. "Stones" in a wide variety of shapes can even be made from cement.

Tobacco Stems—don't use on tomatoes, as they cause mosaic disease.

Vegetable Peelings—good, generally, but don't use old tomatoes or potato peelings or plants. Tomatoes used as a mulch can cause canker and bacterial spot; potatoes can introduce verticillium organisms into the vegetable patch. Compost these waste products instead so that heat will destroy any diseases. One nurseryman reports that composted tomato vines from the previous year used as a mulch greatly increased yields.

Vermiculite—see Perlite.

Water—in recent USDA experiments, 6-ml. clear plastic bags filled with water increased tomato yields by 20 percent. By absorbing intense heat from the summer sun at midday and reducing heat loss at night, a water mulch allows you to plant earlier in the spring and extend your planting into the late fall. Heated water in the bags warms up the soil even more.

Weeds—if weeds haven't gone to seed, they can be used as a mulch. So that they don't root again after a heavy rain, put them atop four or five layers of newspaper, which is a good way to get rid of two "waste products" at the same time.

Wood chips—more attractive than sawdust or shavings, but need the same amount of nitrogen.

Old Christmas tree branches make an excellent winter mulch for evergreens and other foundation plantings.

Irrigating the Garden

For a valuable booklet explaining the proper way to irrigate, send 20¢ for "Irrigation—How Much and How Often?" publication number F-257, from Minnesota Cooperative Extension Service, Bulletin Room, Coffey Hall, University of Minnesota, St. Paul, Minnesota 55101.

Houseplant Watering Tips

• An empty window-cleaner spray bottle makes an excellent indoor sprayer for water, water soluble fertilizers and insecticides. If the bottle is filled with an insecticide, be sure to label it clearly and to store it in a safe place.

• Place small stones over the drainholes of your houseplant pots to permit adequate drainage and eliminate unnecessary moisture. The stones also prevent soil from washing out.

• The best "drink" for houseplants is soft water free from chlorine and other chemicals. Water from ice cubes or ice collected from a defrosted refrigerator will do nicely. But be sure to feed your houseplants such water only after it has melted and risen to room temperature. Treat hard tap water with a little commercial softener before using.

• To waterproof your flower pots, simply dip them into melted paraffin so that it sinks into the pores.

New Watering Technology That Saves $

Soaker hoses with small pinpoints in them are good water savers. A more efficient (and expensive) new variation on these is the deep irrigation systems now available that are patterned on a system developed in Israel. Modern deep irrigation both saves water and results in yield increases of 30 to 100 percent in vegetables by ensuring that plants get exactly the amount of moisture they need at all times. Free literature on the subject can be obtained from Watersaver Systems, Box 2037, Pomona, California 91766, or Chapin Watermatics, Box 298, Watertown, New York 13601. Information about a garden watering kit designed on this principle that covers 625 square feet is available from DuPont Company, Wilmington, Delaware 19898.

Chapin Watermatics (above) offers a semipermanent Spray Stake system, where watering stakes are hammered into the garden near plants. The stakes are adjustable for direction and amount of spray.

New "garden computers," electronic moisture-sensing controllers, monitor soil moisture by remote buried sensors. The sensors feed back information to the control unit, which completely automates watering by watering only when the soil needs it. Some models are priced under $100. Literature can be obtained from Agrotronics Manufacturing Company, Box 1248, Barstow, California 92311.

Ignore the old myth about midday watering being dangerous. The best time to water is at noon.

Free Ways to Drub the Drought

Not only are water rates rising throughout the country, but as the number of home gardeners increases, devastating drought seems to be decreasing the nation's water supply. There is no need for despair, however. Resourceful gardeners and scientists have developed free and low-cost ways to drub the drought, ranging from the use of salt water to the construction of small "solar stills."

A recent government study, for example, reveals that even seltzer is a great help to thirsty plants these drought-ridden days. As a matter of fact, the bubbly liquid is more beneficial to plants than water. Leaf lettuce treated with carbonated water by the Agricultural Research Service of the United States Department of Agriculture produced three times more leaf in six weeks than lettuce sprayed lightly with plain water. Chrysanthemums so treated had ready-to-cut blooms two weeks earlier than untreated plants.

Experiments in this country have also shown that snap beans and other vegetables and fruits, including strawberries, can be saved by irrigating with brackish or slightly salty water during an emergency, although its prolonged use can be detrimental. Asparagus, beets, kale and spinach showed a good tolerance, and broccoli, cabbages, cucumbers, onions, peas, peppers, potatoes, corn and tomatoes proved mildly tolerant to the treatment. Experiment to determine just how salty the water can be on your own vegetables.

Elsewhere in the world, similar experiments are being made with barley, gladioli and sunflowers. The Ministry of Agriculture in Israel has reported that carnations irrigated exclusively with sea water of 3.5 percent salt content easily survived a nine-month drought. The plants actually did better than those treated with plain water, due to the magnesium and nitrogen in the salts.

With the drought, the rainbarrel, far from a modern device, is coming into its own again. Rainbarrels, painted to match either trim or shingles, are best set under gutters to catch runoff water from the roof. The drain downspout is placed inside the barrel, which should be covered to discourage mosquitoes. The water can either be stored to ladle out later, or the barrel can be fitted snugly with a pipe and tap at the bottom. The barrel is often rigged at the top with a pipe, "T" connection and hose, so that overflow from heavy rains will be syphoned off to nearby plants.

Rainbarrels remain an excellent way to collect water, but a newly developed method, originated by the USDA, actually "makes" water. It is a simple matter to build a solar still using polyethylene plastic. Just dig a two-foot hole in the ground in an out-of-the-way area, place a bucket in its center and cover with the plastic, weighing down the edges and center with stones. The sun will draw water from the soil, which will collect on the bottom of the sagging plastic and drip into the bucket. In a week about two and one-half gallons of pure water can be collected.

One scientific advance in water conservation is still in the experimental stage, but promises much. Windham J. Roberts, an engineer on the staff of the Illinois State Water Survey stationed at the University of Illinois in Urbana, has developed a chemical which is said to "substantially inhibit the transpiration of moisture from plants." (Tests were made on hybrid corn and grass.) Certain fatty alcohols in water are applied to the soil just before or after planting. This substance is absorbed by the roots and eventually reduces exhalation from the leaves and other plant parts. The result is a plant that needs less water.

No green thumb need knuckle under to the drought. An excellent idea is to plant drought-resistant stock and to avoid heavy "drinkers," such as willows. Robinson strawberries, for example, do better in hot weather. Petunias have proved to be an excellent drought-resistant flower.

A list of similar plants tolerating dry conditions would include, among many others: French marigolds, nicotiana, gloriosa daisy, candytuft, California poppy, Chinese forget-me-nots, hollyhocks, four-o'clocks, portulaca, heather, rugosa rose, smoke bush, vitex, privet, Japanese barberry, Russian olive, Chinese elm, ailanthus, juniper, gray birch, mungo pine, goldenrain tree and white poplar.

Common-sense expedients include controlling weeds, soaking the ground instead of sprinkling and using cooking, wash and shower water (small amounts of soap and detergent will do most plants no harm). Another method is to recess open-ended No. 10 cans in front of each plant and water into these. Or set inverted bottles of water near plant roots so that watering is gradual and there is no waste. To water deeply and cheaply, when local restrictions are lifted, just tie a sock over the hose nozzle, so that the water seeps out through the sock.

The most important point to remember is to keep the soil in good tilth. Let it shed no water. Aerate it thoroughly. With a little extra effort, improving the soil is a relatively easy matter, too. Cover crops such as inexpensive annual grass seed can be planted and turned under to provide organic matter. Moisture-holding humus like compost, peat moss, manure and well-rotted leaves can be introduced to enrich the earth and make it more friable.

Remember when watering that no water at all is better than shallow sprinkling. Shallow watering causes roots to rise to the surface and dry out, often killing plants in the process.

7

Disease and Pest Control Premiums

Gardening Health Hazards

This authoritative booklet covers the hazards of working a small vegetable plot as well as the back forty. Send $1 for "Health Hazards in Farming and Gardening," from the American Medical Association, Order Handling Department, 535 North Dearborn Street, Chicago, Illinois 60610.

A Colorful Chemical Care Poster

Chevron's valuable free poster giving tips on the proper use of chemicals in the home garden ought to be prominently displayed in the garage, garden shed or wherever you store such chemicals. The 1 × 2-foot poster includes tips on mixing and applying, storing, disposal, spills and first aid. There is even a nationwide number on the chart you can call if you have a question about first aid for chemical misuse. Chevron also offers a free brochure on weeds in the garden. Request "Chemicals and Common Sense" and "Weeds" from Robert L. Hoen, Manager, Consumer Affairs, ORTHO Consumer Products Division,

Chevron Chemical Co., 575 Market St., San Francisco, California 94105.

All About Pesticides

For a free booklet describing the basic pesticides and their safe, effective uses request "Understanding Pesticides," National Agricultural Chemicals Association, 1155 15th Street N.W., Washington, D.C. 20005.

Why not try organic insecticides instead of dangerous chemicals? Spices, certain vegetables mixed in a blender and many other substances are effective in discouraging insects. An excellent book on the subject is Gardening Without Poisons *by Beatrice Trum Hunter.*

Free Home Remedies to Battle the Bugs

To begin with, try companion and trap plants, which combat troublesome insects when planted near more valued plants. These helpful trap plants either repel insects from the general area, or attract insects to them so that they can be trapped and destroyed in considerable numbers. Examples of trap plants are larkspur and white geraniums, which can be used to attract Japanese beetles away from tomatoes; when the beetles congregate on these plants, they can be collected and destroyed. Companion plants, plants that repel insects, include marigolds, which cut down on nematodes in the soil; begonias, which are never approached by aphids; and garlic, which repels many insects. Experiment with other plants, too. Observe combinations that seem to work in the garden. An excellent book on this subject is *The Organic Way to Plant Protection* from *Organic Gardening,* Emmaus, Pennsylvania 18049.

There are also a number of homemade organic repellents that will combat pests and do no ecological harm. They include:

Compost Solution. A spadeful of compost soaked in a bucket of water for an hour or so and sprinkled over plants will both fertilize them and repel a number of insects.

Garlic-Pepper-Soap Spray. Blend together four crushed cloves of garlic, four tablespoons of hot pepper, a cake of strong soap, and a cup of hot water. Dissolve in two gallons of hot water (the size of most watering cans), cool, and use for a general insect spray.

Garlic Spray. Press a garlic clove and mix the oily juice with a gallon of water for an all-purpose spray.

Ground Hot Pepper. Sprinkle on plants for protection against insects.

Hot-pepper Spray. Grind hot pepper pods and mix with an equal amount of water and a little soap powder for use against tomato worms.

Onion Spray. Chop onions finely in an electric blender or by hand and mix one tablespoon with a pint of water for an all-purpose spray.

Pickled Peppers. A pint (or a peck) of pickled peppers put through a blender and sprinkled over plants makes a good general insecticide.

Rhubarb Leaves. Soak three pounds of the leaves in three quarts of water for an hour and sprinkle over plants infected with aphids.

Soapy Water. A soapy solution sprayed or painted on tomato plants serves as a good general-purpose insect repellent. Green soap or soaps made with fish or coconut oils are best, but any will do. Hose off the soap a few minutes after applying it or it might harm plants. Some gardeners mix one cup of green soap with two cloves of garlic and three gallons of water for a soap solution.

Tomato-leaf Spray. Tomato leaves contain solanine, an alkaloid that is a repellent to many insects, including aphids. Boil the leaves and stems in water and spray the solution on plants when it cools.

Vegetable Spray. Grind finely and mix two hot peppers, a large onion, a garlic clove, and a teaspoon of detergent and let this set in a little water for a day or so. Strain it and add the liquid to a pint of water for an all-purpose insect spray. You can use geranium leaves, mint and other strong-flavored plants in the mix, too.

Water. A fine hose spray of water will kill aphids and many other insects, or knock them off the plants. The water also dilutes the juices aphids feed on, thus turning the bugs off so that they do little damage.

The herb camomile is said to help sick plants recover when planted near them.

Fighting Bugs with Bugs

Did you know that the scientist who discovered DDT, now banned in the United States, was awarded a Nobel Prize? This and many other fascinating facts about pesticides can be found in the free booklet "Fighting Pests with Pests," which shows how you can fight bugs in the home garden without using dangerous chemicals, by employing natural means. Complete and easy to understand, the booklet is also an excellent ecology primer for children. Included with our copy were several wonderful wildlife posters in full color very appropriate for a child's room. All free from the National Wildlife Federation, 1412 16th Street N.W., Washington, D.C. 20036.

Ladybugs and Praying Mantises

For a free information kit on how ladybugs and praying mantises can be used instead of chemicals in the garden request "Biological Control Literature," Bio-Control Co., P.O. Box 247, 13451 Highway 174, Cedar Ridge, California 95924.

Insect Allies That Will Work for Nothing in the Garden

Scientists estimate that 99 percent of the 1.6 million known insect species are beneficial to plants. Learn which insects are helpful to plants and don't harm them; in fact, introduce them into the garden where possible. The same applies to birds and other wildlife. An incomplete list of these "good guys" follows. It can be supplemented by a complete book on the subject like C. L. Metcalf and W. P. Flint's *Destructive and Useful Insects—Their Habits and Control* (McGraw-Hill):

Assassin Bugs. Long-legged brown insects ¾ inch long, with wings folded together over the body. They do bite people if bothered, but if left alone devour a good many harmful insects, grabbing them by the front legs and "assassinating" them.

Assassin Flies. Hairy black and gray flies about 1½ inches long with yellowish legs. They prey on many insects.

Birds. Birds can be a problem, but their good qualities usually far outnumber their bad habits. Little birds especially are apt to be meat-eaters and won't harm plants. Most birds feed voraciously on slugs, aphids, and other harmful bugs. (Tips to discourage marauding birds are given further on.)

Centipedes. Flat, brown, many-legged creatures with one pair of legs per segment (unlike the slightly harmful millipede, with two pairs per segment) that often live under rocks. They dine on several types of insects, as well as slugs and snails.

Damsel Bugs. These resemble the assassin bug, but are only about half their size. They feed on aphids and other small, soft-bodied insects.

Doodlebug. A plump brown insect ½ inch long with jaws like forceps. Doodlebugs destroy ants, which often carry aphids. They dig a cone-shaped hole in the ground, hide at the bottom, and wait until an ant falls in.

Dragonflies. Large (2 inches long) insects with big eyes and transparent wings, these fast fliers catch other insects with their legs while airborne.

Flower Flies. Small (⅜-inch-long) insects that resemble bees. Flower flies hover over flowers and pounce on aphids and other harmful insects.

Lacewing Flies. Delicate, ½-inch-long pale-green insects with golden eyes and filmy wings twice the size of their bodies. Lacewing fly larvae are about ⅓ inch long, yellowish and torpedo-shaped, with hairs on the body and jaws shaped like forceps. These larvae are called aphid lions because of the prodigious amount of aphids they eat. Lacewing larvae are also valuable because they devour hard-to-kill mites and other insects.

Ladybugs. Ladybugs, the best known beneficial insects, comprise some 350 species around the world. They feed on aphids, mites, white flies, scale insects, and the eggs of other insects.

Moles. Moles can be destructive in the garden, but they do eat grubs, cutworms, and other harmful insects.

Praying Mantis. Another familiar insect, often kept by kids as a "pet," the praying mantis lives entirely on insects like aphids. Huge by insect standards (they range from 1½ to 5 inches long), they are greenish or brown and have triangular heads that they turn from side to side. Their front legs are held in a "praying" position, ready to seize other insects.

Spiders. Spiders destroy numerous garden pests. They have eight legs, insects six—count the legs if you're in doubt.

Toads. Keep a pet toad in the garden and it will devour many pests, including cutworms, slugs, and stink bugs. Toads can be attracted by keeping a clay pan filled with water in a shady part of the garden.

Trichogramma Wasps. These are tiny microscopic insects whose black eggs are often found in the garden. The wasps deposit these eggs among the eggs of more than 200 harmful insects. When the trichogramma eggs hatch, the larvae kill the embryos of their host eggs. So leave those black eggs alone.

Hornets, ground beetles, and many other insects can also be helpful in the vegetable patch; only the most common benefactors could be mentioned above. If you want to introduce beneficial insects to the garden, there are quite a few insectaries that sell ladybugs, trichogramma wasps, and other good guys. A pint of ladybugs contains about 10,000 of the little insects and costs only three or four dollars (try the Ladybug Beetle & Sierra Bug Company, which really is located on Lady Bug Lane in the town of Rough and Ready, California 95975).

Attracting Hummingbirds

To receive an informative booklet on how to attract the enchanting, beneficial hummingbird to your garden, send 35¢ for postage and handling for "Hummingbirds—Attract and Feed," to Woodsworld, 600 Olive Springs Road, Santa Cruz, California 95060.

Stock Your Backyard with a Menagerie of Wildlife

The National Wildlife Federation pamphlet "Invite Wildlife to Your Backyard" is an attractive, comprehensive guide instructing you how to lure a wide variety of often beneficial wildlife to your backyard, whether it consists of an acre or merely a windowbox. Depending on the size of your plot, you can at minimum cost attract animals ranging from a myriad of birds to ducks, squirrels, raccoons, rabbits, frogs, turtles, butterflies, dragonflies, and even deer by keeping the proper plants and providing for their needs in other ways. Free from National Wildlife Federation, 1412 16th St. N.W., Washington, D.C. 20036.

Put a quick end to ants that are ruining your garden or invading the house itself. Locate the ant hills and pour a kettle of boiling water down each.

A Beat the Bugs Poster

This free four-color wall poster traces insect life from prehistoric times to the present, focusing on insects harmful to man and ways to control them in and out of the garden. Also included are brief biographies of 50 common insects. Request "The Conquest of Insects

Harmful to Man," from Insects, Velsicol Chemical Corporation, 341 East Ohio Street, Chicago, Illinois 60611.

Insect Identification

For a free illustrated booklet that will help you identify and control the bugs that you battle in the garden, request "Lawn and Garden Insect Control Manual," from the CIBA Geigy Chemical Corporation, Ardsley, New York 10502.

Rodent Control

Rats, mice, moles, squirrels and prairie dogs can cause much damage in the garden. A free "Rodent Control Product Guide," available in Spanish as well as English, can be ordered from Bell Laboratories, Inc., 3699 Kinsman Boulevard, Madison, Wisconsin 53704.

Mothballs strewn among your flower and vegetable seedlings in the garden will help repel rabbits and other pests.

Combating Blackbirds

A handsomely illustrated free leaflet that tells how to protect corn plantings from their major avian enemies, red-winged blackbirds and grackles. Request "Protecting Corn from Blackbirds," Wildlife Leaflet 476, U.S. Fish and Wildlife Service, Department of the Interior, Washington, D.C. 20240.

Leaves from the black walnut tree are said to be an excellent flea repellent when placed in an animal's sleeping area.

The Story of Willie Bacteria

Better sanitation through bacteriological research is the slogan of the FX Lab Company, which offers the free booklet "The Story of Willie

Bacteria, or How to Take Care of Your Septic Tank and Cesspool," which should certainly be a concern of every gardener with a cesspool on his property. Write: FX Lab Company, 1275 Bloomfield Avenue, Fairfield, New Jersey 07006.

Free Ways to Eliminate Slugs and Snails in the Garden

Dark, slimy, soft-bodied, snaillike forms up to four inches long that are voracious night feeders, slugs feed on foliage and even on fruit near the ground. They hide under rocks, boards, mulch, and other objects in the daytime and travel at night, lubricating their nocturnal paths with a slimy mucuslike secretion. It takes them about eight days to travel a mile, even when they swing from plant to plant via mucous ropes. Carefully inspect the garden, especially under rocks, mulch, and so on, and destroy any slugs you find by dropping them into kerosene. You can also put boards in the garden to attract them, or use cabbage leaves for the same purpose. As slugs need lubrication to travel, placing a circle of dry sand, sea sand, ashes, sawdust, or hydrated lime around plants will stymie them. Keeping plants staked also helps, as do coarse scratchy mulches like hay. Replacing soil at the base of plants with rocks helps to prevent slugs from crawling up the plants.

To kill slugs: 1) place near plants shallow pans of stale beer that the slugs will crawl into and drown in (beer attracts thirty times as many slugs as commercial baits, says the USDA); 2) use a pan of one tablespoon of flour and ⅛ teaspoon of yeast mixed with a cup of water in the same way as beer; 3) use solutions of grape wine, blackberry wine, or vinegar in the way you would use beer; 4) sprinkle salt on the slugs or spray them with two tablespoons of salt dissolved in a quart of hot water (though excess salt residue in the soil is harmful); 5) in the early spring you can help destroy the slug population by turning over the soil so that slug eggs are exposed and dry out and die in the sun. Try not to have the soil too acid—slugs thrive on an acid soil.

Fighting Fruit Tree Pests Organically

This pamphlet describes the major pests encountered by the home grower of fruits and nuts and gives four ways to combat them without harmful chemicals. Request the price of "Control of Insects on Deciduous Fruit and Nut Trees in the Home Orchard Without Insecticides," publication number G-211, from Superintendent of Documents, Washington, D.C. 20402.

Discourage birds from raiding fruit trees by hanging pieces of fur on the limbs, or by stringing thin thread from branch to branch. The birds will mistake the fur for a natural predator, and brushing up against the thread will frighten them off.

Diagnosing Sick Houseplants

You'll learn how to identify and control common diseases and insect troubles suffered by houseplants from this informative booklet. Send 20¢ for "Houseplant Troubles," publication number BP-1-12, Indiana Cooperative Extension Service, Mailing Room, Agricultural Administration Building, Purdue University, West Lafayette, Indiana 47907.

Houseplant Bugs

The persistent insects that commonly attack houseplants are identified in this thorough illustrated booklet, which also tells how to eliminate or control them. Request the price of "Insects and Related Pests of Houseplants," publication number G-67, from Superintendent of Documents, Washington, D.C. 20402.

Free Houseplant Prescriptions

• A good general treatment for sick plants: put several empty eggshells into a milk bottle filled with water and let stand for a day. Then water the plants with this mixture.

• To revive "sick" ferns, water them with one-half teacup of salt added to six pints of lukewarm water. If ferns are infested with worms, stick matches into the soil, sulfur end down. For an ordinary-sized plant, use four matches; six for a large pot. The sulfur does the trick.

• The best way to remove mealy bugs from African violets is to dip a small swab in alcohol and touch each bug individually. It's time-consuming, but reliable. *Don't touch the leaves;* this will cause brown patches.

• Remove mites and thrips from houseplants by dipping the plants in 110°F. water to which 3 tablespoons of Fels Naphtha has been added per gallon.

• Swab dust from houseplant leaves with Q-tips, which are small enough to get in all the corners.

• If green algae forms on the soil of your houseplants, stir up the surface and water once a month with a solution of potassium permanganate—one-half a teaspoon per gallon.

Controlling Lawn Diseases

For an illustrated booklet that depicts how lawns are ravaged by various diseases and tells how to eliminate or control them, request the price of "Lawn Diseases: How to Control Them," publication number G-61, from Superintendent of Documents, Washington, D.C. 20402.

Bugs on the Lawn

This up-to-date booklet depicts some 30 pests that attack lawns and gives methods of control. Request the price of "Lawn Insects: How to Control Them," publication number G-53, from Superintendent of Documents, Washington, D.C. 20402.

Do not spray the leaves when watering roses; this encourages the spread of disease.

Strawberry Diseases

The major problem with growing strawberries is the number of diseases they are susceptible to, a problem this illustrated booklet helps by depicting the symptoms of many strawberry diseases and suggesting cures or controls for them. Request the price of "Strawberry Diseases," publication number F-2140, from Superintendent of Documents, Washington, D.C. 20402.

Wood or charcoal ashes moistened and painted on tree trunks often discourage borers.

Seven Free Ways to Keep Birds out of the Berry Patch

Birds are probably the worst pests you'll encounter in raising berries. They are harmful to tomatoes and other crops, too, though a berry garden will attract many beautiful species you wouldn't have otherwise seen. To prevent birds from devouring the entire crop, try any of the following methods in addition to the time-honored scarecrow:

• Pieces of rope or garden hose placed at strategic sites are sometimes mistaken for snakes by birds, who keep their distance.

• White string wrapped around bushes looks like spiderwebs to birds and scares them off because birds fear spiders.

• Broken mirrors or aluminum pie plates strung on bushes often frighten birds away.

• Some gardeners leave transistor radios on in the berry patch, since the birds evidently appreciate neither rock nor classical music.

• Another ploy is to plant berries for the birds; that is, plant enough of their favorites, such as mulberry trees, to divert them from precious raspberries and strawberries. Birds have actually been known to get drunk on overripe, fermented wild berries. It is not unusual for waxwings, for example, to get smashed on fermented rowanberries and crash into cars on the road, and ducks can get so drunk on overripe mulberries that they cannot fly.

• All berries and tomatoes can be protected by covering them with cheesecloth or clear plastic. Either can be draped around individual bushes or spread over the strawberry patch. Cheesecloth, because it comes in narrow widths, has to be sewn together to make a piece big enough to cover a strawberry patch. It can be spread right over the plants and anchored down on the sides or attached to a frame constructed around the bed. Clear plastic can be used in the same ways, but punch small holes in it to provide good air circulation for the plants.

Experimenters have found that human hair packed in nylon nets repels deer when the nets are hung on the branches of trees and shrubs.

Vegetable Diseases

Prevent vegetable diseases before planting. Send 30¢ for "Treating Vegetable Seed to Prevent Disease," publication number E-1128, New York State Cooperative Extension Office, Mailing Room, Building 7, Research Park, Cornell University, Ithaca, New York 14850.

Marigolds planted around vegetables are said to discourage numerous insect pests.

Tomato Diseases

Here is an illustrated booklet covering all the principal tomato diseases and their controls. Send 35¢ for "Tomato Diseases: Identification and Control in the Home Garden," publication number IB-28, New York State Cooperative Extension Service, Mailing

Room, Building 7, Research Park, Cornell University, Ithaca, New York 14850.

Cardboard collars from laundered shirts, stapled into a circle, can be inserted in the soil at the base of tomatoes and other plants to protect them from cutworm damage.

8

How to Get Plants for Nothing

How to Get More Shrubs for Nothing

This illustrated pamphlet tells you how to propagate new shrubs from your old established ones by several methods of layering. Send 15¢ for "New Shrubs from Old by Layering," publication number E-1006, New York Cooperative Extension Service, Mailing Room, Building 7, Research Park, Cornell University, Ithaca, New York 14850.

Grow a Free Tree in a Tree, Organically

There are many ways besides planting seeds to propagate plants, including hardwood and softwood cuttings, mounding and several layering methods, all of which can be found in any complete gardening encyclopedia. But a method rarely described and too-little used is air-layering, which is an excellent, easy way to obtain large plants in a short time. While the standard equipment for air-layering (offered in kits at garden supply stores) includes a sharp knife, rooting stimulant, sphagnum moss, polyethylene plastic sheeting, and plastic electrical tape, we have found that only the sharp knife was absolutely essential if we used only materials that we had on hand. For sphagnum moss, we substituted acid peat moss in one case, black peat in another, and rich organic garden soil in the last. The special plastic sheeting was dispensed with in favor of plastic freezer bags for two layerings and burlap for the other. No rooting stimulant was needed and instead of plastic electrical tape, we used black friction tape or string.

Since we were breaking "laws" already, we decided not to use year-old branches, either, but selected older limbs on three 8-year-old Jersey blueberry plants—older limbs usually take longer to root if they root at all. What's more, layering was done late in July, not in cool weather when rooting is most vigorous and air-layering is usually practiced.

The layers were made the proper 18 inches from the tip of each branch, all leaves within six inches being removed. Instead of wounding the wood by slitting or notching, we ringed or girdled the branches half an inch, scraping lightly to remove the slippery cambium, and squeezing the moist peat or soil around each wound to remove excess water. Then the bags and burlap were fixed securely in place with tape or string.

The whole operation took about 15 minutes, and we had little hope for its success, but knew there was nothing to lose except three branches that would have been pruned off anyway. We did watch the wrappings to see that no water seeped in, and made sure that the burlap didn't dry out, but otherwise forgot about the whole matter until fall. Air layers started in spring frequently do not root until the next spring, but we discovered in midautumn, to our surprise, that all three had succeeded. Roots had formed on each of the injured branches and the rooting medium in both plastic bags was filled with fibrous roots, while the growth under the burlap wrap was just as thick.

There are two schools of thought about transplanting air-layers. One claims that the new roots will be injured by freezing if left on the plant over the winter, advising quick transplanting before cold weather. The other holds that the air layer should be left unsevered from the parent plant for a full year. To test both theories, we transplanted the burlap wrapped layer and one from a plastic bag to the nursery bed that fall, and left the third on the shrub until the next spring. Both methods worked—all three new blueberries are thriving today.

When air-layering more conventionally—that is, *not* using our method—notch any young branch 18 inches from its top, sprinkle the wound with rooting hormone, removing all excess powder by shaking the branch, and wrap the wound with moist (but not wet) sphagnum moss. Next fix polyethylene plastic in place with electrical tape. When roots form, the layered growth is removed and given tender care in the nursery bed until ready for transplanting.

Free Mist Propagation Frame Plans

Mist propagation is an excellent technique for propagating cuttings of woody plants both indoors and outdoors. Free plans for an easily constructed 6 × 6-foot mist propagating frame are available from the Agricultural Engineering Department, Virginia Polytechnic Institute, Blacksburg, Virginia 24061.

Mist Propagation Equipment

This is a useful free booklet evaluating mist propagating equipment presently on the market. Request "An Evaluation of Various Equipment and Media Used for Mist Propagation and Their Relative Costs," from the Georgia Agricultural Experiment Station, Athens, Georgia 30601.

Root houseplant cuttings in only about an inch of water instead of the traditional glassful. This allows more space for oxygen and produces healthier roots.

Free Strawberry Plants: Easy Propagation Methods

Unlike wild strawberries, domesticated hybrid strawberries do not come true from seed; that is, strawberry seed will yield plants unlike the plant it came from, plants with characteristics of the hybrid plant's ancestors. But it isn't necessary to grow strawberries from seed. As noted, all strawberries except everbearers take care of propagating themselves admirably by sending out runners or daughter plants that root nearby. These can be used to renew the strawberry patch by holding them in place with a stone, hairpin, clothespin, or small handful of dirt until they root. Or they can be allowed to root and then be transplanted to a new strawberry bed. The best way to do this is to fill peat pots, cut-down milk containers, or small flowerpots with good strawberry soil, sink them in the earth near the runners, and let the runners root once in a pot. Hold each runner in place with a hairpin, clothespin or stone. When the runners are firmly rooted, sever them from the mother plants and transplant elsewhere. Peat pots can, of course, then be transplanted without lifting the plants from them.

Making More Fruit Trees

For an excellent illustrated pamphlet showing the various methods of increasing fruit trees, send 30¢ for "Fruit Tree Propagation," publication number NR.481, Ohio Cooperative Extension Service, Ohio State University, 2120 Fyffe Road, Columbus, Ohio 43210.

Peaches from a Pit for a Pittance, or Budding for the Beginner

Budding is a simple operation that often seems far more difficult than it really is. Probably the easiest tree to bud, and to grow from seed, is the peach. It is also the quickest fruit tree to bear. Other fruits will give you equally good results over a longer period of time, but by following the cultural directions described here, you can be eating home-grown peaches in as little as three years from the time you plant the pit. (By all means, however, try this easy method with other fruit pits and seeds, too.)

To grow your peach tree from seed, first plant the stone of a wild peach, or any named variety, after it has been cleaned of the pulp. Nurserymen generally use a red-leafed variety (to identify budded seedlings) or the Lovell peach for rootstock, and use western sand cherry, Nanking cherry, or beach plum seedlings for dwarfing rootstock.

It is important that any pit has about 12 weeks to "after-ripen" at a temperature of about 41°F. so that it will germinate. But this requirement can easily be met by planting the pit early this fall. Keep the ground moist and don't worry about any growth starting until next spring—the pits have a built-in safety mechanism that prevents them from growing after September. The out-of-doors will supply all the conditions needed for after-ripening and your seedling will come up next spring.

When fall planting is impractical, the pits can be soaked in water 10 to 12 hours, mixed with sawdust or peat moss, and stored in a cool cellar over the winter. Or they may be soaked and sealed in polyethylene envelopes with peat moss at a temperature near 40°F. This last method permits periodic examinations of the seeds, which should be planted before they germinate.

Whether you plant in fall or early spring, give the seedling tender care during its first year, keeping it shaded and well watered, fertilizing sparingly with blood meal, and removing all side branches to encourage growth. You will be ready to bud the tree the following year in late spring or midsummer—depending on the region in which you live—when the tree's diameter is about the thickness of a lead pencil.

June budding, actually performed in May, is the practice of most nurserymen in southern regions, and the budding date for peaches in the New York area is generally toward the end of August. But no really accurate dates can be given, for much depends on many conditions—on how dry the season is, or how light the soil is, for example. The important point to remember is to bud before the bark on the tree tightens, while it still slips easily.

The materials are few for the budding operation. Budsticks from the desired variety are, of course, essential. If you don't have a good peach tree, ask a neighbor for a pruned branch of a peach or a nectarine. Only plump dormant buds should be used—fat, hard buds near the middle of the stick, which should be vigorous current season's growth and firm and woody itself. It is best to cut the budstalks needed, leaves and all, and wrap them in damp burlap until you are ready to use them.

The only equipment needed is a very sharp knife and a rubber band, although both must be used carefully and accurately. There are many methods of budding, but shield or T-budding is probably the easiest for peaches. Simply make a T-shaped cut in the bark of the seedling or stock. Cut upward, starting two inches above the ground line or higher, drawing the knife upward lightly for about an inch and twisting the blade slightly before removing it to loosen the edges. Then make the transverse cut, or the top of the T. Be sure to cut the bark and not the wood of the tree. If the bark has not separated well, use your knife to lift it along both sides of the upward cut.

Now you are ready to cut the bud. Just one bud is needed for each tree. First remove all leaves from the budstick, leaving intact one-half inch of the leaf stem in front of the bud you select for a handle. Invert the budstick. Holding it directly in front of you, make a shallow slanting cut up toward the bud—you'll be cutting downward because the budstock is inverted. Start the cut about one-quarter of an inch below the bud and draw the knife down. With the peach a thin strip of wood may be taken, but cut neither too deep nor too shallow—the object is to avoid injuring the growing tissue between the bark and the wood. Make sure that all the bark is taken at the point of the bud so that it will not crumble when used later. After passing the knife blade under the bud, angle your cut up and out, removing the bud carefully.

The shield bud will be about three-quarters of an inch long, including the bark. The next step is to insert it at the top of the T-cut. Insert it top end up. Using the leaf stem as a handle, push the bud down, making sure it is flush against the wood of the stock. The bud shield should be completely enclosed, with the bud exposed, and any part of the shield protruding above the T should be cut off.

No waxing is required, as is the case in most grafting. The bud is simply tied tightly in place with a rubber band, raffia, plastic sheeting, or even string. .010-gauge rubber strips are best because they expand as the rootstock grows, and will rot out by the time a good union has been effected. Starting at the bottom of the T-cut, wind the wrapping upward, making three or four turns below the bud and three or four turns above it. Do not cover the bud, however, and be certain that the winding is airtight. Then knot the wrapping securely.

In about a month the tie should be cut to prevent girdling. At that time the bud and stock will be united if the budding was successful, but the bud will normally not put forth growth until the following spring. If the leaf stem on the bud falls off, you can be reasonably sure that the union has been successful. But a shriveled leaf stem that still adheres to the bud after a few months is usually a sign of failure and, in that case, budding should be tried again if the bark on the stock still slips readily.

In early spring cut off the top of the tree about two inches above the bud. When the bud sprouts, loosely tie it to the stub left when you cut, so that it will have support. After the new shoot has hardened off somewhat—in a month at the most—untie it and remove the stub close to the budded area where new growth will heal the wound. All growth below the bud should be removed whenever it appears, and the tree should be transplanted to its permanent location in the spring of the next year.

Transplant to a location with full sun, spacing the trees about 15 feet apart. Be sure that the planting hole is deep and wide enough for the root system. Fill in the space around the roots with topsoil or organic matter and tamp the soil down around the roots, adding water to the hole if the soil is dry. Most peaches are self-fertile and need no other varieties nearby to affect pollination. It is important to prune vigorous-growing trees lightly and weak-growing trees vigorously. As the peach generally bears two to three years from the bud, you may well be eating fruit from your new tree in as little as three years, or two years from the budding. The yield will increase in size from year to year—and before you know it, for the price of a pit you'll be enjoying the five to ten bushels which a five-year-old full-bearing tree should produce.

Growing Tree Seedlings

This excellent pamphlet tells how to collect and germinate tree seeds. Send 75¢ for "Growing Trees in Small Nurseries," Cornell Extension Bulletin IB-68, to Distribution Center C, Research Park, Cornell University, Ithaca, New York 14850.

A Tree Almost Free

Think about getting together with a group of neighbors and buying tree seedlings from the USDA for pennies apiece. Some seedlings offered, up to 10 inches tall, cost only $40 per 100, less than 40¢ a tree! For a free price list write the U.S. Department of Agriculture, Forestry Division, Washington, D.C. 20250.

Evergreen Seedlings

For a free twice-a-year catalog offering seedlings and larger transplants of pine, spruce, fir, hemlock and rhododendron, write Musser Forests, Inc., Box 23, Indiana, Pennsylvania 15701.

Wholesale Evergreens

If you need a large number of small evergreens for a planting, you'll find it hard to beat the wholesale prices at Flickingers Nursery, which offers a free catalog. There is a minimum order of 100, but 100 four- to eight-inch-tall Scotch pines, for example, cost only $17. Write Flickingers Nursery, Sagamore, Pennsylvania 16250.

9

Greenhouse Gifts

Greenhouse Gardening

You'll learn a lot from this illustrated booklet on the latest in greenhouse innovations. Send 50¢ for "Give Your Greenhouse a New Look," publication number 74-45, to Agricultural Publications U-35, College of Agriculture and Natural Resources, University of Connecticut, Storrs, Connecticut 06268. Free from the same source is the booklet "Build Your Own Greenhouse," publication number SEB-40.

Plastic Greenhouses

This useful free pamphlet details the latest developments in greenhouses made of plastic instead of glass. Request "Plastic Greenhouses," Circular 905, College of Agriculture, University of Illinois, Urbana, Illinois 61801.

Greenhouse Living

Lord & Burnham's colorful free booklet "Greenhouse Living" gives a score and more ideas on how to use a greenhouse, emphasizing ways to make greenhouses a beautiful part of the house. Write Lord & Burnham, Irvington, New York 10533.

Grow Vegetables 12 Months a Year

Extend the vegetable growing season to 12 months with this illustrated booklet on an often neglected aspect of gardening. Send 30¢ for "Greenhouse Vegetables," publication number NR-517, Ohio State Cooperative Extension Service, Ohio State University, 2120 Fyffe Road, Columbus, Ohio 43210.

Going Commercial?

If you have a large greenhouse you've probably considered cashing in on your gardening expertise at one time or another. An excellent booklet on the subject is "Commercial Production of Vegetable and Flower Plants," publication number IB-82, available for 25¢ from New York State Extension Service, Mailing Room, Building 7, Research Park, Cornell University, Ithaca, New York 14850.

Solar Panel Greenhouses

For free literature, including a colorful catalog, about solar panel greenhouses, which save much money on fuel costs and come in a large variety of types and sizes, write Vegetable Factory Inc., 100 Court Street, Copiague, New York 11726.

Greenhouse Catalog

This free color catalog features redwood greenhouses of many types and sizes, an automatic fog-mist and many other greenhouse controls. Write Santa Barbara Greenhouses, 390 Dawson Drive, Camarillo, California 93010.

18 More Free Greenhouse Booklets

These 18 greenhouse manufacturers, like the others noted here in separate entries, will supply free information about greenhouses along with their price lists, much of this literature devoted to greenhouse tips and even detailed plans for building your own greenhouse:

ALUMINUM GREENHOUSES, INC., 14605 Lorain Avenue, Cleveland, Ohio 44111

ENVIRONMENTAL DYNAMICS, P.O. Box 996, Sunnymead, California 92388

FOUR SEASONS GREENHOUSES (solar type), 672 Sunrise Highway, West Babylon, New York 11704

E.C. GEIGER, P.O. Box 285, Harleysville, Pennsylvania 19438

GOTHIC ARCH GREENHOUSES, P.O. Box 1564, Mobile, Alabama 36601

GREENHOUSES BY BROMACK, Bromack Construction Co., 6554 East 41st Street, Tulsa, Oklahoma 74145

GREENHOUSE GROWING SYSTEMS, P.O. Box 3926, 2214 Loma Avenue, South El Monte, California 91733

GREENHOUSE SPECIALITES, 9849 Kimker Lane, Saint Louis, Missouri 63127

HORTICULTURE ASSOCIATES, INC., P.O. Box 1008, Indian Hills, Colorado 80454

HYDRO-GARDENS, INC., P.O. Box 9707R, Colorado Springs, Colorado 80932

JANCO GREENHOUSES, J.A. Nearing Co., Inc., 9390 Davis Avenue, Laurel, Maryland 20810

NATIONAL GREENHOUSE CO., P.O. Box 100, Pana, Illinois 62557

POLY GROWERS, INC., P.O. Box 359, Muncy, Pennsylvania 11756

ROUGH BROS., INC., P.O. Box 16010, Cincinnati, Ohio 45216

STURDI-BUILT MFG. CO., 11304 S.W. Boones Ferry Road, Portland, Oregon 97219

TEXAS GREENHOUSE CO., 2717 Saint Louis Avenue, Fort Worth, Texas 76110

TROX MFG. CO., 18 Angell Street, Battle Creek, Michigan 49017

WINANDY GREENHOUSE CONSTRUCTION, INC., 2211 Peacock Road, Richmond, Indiana 47374

A Home Greenhouse Building Primer

This free booklet has been hailed as the best introduction to building home greenhouses, furnishing many sources of plans and related materials. Request "Home Greenhouses," Circular 879, Agricultural Information Office, 112 Mumford Hall, Urbana, Illinois 61801.

Greenhouse Building Plans

These finely detailed plans for an 8 × 12-foot backyard greenhouse are clearly written and include a list of all the materials you need to do the job and hints for greenhouse placement as well. Free from Filon, 12333 South Van Ness Avenue, Hawthorne, California 90250.

More Free Greenhouse Plans

Plans for building home greenhouses can also be obtained free from the following sources:

AGRICULTURAL ENGINEERING DEPT., University of Connecticut, Storrs, Connecticut 06268 (Plan 210)

LOUISIANA STATE UNIVERSITY, Baton Rouge, Louisiana 70803 (Plan 48-6)

INFORMATION OFFICE, 112 Mumford Hall, University of Illinois, Urbana, Illinois 61801 (Circular 880)

OREGON STATE UNIVERSITY, Corvallis, Oregon 97330 (Building Plan 73)

JOHNS-MANVILLE CORPORATION, 22 East 40th Street, New York, New York 10016 (Home Greenhouse Plans)

BUILDING MATERIALS DEPT., Union Carbide Corp., 6855 West 65th Street, Chicago, Illinois 60638.

VIRGINIA POLYTECHNIC INSTITUTE, Blacksburg, Virginia 24060 (Circular 892)

Fiberglass Greenhouse Plans

Crystalite fiberglass panels are excellent for building a backyard greenhouse, with top light and heat transmission, long life expectancy, easy installation and low maintenance. Plans for building a small greenhouse with such panels are available free from Lasco Marketing Services Dept., Anaheim, California 92806.

A Free Miniature Greenhouse

A special offer to our readers, this miniature vinyl greenhouse, measuring about a foot long and a foot wide, can be used to display small cactus plants or to start seeds in spring. It will hold three good-sized cactus plants and is attractively designed. Send $1 for postage and handling to Far Out Cactus, 1027 Lenape Road (Rt. 100), West Chester, Pennsylvania 19380.

A 1¢ "Greenhouse"

A plastic greenhouse for only a penny?

Sure it's low in cost, but it's high in performance, and you can build it yourself in almost less time than it takes to read this piece. Once you do, you'll be able to take cuttings and to propagate new plants all year round instead of just for a few weeks in the summer. Here's how to go about it:

Materials needed include a two-quart plastic freezer bag—it costs a penny!—some peat moss and sand. The USDA recommends this common-sense method, which it has found successful with shrubs, trees and all varieties of houseplants.

The schedule for taking or making cuttings lasts all year long. Roses and spring-flowering shrubs are best done in midsummer before succulent growth hardens off. House plants may be done at any time—depending on species and variety—while the evergreens like holly and yew are done in the late fall and early winter.

Using a sharp knife, make the conventional slanting cut about two to six inches below the top of the cutting. Strip off all the lower leaves and wrap the cuttings in a damp towel to keep them fresh.

Next, fill the clean, airtight freezer bag with four inches of the rooting mixture—two parts of peat moss to one part sand—which should be moistened. Then insert 10 to 12 cuttings two to three inches deep, planting so closely that their leaves barely touch. Spray lightly with water, and twist the top of the bag closed, securing it with a rubber band.

You have now made a miniature, vapor-proof "greenhouse" containing cuttings that will need no more water until they are very well-rooted indeed. Set it in a north window where it gets plenty of daylight but never direct sunlight, which could kill the tender young shoots. Put aluminum foil under the bag to protect the sill from dampness.

The cuttings should be rooted by the time they have been in the window for two months. Open the bag gently and then very carefully dig around one of them, inspecting it for roots. If none are visible, replant the cutting, close the bag again, and set it back in the light. Inspect again once a month during the growing season until the cuttings are rooted or turn black, which means they have died. Most will be rooted, and these should either be moved to a cold frame or planted in a shady spot where alternating heat and cold do not have a chance to kill new plants. A variation on the above greenhouse method, recommended by the U.S. Agricultural Research Service, is to insert the cuttings into a six-inch flowerpot containing a rooting medium of one part peat and one part sand, and enclose the whole pot in the plastic bag. Whichever method you choose, however, is well worth the effort.

Cold Frame Plans

Start next year's gardens five or six weeks early and enjoy fresh vegetables all winter long by building a large, 6 × 3-foot cold frame from a single sheet of plywood or standard widths of 1-inch lumber. Excellently detailed, illustrated plans are yours free from Free Plans, % Dalen Products, Inc., 201 Sherlake Drive, Knoxville, Tennessee 37922.

Slitted Row Cover Plans

Earlier production of warm-season vegetables is possible with slitted row covers, which consist of clear polyethylene plastic with a series of short crosswise slits. The plastic is attached to wire hoops along the vegetable row, providing warmth for the plants on cold days, as well as ventilation on sunny days. Plans are free from Ken-Bar, Inc., 24 Gould Street, Reading, Massachusetts 01867. As a special offer Ken-Bar also pays freight on all first orders of material for the row covers.

More Free Row Covers for Early Plants

You can build a free "greenhouse" for a row of plants set out in the garden early by using old storm windows standing lengthwise. Just dig the storm windows about eight inches into the soil on all sides of the row, seal each space where the windows join with tape, and top the "greenhouse" with either more storm windows or clear plastic.

A simple wooden frame built over a row of early plants and covered with clear plastic will serve the same purpose.

Or you can make a plastic tent "greenhouse" by draping clear plastic over tall wire wickets placed in the row, clipping the plastic to the top of each wicket with clothespins, and holding the plastic in place at ground level by covering it with soil.

It is important to remember that adequate ventilation must be provided with any covering used for early plants. This is particularly important in areas where cold or cool spring weather is occasionally broken by temperatures like those on a hot summer day. Plants can be broiled alive under tight coverings on such days. Either be sure to provide small openings that will let excess heat escape on warm spring days (and can be sealed when it gets really cold), or else go out in the garden and remove all coverings, replacing them at night. It's also a good idea to introduce a few beneficial insects (such as ladybugs) under any shelters you make. They will devour those harmful bugs that tend to congregate in warm places in early spring.

Build an Automated Plant Grower

This illustrated booklet shows you how to build a fluorescent light garden featuring automatic watering. Send 35¢ for "Cornell Automated Plant Grower," publication number IB-40, New York Cooperative Extension Service, Mailing Room, Building 7, Research Park, Cornell University, Ithaca, New York 14850.

Hydroponic Basics

This informative booklet describing hydroponics, the science of cultivating plants in a solution of nutrients and water without soil, is by the creators of "The Magic Garden," an almost totally automated greenhouse system. Send $1 to Hydroculture, Inc., P.O. Box 1655, Glendale, Arizona 85311.

10

Free Things from the Garden

Forcing Spring Shrubs to Bloom in Winter

To learn how to cut branches from spring-flowering shrubs and trees late in winter and force them to bloom indoors weeks before they do outside, order this unusual booklet. Send 35¢ for "Forcing Shrubs and Trees for Indoor Bloom," publication number IB-132, New York Cooperative Extension Service, Mailing Room, Building 7, Research Park, Cornell University, Ithaca, New York 14850.

Making Cut Flowers Live Longer

• Cut harvested flowers twice, once when taking them from the garden and again inside. Hold the stems underwater to eliminate air bubbles in the stems. Then make a ½-inch- to 1-inch-long vertical cut through each stem with a sharp knife.

• Double the life of flowers by cutting their stems at a long slant. They'll absorb more water that way and you'll brighten your home with their extra freshness.

• After picking flowers, preferably in the early morning, condition cut flowers in hot or cold water overnight in a dark place, and they'll last much longer. After arranging, display in a spot out of direct sunlight.

• Another authority recommends this way to keep cut flowers fresh: add a lump of sugar or camphor to the water.

• Flowers will keep longer if the leaves below the water are removed. Decaying vegetable matter poisons the water.

• Cut flowers thrive on fresh air. Let fresh air into the room where they are kept daily, but avoid direct drafts. It is safest, also, to keep them away from direct heat, as well as from the direct hot rays of the sun.

• If cut flowers are kept in a very warm room, move them to a cool place each night. Keep them away from warmth whenever they are not on display.

• Even four-day-old roses can keep on radiating beauty in your home if properly cared for. Cut their stems very short, eliminating most of the leaves, and set them in a thick cluster in a shallow bowl. They can be preserved even longer if they are nestled floating in a deep saucer where they can soak up plenty of water.

Arranging Flowers

The basics of floral arrangement, which will serve as an introduction to more complex works, are covered in this illustrated booklet. Send 25¢ for "Principles of Flower Arrangement," publication number HO-73-1, Indiana Cooperative Extension Service, Mailing Room, Agricultural Administration Building, Purdue University, West Lafayette, Indiana 47907.

When making floral arrangements, use containers that can hold enough water to keep the flowers alive and "well fed."

Floral Arrangements

Numerous ways of arranging flowers are depicted, though not explained, in the Flower Selection Guide free from Florists Transworld Delivery Association, International Headquarters, P.O. Box 2227, 29200 Northwestern Highway, Southfield, Michigan 48037.

Radish plants in the vegetable garden that aren't picked and go to flower can be used for interesting floral arrangements.

Free and Easy Dried Flowers

The easiest way to preserve flowers for beautiful arrangements is air-drying. Just strip the leaves off the stems, tie six or so in a bunch (making sure the heads don't touch) and hang them upside down in a dry airy room for 4-14 days (depending on the flowers) until they dry. Plants that do particularly well for this easy type of drying include:

ageratum	dusty miller	pussywillow
allium	globe amaranth	Queen Anne's lace
artemisia	goldenrod	silver dollars
baby's breath	grasses	strawflower
bridal wreath	heather	tamarisk
canna leaves	hydrangea	tansy
cattails	lavender	wheat
cockscomb	oak leaves	yarrow
daisy		

Free Flower Arrangement Catalogs

Flower arrangement fans will be delighted with the unique little catalog offered by the Dorothy Biddle Services featuring aids in flower arranging. Normally costing 10¢, it is available free to our readers from Dorothy Biddle Services, Dept. G, Hawthorne, New York 10532.

A large assortment of holders, wire, stakes, topiary forms and other flower arranging items are also featured in the free 44-page catalog of Floral Art, P.O. Box 1985, Springfield, Massachusetts 01101.

Make Your Own Corsages

This illustrated booklet shows how to make corsages from flowers in the home garden. Send 25¢ for "Corsages from Garden Flowers," publication number H-7-3E, New York Cooperative Extension Service, Mailing Room, Building 7, Research Park, Cornell University, Ithaca, New York 14850.

A Squash "Trumpet"

The hollow leaf stem of a squash can be made into a horn for a child. Cut the leaf stem from the vine and then cut again through the solid part near the leaf. Finally make a slit in the stalk one-half inch up from the solid part. Blow through the slitted end.

Christmas Decorations for Nothing

Ever think of a Christmas wreath made entirely from wild rose hips, or of using sumac seed clusters for red accents in a wreath? These and many other tips are yours in the free illustrated pamphlet "Christmas Decorations Made with Plant Material," which tells you the natural materials to collect and where to collect them, how to preserve the materials and how to make holiday decorations from them. Directions are clear and uncomplicated. Write United States Department of Agriculture, Science and Education Administration, The National Arboretum, Washington, D.C. 20250.

An Unusual Tradition: Free Julie Neg Wheat Bundles

The Julie Neg wheat bundle is a Scandinavian tradition best described by a writer in the catalog of the firm making the offer: "When I was a little girl growing up on a farm in Iowa," she writes, "I remember my mother telling me about a beautiful Christmas tradition from her childhood in Norway. At harvest time, several of the best bundles of grain were stored in a special place until Christmas Eve. When that long anticipated time arrived, birds and animals were all given a special treat. For the birds, it was a golden sheaf of grain, securely attached to a pole out of doors. They were called 'Julie Neg,' which means Christmas bundle. This lovely tradition of the Scandinavian countries spread to other European nations. It was brought to America, but survived chiefly as a folk story, told to youngsters like me. Now this loving custom has been revived. At harvest time wheat and oats are carefully reaped on our farm with an old-fashioned binder, shocked as they were in the early days, then stacked in a barn loft until people start asking for 'bundles for the birds.' Once discovered, the grain is hastily snatched from the sheaves by most birds and a whole variety of wild life."

A minisheaf of the famous "Julie Neg" wheat bundles, with a retail value of $5, is free to our readers from the ABTA Company, 2120 Fox SMPS, Long Lake, Minnesota 55356. Be sure to mention the offer in this book when writing, and include $1 for postage and handling.

More Free Holiday Decorations

A free booklet about creating wreaths, trees, and centerpieces from pine cones, nuts, seed pods, and other materials, this publication includes tips on purchasing a live or cut Christmas tree. Request "Holiday Decorations Made with Plant Materials," item number 643H, Consumer Information Center, Department Z, Pueblo, Colorado 81009. Note FREE on the envelope.

Hoarding Vegetables and Fruits

This valuable booklet shows the many ways garden fruits and vegetables can be stored for long periods, from leaving growing vegetables covered in the ground to vegetable storage in cellars, basements and storage pits dug outside. Request "Storing Vegetables and Fruit," Home and Garden Bulletin No. 119, Office of Information, U.S. Department of Agriculture, Washington, D.C. 20250.

Storing Apples

A number of ways to store apples so they'll last all winter are discussed in this illustrated pamphlet. Send 25¢ for "Apple Storage," publication number A-2209, Wisconsin Cooperative Extension Service, Agricultural Bulletin Building, 1535 Observatory Drive, University of Wisconsin, Madison, Wisconsin 53706.

Six Ways to Save All Those Green Tomatoes

Perhaps you'd like to try this old trick described by a nurseryman in the 1890s to save tomatoes from frost in the fall. He writes: "At the approach of frost the plants will be loaded with full-sized fruits just beginning to put on the first whitish tinge—the first indication of ripening. In a warm situation, with northern protection, dig a 30-inch-deep trench wide and long enough to contain the plants, which should be cut quite close to the ground. Spread out the plants with their green fruit in the trench until about two feet thick, and over them place a covering of straw six inches in depth, which should be held in place by the use of some light brush. The warmth from the earth will ripen the larger fruits perfectly."

But sometimes it is impossible to pick tomatoes ripe from the vine. You may be away for an extended period, or an early killing frost might be predicted before there is a chance to protect the plants. Don't despair if this happens. Partially unripe or green tomatoes can be ripened in several ways. Here are a number of them:

1. Ripen large green tomatoes indoors at temperatures between 60°F. and 72°F. Temperatures below 60°F. delay ripening, while temperatures above 72°F. are likely to cause undesirable color and decay. Light is not necessary, although it will increase the color of tomatoes somewhat. In any case, don't put tomatoes in direct sunlight indoors—the added heat often deteriorates their quality. A north window is best if green tomatoes are ripened in a window. Make sure that the fruits aren't cracked or blemished, and that they don't touch, so that any possible decay can't spread from one fruit to another.

2. Store green tomatoes wrapped in newspaper or packed in individual containers. If the fruits are kept at a temperature of 55°F. using this method, ripening will be slower and they'll last longer. Green tomatoes can be disinfected with a solution of one teaspoon of household bleach to a quart of water before being individually packed. Dry them thoroughly with paper towels before storing.

3. Store tomatoes separately in plastic bags, making small holes for ventilation.

4. Leave a few inches of stem on each tomato when taking the fruits from the vine and store them on trays or racks in a single layer.

5. Pull up an entire tomato vine with green fruits attached and hang it stem up anyplace where the temperature is always between 55°F. and 72°F.—a basement, attic, garage, spare room, etc. An easy way to do this is to string a rope from wall to wall and hang the plant on it. The fruits will continue ripening long after the plant has wilted.

Canning Fruits and Vegetables

For free detailed instructions on how to put up vegetables and fruits from the garden, request the price of "Home Canning," Home and Garden Bulletin No. 8, from Superintendent of Documents, Washington, D.C. 20402.

Home Canning—Read All About It!

Here's a free tabloid publication packed with how-to information on the home canning of fruits and vegetables and recipes for preserves. Write for "Home Canning Tabloid," publication number 1152, Mississippi Cooperative Extension Service, P.O. Box 5404, Mississippi State University, State College, Mississippi 39762.

A Course in Canning

For a free capsule course in home canning from one of the leading canning jar manufacturers, request "10 Short Lessons in Canning and Freezing," Home Economist, Consumer Products Division, Kerr Glass Manufacturing Corporation, Sand Springs, Oklahoma 74063.

Pickle Pointers

Learn all about making various pickles from garden cucumbers in this free publication. Request "Pickle Pointers," Home Economist, Consumer Products Division, Kerr Glass Manufacturing Corporation, Sand Springs, Oklahoma 74063.

Canning Aids

Everything you need for canning fruits and vegetables—from baskets for picking to fruit presses, choppers, canners and containers—is listed in this 48-page illustrated catalog. Send $1 for postage and handling to Garden Way, 1300 Ethan Allen Avenue, Winooski, Vermont 05404.

Freezing Garden Produce

This excellent booklet instructs you how to prepare vegetables and fruits from the home garden for freezing. Request the price of "Home

Freezing," Home and Garden Bulletin No. 10, Superintendent of Documents, Washington, D.C. 20402.

Drying Fruits and Vegetables

The different methods of preserving fruits and vegetables from the home garden are explained in this illustrated booklet. Send 25¢ for "Home Drying of Fruits and Vegetables," publication number ED-332, Utah Cooperative Extension Service, Library 124, Utah State University, Logan, Utah 84321.

Brewing Your Own

You'll prize this valuable booklet telling all about brewing your own wine from various fruits. Send 25¢ for "Homemade Wine," publication number E-1119, New York Cooperative Extension Service, Mailing Room, Building 7, Research Park, Cornell University, Ithaca, New York 14850.

Maple Syruping

This free catalog features 12 pages of all the equipment you'd need to make maple syrup (if you have the trees or know where there are any)—from evaporators and sap buckets to gathering tanks and tubing. Write G. H. Grimm Company, Rutland, Vermont 05701.

Cooking Frozen Garden Vegetables

What's the best way to cook those beans, peas, tomatoes or corn you froze from that bumper crop last summer? The best kitchen-tested methods for cooking frozen vegetables are covered in a free booklet you can order from The California Frozen Vegetable Council, 27 Branan, Suite 501, San Francisco, California 94107.

Nutritious Meals from the Garden

One serving of any of the vegetarian recipes provided free by the nonprofit organization Meals for Millions will supply at least one-third of the recommended daily allowance of protein for an adult. A sample:

RATATOUILLE MONTEREY

1 eggplant, 1¼ lbs.
½ lb. zucchini
1 green pepper
1 onion
2 tbsp. olive oil
¼ cup cooking oil
⅓ cup tomato paste
1½ tsp. salt
1 tsp. thyme
1 tsp. minced garlic
3 tbsp. flour
1 can sliced tomatoes (14½ oz.)
12 oz. sliced jack cheese

Slice eggplant, zucchini, green pepper and onion. Sauté onion in olive oil until cooked. Stirring, add cooking oil, tomato paste, salt, thyme, garlic, flour and tomatoes. In a 3-quart shallow baking dish layer the ingredients as follows: ½ tomato mixture, ½ sliced vegetables, ½ cheese, ½ slices vegetables, ½ tomato mixture and ½ cheese. Bake at 400° F. for 50 minutes (until hot and bubbly). Serves 4.

Write Meals for Millions/Freedom from Hunger Foundation, 1800 Olympic Blvd., P.O. Drawer 680, Santa Monica, California 90406.

Popcorn Pages

Recipes and nutritional information about popcorn are available free to those who grow "popcorn corn" in the garden. Send a request and a stamped self-addressed envelope to the Popcorn Institute, 111 East Wacker Drive, Chicago, Illinois 60601.

11

Free Garden Constructions

Redwood Garden Construction

This illustrated booklet includes detailed plans for fences, decks, dividers and other garden structures made with long-lasting redwood, the best wood for outdoors. Send 40¢ for "Garden Structures You Can Build," California Redwood Association, One Lombard Street, San Francisco, California 94111.

A Strawberry Pyramid Planter for Next to Nothing

Store-bought strawberry pyramids cost up to $60, but you can make your own for next to nothing from either wood or metal. The *circular metal pyramid* is simply a series of three tiers, the bottom one generally six feet in diameter, the second four feet in diameter, and the third two feet in diameter. To construct a strawberry pyramid from aluminum, use corrugated lawn-edging sheets, which are the necessary six inches or so wide. Build the first tier as a circle six feet in diameter, setting it on the ground and filling it with soil. Then add the second and third circular tiers, filling each when it is set in place.

A piece of perforated three-inch pipe can be inserted from the top to water through, or a sprinkler can be placed at the top.

To construct a *square strawberry planter from lumber,* use two-by-eights coated with wood preservative and precut in whatever dimensions you desire—one tier might be five feet square, the other three and a half feet square, and the last two feet square. Join the boards for each tier frame with ½- by 3½-inch corner braces, using 16d nails. Then place each frame atop the other as with the circular metal pyramid.

Either of these terraced planters will hold about 50 plants. They'll grow even more berries than they would on the same space in a strawberry patch if you drill holes in the sides of the wooden or aluminum tiers and plant strawberries therein. Pyramids are also far more convenient to tend than strawberry beds.

Patio, Fence and Carport Plans

The complete detailed plans for these handsome structures include step-by-step directions and a list of all materials you'll have to buy. Free from Filon, 12333 South Van Ness Avenue, Hawthorne, California 90250.

A Backyard Niagara Falls

Free instructions for building a backyard waterfall or fountain to highlight any garden may be obtained on request from Cal Pump, 7051 Hayvenhurst Avenue, Van Nuys, California 91406.

Plexiglass Garden Pools

Pools and many other attractive garden constructions can be made with Plexiglass. Send 25¢ for the informative booklet "Do It Yourself with Plexiglass Acrylic Sheet," P.O. Box 4470, Philadelphia, Pennsylvania 19140.

Dig Your Own Shallow Well for Next to Nothing

Depending on the type of drilling required, professional well diggers generally charge up to $20 an hour to install a shallow well. But by renting an auger-type post-hole digger from a plumbing supply or hardware dealer, you can dig the same well (13 to 25 feet) for a fraction of the cost. How expensive the well will be after it is dug depends of course on whether you install an inexpensive hand pump or an electric pump, but either way you'll save a lot of money doing it yourself.

The materials required, assuming that the well is sunk the average 20 feet, are three or four five-foot lengths of 1¼-inch galvanized pipe and couplings (both of which you may have on hand or may be able to scrounge somewhere) and a well point ($20). One long length of pipe may of course be used instead of the five-foot lengths; this may prove cumbersome, but it does reduce the number of couplings needed and the chances of breakage from the pipe. If you intend to install an electric pump for the well, be sure to select a site convenient to an electrical outlet, or one easily reached with an extension cord. Before digging, ascertain all the licensing requirements in your area and take care that the location you choose contains no old foundations, boulders, sewer lines or similar obstacles.

In choosing a place to dig, remember that the water table tends to follow the contours of the land, sloping downward from hilly areas to low points. There are two basic types of water-bearing formations. One is sand, or a mixture of sand and gravel, the space between individual particles being filled with water. The other, deeper down, is rock interlaced with fissures. Only the first formation is appropriate for driven wells, which include those dug with an auger-type post-hole digger. Driven wells consist of a series of tightly coupled pipe lengths (or a single pipe) fitted with a well point at the lower end, water flowing into the pipe through a screened opening on the shank of the well point when the point reaches the water table. The pipe can be driven down 20 feet with a sledgehammer or a motorized (or manual) driving weight, but the auger-type post-hole digger method offers several advantages. First, it takes less time than driving; second, it requires much less effort; and third, there is no chance of the well point breaking on a rock or other solid object while being driven. The device is suited to most localities, being impractical only in those few areas where the subsoil is so hard that it cannot be dug. Your plumbing supply dealer will probably let you use one free if you buy pipe or anything else from him.

Before using the auger-type post-hole digger, dig down a few feet with pick and shovel until you pass all tree roots and other encumbrances. The auger-type post-hole digger is then inserted into the soil, leaned on and turned in a circle. When the auger is filled with a core of soil it is lifted gently (so that it misses the sides of the hole) and emptied into a wheelbarrow or a pile somewhere out of the way. As the hole sinks deeper, the extensions of old pipe that will be supplied with the auger-type post-hole digger must be coupled securely onto the device. At first the operation is easy, but by the time you hit wet sand at 13 feet or more, you'll be lifting heavy earth out of the hole hand over hand at a height that may tower over your garage. Here another pair of hands is called for and the assistance of a relative, friend or neighbor will save a lot of trouble.

Once you hit really wet sand or a small glimmering puddle of water (at 13 to 20 feet) and the sand is too slippery to lift, put the auger-type post-hole digger aside. It is important to stop digging at this stage, for eager homeowners all too often bore down past the water table. The next step is to drive the four-foot well point all the way into the water-bearing strata. The well point should have its brass filler screen (which keeps sand from entering with the water being pumped) built inside so that it will be protected by the steel skeleton during driving. Use your one long length of well pipe or couple together tightly as many five-foot lengths of 1½-inch pipe as is necessary and then couple the well point onto the pipe. Apply ample good-quality pipe compound and be sure that the connection is tight or the well point may be lost in the sand. Then lower the pipe and attached well point into the hole, easily. Another method here is to insert a larger bore pipe first and use it as a casing, but this is more expensive and is not essential if you are careful.

When the pipe is set in place, attach a driving coupling or cap and sledge the well point down four feet or so, hitting the coupling squarely. A heavy wooden maul may be used in place of the sledge-hammer but a sledge does a better job. Definitely be sure to attach a driving coupling, though, or the pipe will have to be rethreaded, and *stop driving and begin digging elsewhere should your well point somehow strike a rock or solid object.*

Next, prime the sunken pipe with water, filling it with the garden hose, and attach a rented hand pump, priming this in turn. You should have sandy water as soon as the pump is primed, and after a half hour or so of pumping, the water will be clear and ready to be tasted. If you intend to install a ⅓ H.P. electric pump, make certain that there is about five feet of water in the pipe, measuring this by carefully lowering a tape measure and weight down the pipe. If there is five feet or more of water present, the electric pump will operate efficiently and you can fill in the hole around the pipe. Where surface-water contamination is a problem, especially in low-lying areas with no natural drainage, fill the space between the oversize borehole and pipe with cement grout to a depth of 15 feet.

Should you fail to reach water, as is infrequently the case, there is no choice but to attach another extension of pipe and drive deeper. In no event, however, is it advisable to go deeper than 25 feet, unless you are prepared to expend a lot more energy and to buy a more expensive electric pump powerful enough to handle a deep well. The practical limit for all shallow-well pumps is a lift of 25 feet; though theoretically water could be drawn up 34 feet, this is not possible because the pump cannot create a perfect vacuum and there is friction loss in the suction pipe. The only alternative if no water is reached by about 25 feet is to take up the pipe and begin the process all over again at another site. Most people generally find water the first time at 13 to 20 feet, but it isn't impossible that you'll have to dig two or three times before you're successful.

After you hit water, what you do is a matter of your own bank account or credit standing. Jet, piston, centrifugal, and turbine pumps are all satisfactory. The jet-action pump is popular because it is easy to install, doesn't have to be installed over the well, and is simple in operation. Its only real disadvantage is that its capacity reduces as the lift increases. There are adequate self-priming, jet-action pumps (⅓ H.P.) complete with 20-gallon tanks for as low as $125, and there are far more elaborate setups costing many times more. The cost of an electric pump without storage tank is less, but a pump without a tank is not fully automatic and must be activated each time it is used. It would be a good idea to buy the pump through a plumbing supply dealer and have him install it, or at least get the benefit of his advice.

Follow directions carefully when installing any electric pump, making sure all connections are tight to prevent air leakage. You can chlorinate the water if you like (chlorine and instructions are often provided with the pump) and should definitely have the water tested if you intend to drink it, even if there are no health regulations regarding well water in your locality. The pump should be covered when it rains and disconnected and stored for the winter, unless you decide to build a pump house. The water, generally higher in mineral content, will probably prove more beneficial to garden plants than tap water and the well will of course enable you to cut down on your water bills and give you insurance against any watering restrictions that might be imposed during a drought.

Turn Your Edger into a Motorized Hoe for Nothing

An ordinary lawn edger powered by an internal combustion engine can easily be turned into a garden hoe and trimmer that eliminates much backbreaking work in the garden. Just add a "Trim and Hoe" edger blade. If you can get your local hardware store or lawn and garden center, etc., to order a dozen of these handy gadgets, a free one worth $5.95 retail will be mailed to you. Write for details to Trim and Hoe Manufacturing Company, P.O. Box 719, Pearland, Texas 77581.

Free Stakes and Supports for the Garden

• Cut off two sides of the wooden frame that supports the inside of large packing crates such as those used for refrigerators and stoves. Set what's left of the frame in the garden like an arch and grow plants along the sides of it.

• Make a tomato or cucumber fence from old four-paned window frames with the glass knocked out. Just nail the old frames to posts sunk in the ground.

• Use sunflowers as living stakes for tomatoes and other plants. Plant sunflowers close by at the same time tomatoes are set out. Let the tomatoes grow up three-foot wooden stakes at first. By the time the tomato plants reach the top of these wooden stakes, the sunflowers will be ready to use as natural stakes for the rest of the season. Tie the tomato stems to the sunflower stalk with soft cloth ties. Fertilize and water heavily to provide for the needs of both plants. Besides providing natural stakes, the sunflowers will shade the tomato plants and help prevent sunscalded fruit.

• In staking climbing plants—some of which grow over 20 feet high—use your imagination. One gardener trains his giant plants to wooden and aluminum extension ladders propped against his garage. No matter what kind of staking is devised for climbing plants (large stakes made by nailing boards together, long tree limbs, etc.) be sure that they're anchored at least three feet in the ground so that they won't topple over. Don't forget that you'll have to use at least a ten-foot stepladder to care for giant plants and to pick any fruit off them as they grow up into the stratosphere.

• All the free stakes needed can also be *grown* in your own yard if you plant shrubby willows like *Salix viminalis, Salix purpurea, Salix caprea, Salix discolor* and *Salix gracilistyla.* If these bushes are cut back hard, eight-foot shoots can often be grown in one year, though it is best to leave the shoots on the plant for another year until they thicken and harden. Willow sticks root very easily; they should be cut early in the winter so that they'll dry out before being used. Nurseries offering shrubby willows to grow stakes from include: Zilke Brothers, Baroda, Michigan 49101; Waynesboro Nurseries, Waynesboro, Virginia 22080; and Girard Nurseries, Geneva, Ohio 44041.

Garden Handcraft Supplies

Sources for supplies for garden handcrafts from sculptures to strawberry pots will be furnished on request from The American Craftsmen's Council, 29 West 53rd Street, New York, New York 10019.

A Full-Length Book on Straw Tying

Bits of Scandia, a full-length illustrated how-to book on the little-known art of tying straw decorations for halls, walls and trees by Marcy Farber, was published at $2.95. It is free to our readers from the ABTA Co., 2120 Fox SMPB, Long Lake, Minnesota 55356. Be sure to mention this offer when writing and include $1 for shipping costs.

A Free Strawberry or Flower Barrel

Save $30 to $40 making your own strawberry or flower barrel. The old-fashioned strawberry barrel is a great space saver and is portable as well. Berries grown in this way will always be clean and ripen evenly. Strawberry barrels can be made out of anything from a small wooden nail keg to steel oil drums. Starting at the bottom, simply drill from two- to four-inch diameter holes in circles around the barrel. Stagger each circle of holes 6 to 12 inches from the preceding one. Make the holes in each circle 6 to 12 inches apart from center to center. Finally, drill small holes in the bottom for drainage, and paint or decorate the container for use on the lawn, terrace, or patio. Attach coasters to the bottom so that the barrel can be moved about, or set it on a wagon wheel that spins around, or simply place the barrel on bricks or wooden blocks. Each of these methods provides good air circulation.

When ready to plant, put stones or gravel in the bottom for drainage and fill the barrel with your soil mix. Plant as you fill the barrel with soil, inserting the plants from the inside of the barrel, guiding the leaves and crown outside through the holes and fanning out the roots inside. When the barrel is planted, insert a piece of perforated drainpipe that has been cut to the height of the barrel (rolled screen can also be used). Fill this with pure sand and water through it.

Strawberry barrels can be winter-protected by bringing them into the garage or a cool cellar, or by mulching them heavily with straw or leaves held in place with chicken wire. It is worth a try to save them for next year, but generally the plants should be replaced with new ones after they have fruited, for they bear very sparsely after the first year.

In addition to strawberries, almost all flowers can be planted in these barrels.

Quick Free Things You Can Make for the Garden

• The shallow upper drawers from unsalvageable dressers and coffee tables can be made into seed flats by drilling holes in the bottom for drainage and filling them three-quarters with soil.

• Egg cartons, tops removed, and soil added, become ready-made compartmentalized flats in which to start a dozen plants from seed.

• The bottom thirds of empty milk containers make excellent pots for young plants started from seed indoors.

• Use spring-clip type clothespins to seal partly used seed packets.

• A plastic milk container with the cap left on and the bottom cut out makes a fine hot cap for plants.

• Save ice cream sticks for plant markers.

• Discarded nylon stockings—toes and heels cut off—make the best plant ties. Pipe cleaners and old plastic bags cut in strips are also good. Always tie them loosely, using as a sling support.

• Metal clothes hangers make excellent iris stakes. Straighten out all but the hanger hook and push the straight part into the ground. Then bend the hook over and encircle the plant with it.

• Use old tires for attractive flower planters. Simply scallop the edges with a sharp knife, paint, and fill with rich soil.

• Old milk cans make excellent decorative planting containers for the lawn. Save money by buying an old one and painting and decorating it yourself.

• To beautify a bare unsightly fence, paint ordinary gallon cans and drill holes in the bottoms. Attach them to the fence and place wood blocks under potted plants—like begonias—in the cans. This will raise the plants above the fence top and make it "bloom."

• Hang baskets of flowers on fishing tackle swivels so that they can be rotated without being unhooked.

• Tile flues filled with soil can be used to grow herbs like chives, rosemary or mint on the patio close by the barbecue.

• Weathered logs with natural crevices make beautiful natural plant containers for plants such as low-growing junipers. If no adequate depressions exist, drill flowerpot-size holes into the logs.

• The tool belts used by telephone company linesmen and electricians make excellent tool belts for the garden.

• Garden tools will repay the care you give them. Protect your smaller tools from rusting by keeping a pail of sand near the garage or cellar door and plunging the tools into the sand when you are through with them.

• Be your own surgeon when your garden hose develops a leak. Here's how to "operate." If the hose is torn, cut at the break, remove the damaged portion, and join together with metal hose mender inserted inside the hose and held in place with twisted wire (or a hose clamp) on the outside. Small leaks can usually be fixed with plastic cement or friction tape.

• Observe these rules and you'll lengthen the life of your garden hose: 1. Drain thoroughly after use. 2. Roll into large, loose coils. 3. Store in a cool place. (If hung, place over a rounded object to prevent sharp bends.) 4. Don't drag the hose near oil drippings; oil rots rubber. 5. Don't turn off the water by pinching on the hose, even for a minute; this strains and weakens the rubber. 6. Never step on or drive over your hose. 7. Don't leave hose exposed to the sun for any length of time; heat deteriorates rubber.

• A teaspoon of salt added to the soap lather will clean the grimiest of gardener's hands.

A Horticultural Equipment Catalog

For a free 72-page catalog featuring hundreds of horticultural tools, from horticultural knives to a large selection of gardening books, write A. M. Leonard, Inc., P.O. Box 816, Piqua, Ohio 45356.

Hard-to-Find Garden Aids

Everything from glass tents and gooseneck hoes to seeding guards and Danish tools are featured in this 48-page catalog. Send 25¢ for postage and handling to Walter Nicke, 19 Columbia Turnpike, P.O. Box 667, Hudson, New York 12534.

Forestry Items

Here is a huge 500-page free catalog featuring hundreds of unusual items used in forestry, many of which can be employed by home gardeners. The illustrated book includes animal traps, horticultural knives, soil samplers, budding and grafting products, and much, much more. Write Forest Supplies, Inc., 205 West Rankin Street, Box 8397 Jackson, Michigan 39204.

Tree Trimming

This free illustrated 32-page catalog features all the tree trimming equipment you'd ever need, from pruning saws to ladders. Write Bartlett Manufacturing Company, 3003 East Grand Boulevard, Detroit, Michigan 48202.

Senior Citizen Garden Tools

Garden tools such as spades, rakes and hoes made with consideration for the older gardener's sacroiliac are the specialty of this free illustrated catalog. Write Gardening Naturally, Inc., Route 102, Stockbridge, Massachusetts 01262.

Unusual Tools

This free illustrated catalog features a full 68 pages of gardening tools, such as seeding wheels, that aren't found in ordinary hardware stores or even in garden supply stores. Write Brookstone Company, 498 Vose Farm Road, Peterborough, New Hampshire 03458.

101 Useful Ways to Use a Chain Saw

The illustrated booklet "101 Good Ideas For Using Chain," which retails for $1, is available free to our readers from Acco Industries Inc., American Chain Division, 454 E. Princess St., York, Pennsylvania 17403.

Safety Savvy

Pushing forward is always wise;
Mowing backward may be a surprise!

Above is one of the many rhymes captioning amusing cartoons in a free garden safety booklet offered by one of America's oldest farm and garden equipment manufacturers. "Lawn and Garden Safety Savvy" emphasizes safety precautions to be taken with lawn mowers, tillers, chain saws and snow blowers. Write John Deere, Dept. D-574, Moline, Illinois 61265.

Wood Stove Safety

This free pamphlet, stressing safety precautions when buying, installing and using wood stoves, should be read by everyone considering this method of heating. Write for "Wood Stove Safety" to Insurance Information Institute, 110 William Street, New York, New York 10038.

12

Free Gardens to Visit and Places to Learn From

100 Free Gardens to Visit

This list of free gardens to visit in every state, U.S. territory and Canada is not complete by any means, but is one of the largest collections of free gardens you'll find anywhere. We only wish there were room to describe the natural beauties of these places here, but that might be impossible for anyone to do adequately, anyway. No gardens charging a fee have anything on these, and the experts always on hand in these gardens will be glad to answer any horticultural questions.

Alabama
BIRMINGHAM BOTANICAL GARDENS, 2612 Lane Park Road, Birmingham, 35223

Alaska
MT. McKINLEY NATIONAL PARK, Anchorage, Alaska

Arizona
SONORA DESERT MUSEUM, P.O. Box 5607, Tucson Mount Park, Tucson 85703

Arkansas
QUEEN WILHELMINA STATE PARK, Mena 71953

California
BOTANICAL GARDEN, University of California, Berkeley 94720
BOTANICAL GARDENS—HERBARIUM, University of California, Los Angeles 90024
DESCANSO GARDENS, 1418 Descanso Drive, La Canada 91011
GOLDEN GATE PARK, San Francisco 94122
HUNTINGTON BOTANICAL GARDENS, San Marino 91108
QUAIL GARDENS, P.O. Box 5, Encinitas 92024
THE SANTA BARBARA BOTANIC GARDEN, 1212 Mission Canyon Road, Santa Barbara 93103
SHERMAN FOUNDATION EDUCATION PROGRAM, Sherman Foundation Center, 2647 East Coast Highway, Corona Del Mar 92625
THE STRYBING ARBORETUM, 9th Avenue and Lincoln Way, San Francisco 94122
SOUTH COAST BOTANIC GARDENS, 26701 Rolling Hills Road, Palos Verdes 90274

Colorado
DENVER BOTANIC GARDENS, 909 York Street, Denver 80206

Connecticut
THE CONNECTICUT ARBORETUM, Connecticut College, New London 06320
BARTLETT ARBORETUM, 151 Brookdale Road, Stamford 06903

Delaware
THE WINTERTHUR GARDENS, The Henry Francis du Pont Winterthur Museum, Winterthur 19735

District of Columbia
UNITED STATES BOTANIC GARDENS, 20024
U. S. NATIONAL ARBORETUM, United States Department of Agriculture, 20002
DUMBARTON OAKS, 1703 32nd Street N.W., 20007
KENILWORTH AQUATIC GARDENS, Douglas Street N.E., 20250

Florida
MIAMI BEACH GARDEN CENTER, 3000 Garden Center Drive, Miami Beach 33139

Georgia
SEARS GARDEN—CIVIC CENTER, 3012 Bacon Road, Columbus 31906

Hawaii
HAROLD L. LYON ARBORETUM, University of Hawaii at Manoa, 3860 Manoa Road, Honolulu 96822

Idaho
ROTARY ROSE GARDEN, Pocatello 83204

Illinois
CHICAGO BOTANIC GARDEN, 715 Dundee Road, Glencoe, Illinois 60022
THE MORTON ARBORETUM, Lisle 60532

Indiana
HAYES REGIONAL ARBORETUM, 801 Elks Road, Richmond, Indiana 47374
HONEYWELL GARDENS, P.O. Box 432, Wabash 46992

Kentucky
BERNHEIM FOREST, Clermont 40110

Louisiana
LOUISIANA STATE ARBORETUM, Ville Platte 70586

Maine
UNIVERSITY OF MAINE AT ORONO, Department of Botany and Plant Pathology, Deering Hall, Orono 04473
THUYA GARDENS, Asticou Terrace, Northeast Harbor 04662

Maryland
CYLBURN WILDFLOWER PRESERVE AND GARDEN CENTER, Cylburn Park, 4915 Greenspring Avenue, Baltimore 21209

Massachusetts

THE ARNOLD ARBORETUM, Jamaica Plain 02130
BERKSHIRE GARDEN CENTER, Routes 102 and 183, Stockbridge 01262
BOSTON PUBLIC GARDEN, Boston 02101
THE BOTANIC GARDEN OF SMITH COLLEGE, Northampton 01060
ISABELLA STEWART GARDNER MUSEUM GREENHOUSES, 2 Palace Road, Boston 02115

Michigan

IVA DOTY NATIVE FLOWER TRAIL, Bellevue 49021
GARDEN CENTER, Grand Rapids Public Museum, 54 Jefferson S.E., Grand Rapids 49502
MATTHAEL BOTANICAL GARDENS, The University of Michigan, 1800 North Dixboro Road, Ann Arbor 48105

Minnesota

COMO PARK CONSERVATORY, 1224 North Lexington, St. Paul 55103
ELOISE BUTLER WILDFLOWER GARDEN, 250 S. Fourth Street, Minneapolis 55145
THE MINNESOTA LANDSCAPE ARBORETUM, 3675 Arboretum Drive, Chaska 55318

Mississippi

NATCHEZ TRACE PARKWAY, Tupelo 38801

Missouri

THE MISSOURI BOTANICAL GARDEN, 2345 Tower Grove Avenue, St. Louis 63110

Nebraska

MOUNT VERNON MUNICIPAL GARDENS, Omaha 68501

Nevada

SQUIRE PARK, Las Vegas 89114

New Hampshire

MOUNT WASHINGTON ARCTIC GARDENS, Mount Washington 03589

New Jersey
CEDAR BROOK PARK, Plainfield 07061
SKYLAND, Ringwood State Park, P.O. Box 1304, Ringwood 07456
FRELINGHUYSEN ARBORETUM, 53 East Hanover Avenue, Morristown 07960

New Mexico
LIVING DESERT STATE PARK, Carlsbad 88220

New York
BARTOW-PELL MANSION, Shore Road, Pelham Bay Park, Bronx 10464
BROOKLYN BOTANIC GARDEN, 1000 Washington Avenue, Brooklyn 11225
CENTRAL PARK, 59th to 110th Streets, New York City
THE CLOISTERS, The Metropolitan Museum of Art, Fort Tryon Park, New
    York City 10034
THE CORNELL PLANTATIONS, Cornell University, 100 Judd Falls Road,
    Ithaca 14853
GEORGE LANDIS ARBORETUM, Esperance 12066
THE NEW YORK BOTANICAL GARDEN, Southern Boulevard and 200th
    Street, Bronx 10454
THE PARRISH ART MUSEUM ARBORETUM, Southampton 11968
QUEENS BOTANICAL GARDEN, 43-50 Main Street, Flushing 11355
READERS DIGEST GARDENS, Pleasantville 10570
THE ROOT GLEN, Hamilton and Kirkland Colleges, Clinton 13323
WAVE HILL CENTER FOR ENVIRONMENTAL STUDIES, 675 W. 252nd Street,
    Bronx 10471

North Carolina
CLARENDON GARDENS, Linden Road, Pinehurst 28374

North Dakota
INTERNATIONAL PEACE GARDEN, Dunseith 58329

Ohio
CANTON GARDEN CENTER, 1615 Stadium Park, N.W., Canton 44718
COX ARBORETUM, 6733 Springboro Pike, Dayton 45449
THE DAWES ARBORETUM, R.F.D. 5, Newark 43055

THE GARDEN CENTER OF GREATER CLEVELAND, 110 East Boulevard, Cleveland 44106

GARDENVIEW HORTICULTURAL PARK, 16711 Pearl Road, Strongville 44136

KINGWOOD CENTER, 900 Park Avenue, West, Mansfield 44906

IRWIN M. KROHM CONSERVATORY, 950 Eden Park Drive, Cincinnati 45200

SECOR PARK, Route 1, Berkey 43504

Oklahoma
WILL ROGERS GARDEN, Will Rogers Park, 3500 N.W. 36th Street, Oklahoma City 73112

Oregon
INTERNATIONAL ROSE TEST GARDEN, 400 S.W. Kingston Street, Portland 97201

HOYT ARBORETUM, 4000 S.W. Fairview Boulevard, Portland 91201

Pennsylvania
ARBORETUM OF THE BARNES FOUNDATION, Merion 19066

ARTHUR HOYT SCOTT HORTICULTURAL FOUNDATION, Swarthmore College, Swarthmore 19081

GARDENS OF JAPAN, Swiss Pines, R.D. 1, Malvern 19355

Rhode Island
DIALOGUE GARDENS, Cranston 02910

South Carolina
CLEMSON UNIVERSITY GARDENS, Clemson 29631

South Dakota
McCRORY GARDENS, Highway 14, Brookings 57006

Tennessee
MEMPHIS BOTANIC GARDEN, 750 Cherry Road, Memphis 38117

THE UNIVERSITY OF TENNESSEE, AGRICULTURAL EXPERIMENT STATION,

Forestry Stations and Arboretum, 901 Kerr Hollow Road, Oak Ridge 37830

Texas
DALLAS GARDEN CENTER, Forest and First Street, Dallas 75226
SAN ANTONIO GARDEN CENTER, 3310 N. New Braunfels Avenue, San Antonio 78201

Vermont
GARDEN IN THE WOODS, Peacham 05862

Virginia
NORFOLK BOTANICAL GARDEN, Airport Road, Norfolk 23518

Washington
THE FINCH ARBORETUM, 3404 W. Woodland Boulevard, Spokane 98195
SEYMOUR CONSERVATORY, P.O. Box 7014, Tacoma 98406
THE UNIVERSITY OF WASHINGTON ARBORETUM, Seattle 98195

West Virginia
WEST VIRGINIA UNIVERSITY ARBORETUM, West Virginia University, Morgantown 26506

Wisconsin
BOERNER BOTANICAL GARDENS, Whitehall Park, 5879 S. 92nd Street, Hales Corner 53130
MITCHELL PARK HORTICULTURAL CONSERVATORY, 524 S. Layton Boulevard, Milwaukee 53215
UNIVERSITY OF WISCONSIN MADISON ARBORETUM, Madison 53706

Wyoming
YELLOWSTONE NATIONAL PARK 82190
GRAND TETON NATIONAL PARK, Jackson Hole 82190

Puerto Rico
CASA MARIA GARDENS, San Germán 00753

Virgin Islands
SAINT THOMAS GARDENS, The Orchidiarium, 6-37 Constant, St. Thomas 00801
WATER ISLE BOTANICAL GARDEN, P.O. Box 570, St. Thomas 00801

Canada
THE NIAGARA PARK COMMISSION, School of Horticulture, P.O. Box 150, Niagara Falls, Ontario L2E 6T2
ROYAL BOTANICAL GARDENS, P.O. Box 399, Hamilton, Ontario L8N 3H8
THE UNIVERSITY OF BRITISH COLUMBIA, BOTANICAL GARDEN, 6501 Northwest Marine Drive, Vancouver, British Columbia V62 1W5

The Seven Natural Wonders of the World: All Yours to Visit—Free

Surrounded by a seemingly endless abundance of natural beauty, the ancients, much like ourselves, often ignored the natural world. Except possibly for the Hanging Gardens of Semiramis at Babylon, even Antipater's proverbial seven wonders of the Alexandrian era celebrated the works of man rather than nature. Antipater's list, compiled in the second century, included the Egyptian pyramids, the Olympian statue of Zeus, the temple of Artemis, the mausoleum at Halicarnassus, the Colossus at Rhodes, the lighthouse of Alexandria, and the fabled walls of Babylon. Excluding the pyramids, not one remains today, whereas, unless they "make way for civiliation," many of the natural wonders Antipater missed seeing will endure for centuries to come. In North America, especially in the western U.S., nature has been prodigal of superlatives and nowhere can this be seen better than in our great and grandiose plants, whose size and age are unequaled anywhere else on earth. These are sights every traveler should make a point to see.

When Antipater compiled his list, for example, the bristlecone pines on California's Iyno National Forest were already thousands of years old. The oldest *Pinus arista* or "living driftwood," as the bristlecones have aptly been called, has endured for more than 4800 years on the high windswept slopes of the White Mountains northeast of

Bishop, California. Named "Methuselah" or "Great-Grandad Picka-back," and with its birth dating back to c. 2000 B.C., this venerable bristlecone is found in the Methuselah Grove, where many of the other trees approach it in age. There is no doubt that the Methuselah Grove contains the oldest living things on earth, trees that were growing before Moses received the Ten Commandments. Amazingly, these trees still produce seed from which new trees can grow. All the bristlecones hold tenaciously to life. Gnarled, burled, and bent, the epitome of the strange beauty that comes from age and suffering, they endure the elevation of 11,000 feet on an arid limestone soil totally unsuitable for most plants. Wind, fire, and ice have sculpted these trees through the ages, and so fierce is their will to live that they are sometimes found, roots mostly bared, growing almost parallel to the ground, as if praying for one more tomorrow. Most grow at the rate of only one inch in diameter every century, and although great sections of the knotted giants are dead, when bristlecones partially die, the reduced living portion stands a better chance against low pre-cipitation and other extremes of weather.

Probably the best known of all spectacular plants on earth is the 272.4-foot tall "General Sherman," a sequoia in California's Sequoia National Park. This *Sequoia Gigantea* has a 79.1-foot girth (at five feet above the ground), and it contains enough timber to make 35 five-room houses. From its beginnings as a minuscule seed nearly 40 cen-turies ago, the massive "General Sherman" has increased in weight over 250-billion fold. In combined height and girth it is by far the largest living thing on earth, a line of relatively young redwoods called the "Sentinel Trees" forming a perfect path to its base.

America is also the home of the tallest living thing. Towering above any other plant on earth is the "Howard Libby" or "Tall Tree" redwood growing along Redwood Creek in California's Redwood Na-tional Park. A *Sequoia sempervirens* that stands 367.8 feet tall, the "Tall Tree" may be the tallest tree of all times, although there are unconfirmed reports that an Australian mountain ash *(Eucalyptus reg-nans)* felled in 1868 reached 464 feet. The "Howard Libbey" was named after the president of the Arcata Redwood Company, on whose land it was located until the park was established. The "Tall Tree" can barely be seen in the Tall Trees Grove, which contains several other brobdingnagians almost matching it in height. It is a double-formation specimen (two trees grown together) with a dead top.

Mexico has the honor of being home to the widest living plant. Its girth far greater than even the "General Sherman" redwood, the imposing Montezuma cypress *(Taxodium mucronatum)* holding the title is found in the state of Oaxaca in Mexico and in 1949 it had a circumference of 112 to 113 feet (at five feet above the ground). It is called the "Santa Maria del Tule" tree, after the mission near which it is located. Its only challenger was a European chestnut in Italy (c. 1770) reported as 204 feet in circumference, an unsubstantiated figure. In top spread, a southern red oak in Como, Mississippi, takes world honors, with a 115-foot spread. The largest spreading plant from a single clonal growth is the wild box huckleberry *(Gaylussacia brachyera)* found in eastern Pennsylvania, which covers up to 100 acres.

As for flowering plants, the rose remains the most celebrated of flowers, and the largest living rose tree is a little-known "Lady Banksia" at Tombstone, Arizona. Located in the patio of the Rose Tree Inn Museum at 4th and Toughnut Streets, an unlikely location, this "Lady Banksia" requires some 68 posts and thousands of feet of iron piping to support it. Started from a cutting imported from Scotland in 1884, it has a main trunk measuring 40 feet thick, stands over 9 feet high, and covers over 5,380 square feet. Its blooms would easily fill a palace ballroom. However, the world's largest flowering plant is a giant Chinese wisteria at Sierra Madre, California, that suggests a vast field filled with delicate flowers. Planted in 1892, today it covers almost one acre, has branches surpassing 500 feet in length, and weighs over 252 tons. Thirty thousand people a year come to see this fabulous plant, which is located near the Los Angeles State and County Arboretum, and which, no matter how depressing the morning headlines, never fails to display its 1.5 million blossoms for a full five weeks each year.

To view our seventh and final natural wonder of the world, one need travel only to Arizona, where the world's largest cactus is found. Called "apartment houses of the desert" because they provide living quarters for so many bird species, the huge saguaros of the Saguaro National Monument in Arizona's small part of the Sonoran desert justly claim this title. Saguaros often reach a height of 50 feet before dying. The slender-ribbed plant, which sometimes lives two centuries, takes 75 years to develop its first blunt branches and years more before it weighs from six to ten tons and resembles a giant candelabrum or fingers afire when hit by the sun. It is a wondrous thing that thrives against great odds in the desert, supplying both food and lodging to many animals, as well as to the Papago Indians of the region, who still harvest its fruit for cakes and syrup. During extended dry periods, the saguaro gradually uses up to a ton of stored water and decreases in girth and weight until the next rains, when it swells to its proud dimensions once again.

Free Garden Information from State Tourist Bureaus

Before visiting any state be sure to write the state tourist bureau, which on request will often provide you with lists of free gardens to visit and local garden pilgrimages to make. Use this information to supplement the lists you already have, for it will probably be more up-to-date and cover small gardens otherwise overlooked.

Alabama
BUREAU OF PUBLICITY AND INFORMATION, State Capitol, Montgomery 36104

Alaska
ALASKA TRAVEL DIVISION, Pouch E, Juneau 99801

Arizona
DEPT. OF ECONOMIC PLANNING AND DEVELOPMENT, 3303 N. Central Avenue, Phoenix 85012

Arkansas
PUBLICITY AND PARKS COMMISSION, 149 State Capitol, Little Rock 72201

California
STATE OFFICE OF TOURISM, 1400 Tenth Street, Sacramento 95814

Colorado
STATE DIVISION OF COMMERCE AND DEVELOPMENT, 600 State Service Building, Denver 80203

Connecticut
CONNECTICUT DEVELOPMENT COMMISSION, Research and Information Division, 102 State Office Building, Hartford 06115

Delaware
STATE DEVELOPMENT DEPT., 45 The Green, Dover 19901

District of Columbia
WASHINGTON CONVENTION AND VISITORS BUREAU, 1616 K Street N.W., Washington 20006

Florida
FLORIDA DEPARTMENT OF COMMERCE, TOURIST AND MARKETING, Caldwell Building, Tallahassee 32304

Georgia
DEPARTMENT OF INDUSTRY AND TRADE, Tourist Division, Box 38097, Atlanta 30334

Hawaii
HAWAII VISITORS BUREAU, 609 Fifth Avenue, New York, New York 10017

Idaho
DEPARTMENT OF COMMERCE AND DEVELOPMENT, Room 108, Capitol Building, Boise 83701

Illinois
DIVISION OF TOURISM, 222 College, Springfield 62706

Indiana
DEPARTMENT OF COMMERCE, TOURIST DIVISION, 333 State House, Indianapolis 46204

Iowa
DEVELOPMENT COMMISSION, 250 Jewett Building, Des Moines 50309

Kansas
DEPARTMENT OF ECONOMIC DEVELOPMENT, State Office Building, Room 122-S, Topeka 66612

Kentucky
DEPARTMENT OF PUBLIC INFORMATION, Travel Division, 410 Ann Street, Frankfort 40601

Louisiana
TOURIST DEVELOPMENT COMMISSION, State Capitol, Baton Rouge 70804

Maine
MAINE PUBLICITY BUREAU, Gateway Circle, Portland 04102

Maryland
DEPARTMENT OF ECONOMIC DEVELOPMENT, Travel Department, Division State Office Building, Annapolis 21401

Massachusetts
DEPARTMENT OF COMMERCE AND DEVELOPMENT, 100 Cambridge Street, Boston 02202

Michigan
MICHIGAN TOURIST COUNCIL, Stevens T. Mason Building, Lansing 48926

Minnesota
DEPARTMENT OF ECONOMIC DEVELOPMENT, 57 W. Seventh Street, St. Paul 55102

Mississippi
TRAVEL DEPARTMENT, Agricultural & Industrial Board, 1504 State Office Building, Jackson 39205

Missouri
DIVISION OF COMMERCE AND INDUSTRIAL DEVELOPMENT, Jefferson Building, Jefferson City 65101

Montana
STATE HIGHWAY COMMISSION, Advertising Department, Helena 59601

Nebraska
NEBRASKA LAND, State Capitol, Lincoln 68509

Nevada
DEPARTMENT OF ECONOMIC DEVELOPMENT, Carson City 89701

New Hampshire
DIVISION OF ECONOMIC DEVELOPMENT 856, Concord 03301

New Jersey
DEPARTMENT OF CONSERVATION AND ECONOMIC DEVELOPMENT, Box 1889, Trenton 08625

New Mexico
TOURIST DIVISION DEPARTMENT OF DEVELOPMENT, 113 Washington Avenue, Santa Fe 87501

New York
DEPARTMENT OF COMMERCE, TRAVEL BUREAU, 112 State Street, Albany 12207

North Carolina
DEPARTMENT OF CONSERVATION AND DEVELOPMENT, Travel and Promotion Division, 211 Administration Building, Raleigh 27611

North Dakota
GREATER NORTH DAKOTA ASSOCIATION, Box 1781, Fargo 58102

Ohio
DEPARTMENT OF DEVELOPMENT, 65 S. Front Street, Box 1001, Columbus 43215

Oklahoma
INDUSTRIAL DEVELOPMENT AND PARK DEPARTMENT TOURIST DIVISION, 500 Will Rogers Memorial Building, Oklahoma City 73105

Oregon
TRAVEL INFORMATION, STATE HIGHWAY DEPARTMENT, 101 Highway Building, Salem 97310

Pennsylvania
DEPARTMENT OF COMMERCE, Travel Development Bureau, 400 S. Office Building, Harrisburg 17120

Rhode Island
TOURIST PROMOTION DIVISION, Development Council, 49 Hayes Street, Providence 02908

South Carolina
STATE DEVELOPMENT BOARD, Box 929, Columbia 29205

South Dakota
TRAVEL DIVISION, DEPARTMENT OF HIGHWAYS, Highways Building, Pierre 57501

Tennessee
DIVISION OF TOURIST PROMOTION, Department of Conservation, 2611 West End Avenue, Nashville 37203

Texas
TEXAS HIGHWAY DEPARTMENT, TRAVEL DIVISION, Box 5064, Austin 78701

Utah
UTAH TRAVEL COUNCIL, Council Hall, Capitol Hill, Salt Lake City 84114

Vermont
DEVELOPMENT DEPARTMENT PROMOTION AND TRAVEL, State Office Building, Montpelier 05602

Virginia
VIRGINIA STATE TRAVEL SERVICE, 911 E. Broad Street, Richmond 23219

Washington
TOURIST PROMOTION DIVISION, Department of Commerce and Economic Development, General Administration Building, Olympia 98501

West Virginia
WEST VIRGINIA DEPARTMENT OF COMMERCE, Travel Development Division, Room E-404, State Capitol, Charleston 25305

Wisconsin
DEPARTMENT OF NATURAL RESOURCES, Vacation and Travel Service, Box 450, Madison 53701

Wyoming
TRAVEL COMMISSION, 2320 Capitol Avenue, Cheyenne 82001

Virgin Islands
GOVERNMENT TOURIST INFORMATION OFFICE, 16 W. 49th Street, New York, New York 10020

Canada
CANADIAN GOVERNMENT TRAVEL BUREAU, Ottawa, Ontario, 680 Fifth Avenue, New York, New York 10019

I Never Promised You a Free Rose Garden, But . . .

Here is a list of over 100 gardens throughout the U.S. where award-winning AARS roses are grown every year, according to the American Rose Society. All of these public gardens are free and you should take the opportunity to visit the ones nearest you.

California

ARCADIA COUNTY PARK ROSE GARDEN, Arcadia
BERKELEY MUNICIPAL ROSE GARDEN, Berkeley
FRESNO MUNICIPAL ROSE GARDEN, Roeding Park, Fresno
DESCANSO GARDENS, LaCanada
EXPOSITION PARK ROSE GARDEN, Los Angeles
MORCUM AMPHITHEATRE OF ROSES, Oakland
FAIRMONT PARK ROSE GARDEN, Riverside
CAPITOL PARK ROSE GARDEN, Sacramento
GOLDEN GATE PARK ROSE GARDEN, San Francisco
SAN JOSE MUNICIPAL ROSE GARDEN, San Jose
HUNTINGTON BOTANICAL GARDENS, San Marino
MEMORIAL ROSE GARDENS, Santa Barbara
VISALIA GARDEN CLUB PUBLIC ROSE GARDENS, Visalia

Colorado

LONGMONT MEMORIAL ROSE GARDEN, Longmont

Connecticut

NORWICH MEMORIAL ROSE GARDEN, Norwich
HAMILTON PARK ROSE GARDEN, Waterbury
ELIZABETH PARK ROSE GARDEN, West Hartford

Georgia

GREATER ATLANTA ROSE GARDEN, Atlanta
THOMASVILLE ROSE TEST GARDEN, Thomasville

Hawaii

UNIVERSITY OF HAWAII COLLEGE OF TROPICAL AGRICULTURE, Kula

Idaho

MEMORIAL BRIDGE ROSE GARDEN, Lewiston

Illinois

GRANT PARK ROSE GARDEN, Chicago
MARQUETTE PARK ROSE GARDEN, Chicago
GARDENER'S MEMORIAL GARDEN, Highland Park
COOK MEMORIAL ROSE GARDEN, Libertyville

PEORIA PARK ROSE GARDEN, Peoria
SINISSIPPI SUNKEN GARDENS, Rockford
ROBERT R. McCORMICK MEMORIAL GARDENS, Wheaton

Indiana
LAKESIDE ROSE GARDEN, Fort Wayne
GLEN MILLER PARK, Richmond

Iowa
IOWA STATE UNIVERSITY ROSE GARDEN, Ames
BETTENDORF COMMUNITY CENTER ROSE GARDEN, Bettendorf
HUSTON PARK ROSE GARDEN, Cedar Rapids
VANDERVEER PARK MUNICIPAL ROSE GARDEN, Davenport
GREENWOOD PARK MUNICIPAL ROSE GARDEN, Des Moines
WEED PARK MEMORIAL ROSE GARDEN, Muscatine
MOUNT ARBOR DEMONSTRATION GARDEN, Shenandoah
IOWA ROSE SOCIETY GARDEN, State Center
BYRNES PARK MUNICIPAL ROSE GARDEN, Waterloo

Kansas
KANSAS STATE UNIVERSITY ROSE GARDEN, Manhattan
E. F. A. REINISCH ROSE AND TEST GARDENS, Topeka

Louisiana
LOUISIANA STATE UNIVERSITY ROSE AND TEST GARDEN, Baton Rouge
PAULINE WORTHINGTON MEMORIAL ROSE GARDEN, New Orleans
THE AMERICAN ROSE CENTER, Shreveport

Massachusetts
STANLEY PARK, Westfield

Michigan
MICHIGAN STATE UNIVERSITY HORTICULTURE GARDENS, East Lansing
FRANCES PARK MEMORIAL ROSE GARDEN, Lansing

Minnesota
DULUTH ROSE GARDEN, Duluth

MINNEAPOLIS MUNICIPAL ROSE GARDEN, Minneapolis

Missouri
CAPE GIRARDEAU ROSE GARDEN, Cape Girardeau
JACKSON COUNTY ROSE SOCIETY, Laura Conyers Smith Memorial Rose Garden, Kansas City
MISSOURI BOTANICAL ROSE GARDEN, St. Louis

Montana
MISSOULA MEMORIAL ROSE GARDEN, Sunset Park, Missoula

Nebraska
LINCOLN MUNICIPAL ROSE GARDEN, Lincoln
OMAHA MEMORIAL PARK ROSE GARDEN, Omaha

Nevada
RENO MUNICIPAL ROSE GARDEN, Reno

New Jersey
BROOKDALE PARK ROSE GARDEN, Bloomfield

New Mexico
PROSPECT PARK ROSE GARDEN, Albuquerque

New York
CRANFORD MEMORIAL ROSE GARDEN, Brooklyn Botanic Gardens, Brooklyn
NIAGARA FRONTIER TRAIL ROSE GARDEN, Buffalo
THE NATIONAL ROSE GARDEN, Newark
UNITED NATIONS ROSE GARDEN, New York
MAPLEWOOD ROSE GARDEN, Rochester
CENTRAL PARK ROSE GARDEN, Schenectady

North Carolina
RALEIGH MUNICIPAL ROSE GARDEN, Raleigh

Ohio
COLUMBUS PARK OF ROSES, Ohio State University, Rose Garden, Columbus

Oklahoma
CONRAD MUNICIPAL ROSE GARDEN, Muskogee
MUNICIPAL ROSE GARDEN, Will Rogers Park, Oklahoma City
TULSA MUNICIPAL ROSE GARDEN, Tulsa

Oregon
CORVALLIS MUNICIPAL ROSE GARDEN, Avery Park
GEORGE E. OWEN MUNICIPAL ROSE GARDEN, Eugene
INTERNATIONAL ROSE TEST GARDEN, Portland

Pennsylvania
MALCOLM GROSS MEMORIAL ROSE GARDEN, Allentown
HERSHEY ROSE GARDENS AND ARBORETUM, Hershey
LONGWOOD GARDENS, Renziehausen Park Arboretum, McKeesport
MELLON PARK ROSE GARDEN, Pittsburgh
POTTSTOWN MEMORIAL ROSE GARDEN, Pottstown
READING MUNICIPAL ROSE GARDEN, Reading
PENN STATE UNIVERSITY ROSE GARDEN, State College
THE ROBERT PYLE MEMORIAL ROSE GARDEN, West Grove

South Carolina
EDISTO ROSE GARDEN, Orangeburg

Tennessee
MUNICIPAL ROSE GARDENS, Warner Park, Chattanooga
MEMPHIS MUNICIPAL ROSE GARDEN, Audubon Park, Memphis

Texas
CORPUS CHRISTI ROSE SOCIETY DISPLAY GARDEN, Corpus Christi
SAMUEL-GRAND MUNICIPAL ROSE GARDEN, Dallas
EL PASO MUNICIPAL ROSE GARDEN, El Paso
FORT WORTH BOTANIC GARDEN, Fort Worth
HOUSTON MUNICIPAL ROSE GARDEN, Houston
MUNICIPAL ROSE GARDEN, San Angelo
TYLER ROSE GARDEN PARK, Tyler

Utah
TERRITORIAL STATEHOUSE ROSE GARDENS, Old Capitol State Park, Fillmore

MUNICIPAL MEMORIAL ROSE GARDEN, Nephi
SALT LAKE CITY MUNICIPAL ROSE GARDEN, Salt Lake City

Virginia
ARLINGTON MEMORIAL ROSE GARDEN, Arlington
MOUNTAIN VIEW GARDEN, Roanoke

Washington
CORNWALL PARK ROSE GARDEN, Bellingham
CHEHALIS MUNICIPAL ROSE GARDEN, Chehalis
WOODLAND PARK ROSE GARDEN, Seattle
ROSE HILL–MANITO PARK ROSE GARDEN, Spokane
POINT DEFIANCE PARK ROSE GARDEN, Tacoma

West Virginia
RITTER PARK ROSE GARDEN, Huntington

Wisconsin
BOERNER BOTANICAL GARDENS, Hales Corners

Free Agricultural Experiment Station Tours

Our Agricultural Experiment Stations were established by the federal government and states to do scientific research in agriculture and horticulture. There is often more than one station in a state and you should certainly visit the one nearest you to witness the plantings and interesting experiments being conducted there. Take time out to visit these stations while traveling, too. Many, such as the stations at Beltsville, Maryland, are more elaborate than others, *and you are sure to find a station on this list with a specialty that whets your interest.* Free tours are usually available. Write or call to make sure.

Alabama
ALABAMA AGRICULTURAL EXPERIMENT STATION, Auburn Univeristy, Auburn 36830
CHILTON AREA HORTICULTURAL SUBSTATION, Clanton 36045
GULF COAST SUBSTATION, Auburn University, Fairhope 36532

N. ALABAMA HORTICULTURAL SUBSTATION, Alabama Agricultural Experiment Station System, Route 7, Box 508, Cullman 35055

ORNAMENTAL HORTICULTURE FIELD STATION, Box 8276, Spring Hill Station, Mobile 36608

PIEDMONT SUBSTATION, Auburn University, Camp Hill 36850

SAND MOUNTAIN SUBSTATION, Crossville 35962

TENNESSEE VALLEY SUBSTATION, Belle Mina 35615

WIREGRAPP SUBSTATION, Headland 36345

Alaska

ALASKA AGRICULTURAL EXPERIMENT STATION, University of Alaska, College 99701

ALASKA AGRICULTURAL EXPERIMENT STATION, Box AE, Palmer 99645

Arizona

ARIZONA AGRICULTURAL EXPERIMENT STATION, University of Arizona, Tucson 85721

CITRUS BRANCH EXPERIMENT STATION, University of Arizona, Rt. 1, Box 715, Tempe 85281

MESA BRANCH STATION, University of Arizona, Mesa 85202

SAFFORD EXPERIMENT STATION, University of Arizona, Box 1015, Safford 85546

YUMA BRANCH STATION, University of Arizona, Rt. 1, Box 587, Yuma 85364

Arkansas

ARKANSAS AGRICULTURAL EXPERIMENT STATION, University of Arkansas, Fayetteville 72701

COTTON BRANCH EXPERIMENT STATION, University of Arkansas, P.O. Box 522, Marianna 72360

FRUIT SUBSTATION, University of Arkansas, Clarksville 72830

PEACH SUBSTATION, University of Arkansas, Nashville 71852

SOUTHWEST BRANCH EXPERIMENT STATION, University of Arkansas, Rt. 3, Box 218, Hope 71801

STRAWBERRY SUBSTATION, University of Arkansas, Box 543, Bold Knob 72010

VEGETABLE SUBSTATION, University of Arkansas, Box 358, Van Buren 72956

California

CALIFORNIA AGRICULTURAL EXPERIMENT STATION, University of California at Davis, Davis 95616

CALIFORNIA AGRICULTURAL EXPERIMENT STATION, University of California at Los Angeles, Los Angeles 90024

CALIFORNIA AGRICULTURAL EXPERIMENT STATION, University of California at Riverside, Riverside 95202

DECIDUOUS FRUIT FIELD STATION, University of California, 125 North Winchester Boulevard, San Jose 95128

IMPERIAL VALLEY FIELD STATION, University of California, 1004 East Holton Road, El Centro 92243

LINDCOVE FIELD STATION, University of California, 22963 Carson Avenue, Exeter 93221

SOUTH COAST FIELD STATION, University of California, 7601 Irvine Boulevard, Santa Ana 92705

TULELAKA AGRICULTURAL FIELD STATION, University of California, Tulelaka 96134

U.S. PLANT INTRODUCTION STATION, Box 1040, Chico 95927

U.S. DATE AND CITRUS STATION, USDA-ARS, 40-455 Clinton Street, Indio 92201

USDA HORTICULTURAL STATION, Plant Science Research Division, 2021 South Peach Avenue, Fresno 93727

USDA-ARS PLANT SCIENCE RESEARCH DIVISION, 1636 East Alisal Street, P.O. Box 5098, Salinas 93901

WEST SIDE FIELD STATION, University of California, Box 158, Five Points 93624

WESTERN REGION, USDA-ARS, 2850 Telegraph Avenue, Berkeley 94706

Colorado

ARKANSAS VALLEY BRANCH STATION, Colorado State University, Rocky Ford 81067

COLORADO AGRICULTURAL EXPERIMENT STATION, Colorado State University, Fort Collins 80521

NATIONAL SEED STORAGE LABORATORY, Colorado State University Campus, Fort Collins 80521

SAN LUIS VALLEY STATION, Colorado State University, Route 2, Center 81125

WESTERN SLOPE BRANCH STATION, Colorado State University, 31688 ½ Road, Grand Junction 81501

Connecticut

CONNECTICUT AGRICULTURAL EXPERIMENT STATION, University of Connecticut, Storrs 06268

CONNECTICUT AGRICULTURAL EXPERIMENT STATION, Valley Laboratory, Box 248, Windsor 06095

CONNECTICUT AGRICULTURAL EXPERIMENT STATION, 123 Huntington Street, Box 1106, New Haven 06504

Delaware

DELAWARE AGRICULTURAL EXPERIMENT STATION, University of Delaware, Newark 19711

District of Columbia

ARS—INFORMATION DIVISION, Office of the Director 20250

CHESAPEAKE AND POTOMAC AREA, U.S. National Arboretum, 28th and M Streets N.E. 20002

NATIONAL PROGRAM STAFF, Plant and Entomology Sciences, USDA-ARS Administration Building 20250

OFFICE OF ADMINISTRATOR, ARS Administration Building 20250

PROGRAM ANALYSIS AND COORDINATION STAFF, USDA-ARS 20250

Florida

AGRICULTURAL RESEARCH CENTER MONTICELLO, Box 539, Monticello 32344

ARS, SOUTHERN REGION, USDA Horticultural Research Laboratory, 2120 Camden Road, Orlando 32803

BIG BEND HORTICULTURAL LABORATORY, University of Florida, Box 539, Monticello 32344

CITRUS EXPERIMENT STATION, University of Florida, Lake Alfred 33850

EVERGLADES EXPERIMENT STATION, University of Florida, Gainesville 32601

FLORIDA AGRICULTURAL EXPERIMENT STATION, University of Florida, Watermelon and Grape Investigation Laboratory, Leesburg 32748

GULF COAST EXPERIMENT STATION, IFAS, University of Florida, 5007 60th Street East, P.O. Box 2125, Brandenton 33505

POTATO INVESTIGATION LABORATORY, Box 728, Hastings 32045

RIDGE ORNAMENTAL HORTICULTURAL LABORATORY, Rt. 1, Box 980, Apopka 37203

SUB-TROPICAL EXPERIMENT STATION, IFAS, University of Florida, 18905 S.W. 280th Street, Homestead 33030

SUB-TROPICAL HORTICULTURE RESEARCH STATION, 13601 Old Cutler Road, Miami 33158

U.S. HORTICULTURAL FIELD LABORATORY, 2120 Camden Road, Orlando 32803

U.S. PLANT INTRODUCTION STATION, 13601 Old Cutler Road, Miami 33158

UNIVERSITY OF FLORIDA AGRICULTURAL EXPERIMENT STATION, Plantation Field Laboratory, 3205 S.W. 70th Avenue, Fort Lauderdale 33134

Georgia

AMERICUS PLANT MATERIALS CENTER, University of Georgia, Box 688, Americus 31709

GEORGIA AGRICULTURAL EXPERIMENT STATION, University of Georgia, Athens 30601

GEORGIA COASTAL PLAIN EXPERIMENT STATION, University of Georgia, Tifton 31794

GEORGIA MOUNTAIN BRANCH EXPERIMENT STATION, University of Georgia, Blairsville 30512

SOUTHWEST GEORGIA BRANCH EXPERIMENT STATION, University of Georgia, Plains 31780

U.S. PLANT INTRODUCTION STATION, Rt. 4, Box 433, Savannah 31405

Hawaii

HAWAII AGRICULTURAL EXPERIMENT STATION, College of Tropical Agriculture, University of Hawaii, Honolulu 96822

HAWAII BRANCH STATION, HAES, University of Hawaii, Hilo, Hawaii 96720

KAUAI BRANCH STATION, HAES, University of Hawaii, Kapaa, Kauai 96746

KONA BRANCH STATION, HAES, University of Hawaii, Kealakekua, Kona, 96750

MAUI BRANCH STATION, HAES, University of Hawaii, Kula, Maui 96790

Idaho

IDAHO AGRICULTURAL EXPERIMENT STATION, University of Idaho, Moscow 83843

IDAHO BRANCH EXPERIMENT STATION, University of Idaho, Parma 83660
IDAHO BRANCH EXPERIMENT STATION, University of Idaho, Aberdeen
  83210

Illinois

ILLINOIS AGRICULTURAL EXPERIMENT STATION, University of Illinois, Urbana 61801
SMALL FRUIT AND GRAPE INVESTIGATIONS, Southern Illinois University, Plant Industries Department, Carbondale 62903
USDA-ARS NORTH CENTRAL REGION, 2000 West Pioneer Parkway, Peoria 61614

Indiana

AGRICULTURAL RESEARCH SERVICE, USDA Location Leader, 2336 Northwestern Avenue, West Lafayette 47906
FELDUNPURDUE AGRICULTURAL CENTER, Purdue University, RR2, Bedford 47421
PURDUE UNIVERSITY AGRICULTURAL EXPERIMENT STATION, Purdue University, Lafayette 47907

Iowa

AGRICULTURAL EXPERIMENT STATION, Iowa State University, Plant Materials Investigations, Ames 50010

Idaho

IDAHO BRANCH EXPERIMENT STATION, University of Idaho, Parma 83660
IDAHO BRANCH EXPERIMENT STATION, University of Idaho, Aberdeen
  83210

Kansas

GARDEN CITY EXPERIMENT STATION, Kansas State University, Box L, Garden City 67846
KANSAS AGRICULTURAL EXPERIMENT STATION, Kansas State University, Manhattan 66502
NORTHEAST KANSAS EXPERIMENTAL FIELDS, Kansas State University, Wathena 66090
SOUTHEAST KANSAS BRANCH EXPERIMENT STATION, Kansas State University, Mound Valley 67354

SOUTHWEST KANSAS EXPERIMENTAL FIELD, Department of Horticulture and Forestry, Kansas State University, Box 245, Chetopa 67336
TRIBUNE BRANCH EXPERIMENT STATION, Kansas State University, P.O. Box 307, Tribune 67869

Kentucky
KENTUCKY AGRICULTURAL EXPERIMENT STATION, University of Kentucky, Lexington 40506
ROBINSON SUBSTATION, University of Kentucky, Quicksand 41363
UNIVERSITY OF KENTUCKY RESEARCH AND EXTENSION CENTER, Princeton 42445

Louisiana
ARS SOUTHERN REGIONAL OFFICE, 701 Loyola Avenue, P.O. Box 53326, New Orleans 70153
FRUIT AND TRUCK EXPERIMENT STATION, Louisiana State University, Route 2, Box 71, Hammond 70401
LOUISIANA AGRICULTURAL EXPERIMENT STATION, Louisiana State University, Baton Rouge 70803
NORTH LOUISIANA EXPERIMENT STATION, Louisiana State University, Calhoun 71225
PLAQUEMINES PARISH EXPERIMENT STATION, Louisiana State University, Rt. 1, Box 437, Port Sulphur 70083
U.S. PECAN FIELD LABORATORY, Rt. 1, Box 223, Shrevesport 71105

Maine
BLUEBERRY HILL EXPERIMENTAL FARM, Maine Agricultural Experiment Station, Addison 04606
MAINE AGRICULTURAL EXPERIMENT STATION, Highmoor Farm, Monmouth 04259
MAINE AGRICULTURAL EXPERIMENT STATION, University of Maine, Orono 04473
MAINE AGRICULTURAL EXPERIMENT STATION, Aroostock Experiment Farm, Presque Isle 04769

Maryland
AGRICULTURAL ENVIRONMENTAL QUALITY INSTITUTE, Beltsville Agricultural Research Center, Beltsville 20705

ARS/IPD FEDERAL CENTER, Building 1, Hyattsville 20782

ARS PLANT SCIENCE RESEARCH DIVISION, U.S. Plant Introduction Station, Box 88, Glenn Dale 20769

DIRECTOR'S OFFICE, BELTSVILLE AREA, Beltsville Research Center, Beltsville 20705

CHESAPEAKE AND POTOMAC AREA, OFFICE OF DIRECTOR, 6505 Belcrest Road, Hyattsville 20782

DEPUTY ADMINISTRATION OFFICE, NORTHEAST REGION AREA, Beltsville Agricultural Research Center, Beltsville 20705

FRUIT LABORATORY, P.G.G.I. Institute—USDA-ARS, Beltsville Research Center, Beltsville 20705

GERMPLASM RESOURCES LABORATORY, P.G.G.I. Institute—USDA-ARS, Beltsville Research Center, Beltsville 20705

MARYLAND AGRICULTURAL EXPERIMENT STATION, University of Maryland, College Park 20742

MEDICINAL PLANT RESOURCES, P.G.G.I. Institute—USDA-ARS, Beltsville Research Center, Beltsville 20705

NATIONAL PROGRAM STAFF, PLANT AND ENTOMOLOGY SCIENCES, USDA-ARS West, North Building, Beltsville 20705

ORNAMENTALS LABORATORY, P.G.G.I. Institute—USDA-ARS, Beltsville Research Center, Beltsville 20705

PLANT AND ENTOMOLOGY SCIENCES, USDA-ARS West, North Building, Beltsville 20705

PLANT PROTECTION INSTITUTE, Beltsville Research Center, Beltsville 20705

PLANT TAXONOMY LABORATORY, P.G.G.I. Institute—USDA-ARS, Beltsville Research Center, Beltsville 20705

TURFGRASS LABORATORY, P.G.G.I. Institute—USDA-ARS, Beltsville Research Center, Beltsville 20705

USDA PLANT INDUSTRY STATION, Plant Science Research Division, Beltsville 20705

VEGETABLE RESEARCH FARM, University of Maryland, Route 5, Salisbury 20861

Massachusetts

CRANBERRY STATION, University of Massachusetts, East Wareham 02538

MASSACHUSETTS AGRICULTURAL EXPERIMENT STATION, University of Massachusetts, Amherst 01002

WALTHAM FIELD STATION, University of Massachusetts, 240 Beaver Street, Waltham 02154

Michigan
GRAHAM HORTICULTURAL EXPERIMENT STATION, 2989 Lake Michigan Drive, N.W., Grand Rapids 49501

MICHIGAN AGRICULTURAL EXPERIMENT STATION, Michigan State University, East Lansing 49090

UPPER PENINSULA EXPERIMENT STATION, Michigan State University, Chatham 49816

W. K. KELLOGG FOREST, Michigan State University, Route 1, Augusta 49012

Minnesota
MINNESOTA AGRICULTURAL EXPERIMENT STATION, University of Minnesota, St. Paul 55101

NORTHWEST EXPERIMENT STATION, University of Minnesota, Crookston 56716

SOIL SCIENCE BUILDING, University of Minnesota, St. Paul 55101

WEST CENTRAL EXPERIMENT STATION, University of Minnesota, Morris 56267

Mississippi
COASTAL PLAIN BRANCH STATION, Mississippi State University, Newton 39345

DELTA BRANCH STATION, Mississippi Agricultural Experiment Station, Mississippi State University, Holly Springs 38635

NORTH MISSISSIPPI BRANCH EXPERIMENT STATION, Mississippi State University, Holly Springs 38635

PONTOTOC RIDGE–FLATWOODS BRANCH EXPERIMENT STATION, Mississippi State University, Pontotoc 38863

SOUTH MISSISSIPPI BRANCH STATION, Mississippi State University, Poplarville 39470

TRUCK CROPS BRANCH STATION, Mississippi State University, Crystal Springs 39059

Missouri
AGRICULTURAL RESEARCH SERVICE, USDA AREA DIRECTOR, 800 N. Providence Road, Columbia 65201

MISSOURI AGRICULTURAL EXPERIMENT STATION, University of Missouri, Columbia 65201

Montana
CENTRAL MONTANA BRANCH STATION, Montana State University, Moccasin 59462

EASTERN MONTANA STATION, Montana State University, Sidney 59270

HUNTLEY BRANCH STATION, Montana State University, Huntley 59037

MONTANA AGRICULTURAL EXPERIMENT STATION, Montana State University, Bozeman 59715

NORTH MONTANA BRANCH STATION, Montana State University, Havre 59501

NORTHWESTERN MONTANA BRANCH STATION, Montana State University, Kalispell 59901

WESTERN MONTANA BRANCH STATION, Montana State University, Corvallis 59828

Nebraska
NEBRASKA AGRICULTURAL EXPERIMENT STATION, University of Nebraska, Lincoln 68503

NORTH CENTRAL REGION, Kansas-Nebraska Area, P.O. Box 166, Clay Center 68933

NORTH PLATTE STATION, University of Nebraska, Rt. 4, North Platte 69101

SCOTTSBLUFF STATION, University of Nebraska, Mitchell 69357

New Hampshire
NEW HAMPSHIRE AGRICULTURAL EXPERIMENT STATION, University of New Hampshire, Durham 03824

New Jersey
CRANBERRY AND BLUEBERRY RESEARCH LABORATORY, Rutgers State University, New Lisbon 08064

NEW JERSEY AGRICULTURAL EXPERIMENT STATION, Rutgers State University, New Brunswick 08903

New Mexico
MIDDLE RIO GRANDE BRANCH STATION, New Mexico State University, Rt. 1, Box 28, Los Lunas 87031

NEW MEXICO AGRICULTURAL EXPERIMENT STATION, New Mexico State University, Las Cruces 88001

SAN JUAN BRANCH STATION, New Mexico State University, Box 1018, Farmington 87401

Nevada

NEVADA AGRICULTURAL EXPERIMENT STATION, University of Nevada, Reno 89007

New York

AGRICULTURAL EXPERIMENT STATION, Cornell University, Ithaca 14850

CORNELL ORNAMENTALS RESEARCH LABORATORY, Melville Road, Farmingdale 11735

CORNELL UNIVERSITY, Tower Road, Plant Soil and Nutrition Laboratory, Ithaca 14850

CORNELL UNIVERSITY BRANCH EXPERIMENT STATION, Riverhead 11901

GRAPE RESEARCH LABORATORY, New York State Agricultural Experiment Station, Fredonia 14063

NEW YORK STATE AGRICULTURAL EXPERIMENT STATION, USDA New Crops Research Branch, Plant Materials Investigation, Geneva 14456

NEW YORK STATE AGRICULTURAL EXPERIMENT STATION, Geneva 14456

NEW YORK STATE AGRICULTURAL EXPERIMENT STATION, Hudson Valley Laboratory, Highland 12528

North Carolina

COASTAL PLAIN VEGETABLE RESEARCH STATION, Route 5, Box 43, Clinton 28238

HORTICULTURE CROPS RESEARCH STATION, P.O. Box 397, Castle Hayne 28429

MOUNTAIN HORTICULTURE CROPS RESEARCH STATION, RFD 2, Box 250, Fletcher 28732

NORTH CAROLINA AGRICULTURAL EXPERIMENT STATION, North Carolina State University, Raleigh 27607

PIEDMONT RESEARCH STATION, Rt. 6, Box 420, Salisbury 28144

SANDHILLS RESEARCH STATION, Rt. 1, Jackson Springs 27281

TIDEWATER RESEARCH STATION, Rt. 2, Box 106, Plymouth 27962

North Dakota

CARRINGTON IRRIGATION STATION, Box 95, Carrington 58421

NORTH DAKOTA AGRICULTURAL EXPERIMENT STATION, North Dakota State University, Fargo 58102

USDA-ARS Area Office, P.O. Box 5033, State University Station, Fargo 58102

Ohio

AGRICULTURAL RESEARCH AND DEVELOPMENT CENTER, Ohio State University, Northwestern Branch, RD 1, Custar 43511

MUCK CROPS BRANCH STATION, Ohio State University, Willard 44890

OHIO AGRICULTURAL EXPERIMENT STATION, Ohio State University, Columbus 43210

OHIO AGRICULTURAL RESEARCH AND DEVELOPMENT CENTER, SOUTHERN BRANCH, RD 1, Box 101, Ripley 45167

OHIO AGRICULTURAL RESEARCH AND DEVELOPMENT CENTER, Wooster 44691

SHADE TREE AND ORNAMENTAL PLANTS LABORATORY, USDA-ARS Plant Science Research Division, Box 365, Delaware 43015

VEGETABLE CROPS BRANCH STATION, Ohio State University, Marietta 45750

Oklahoma

EASTERN OKLAHOMA FIELD STATION, Rt. 2, Westville 74965

PECAN RESEARCH STATION, Oklahoma State University, Sparks 74869

VEGETABLE RESEARCH STATION, Oklahoma State University, Bixby 74008

Oregon

MALHEUR EXPERIMENT STATION, Oregon State University, Rt. 1, Box 302, Ontario 97914

MID-COLUMBIA EXPERIMENT STATION, Oregon State University, Rt. 4, Box 176, Hood River 97031

NORTH WILLAMETTE EXPERIMENT STATION, Oregon State University, Aurora 97002

OREGON AGRICULTURAL EXPERIMENT STATION, Oregon State University, Corvallis 97331

OREGON STATE UNIVERSITY, Cordley Hall, Corvallis 97331

PACIFIC BULB GROWERS RESEARCH AND DEVELOPMENT STATION, Oregon State University, Pendleton 97801

SOUTHERN OREGON EXPERIMENT STATION, Oregon State University, 569 Hanley Road, Medford 97501

Pennsylvania

AGRICULTURAL EXPERIMENT STATION FRUIT RESEARCH LABORATORY, Pennsylvania State University, Arendtsville 17303

AGRICULTURAL EXPERIMENT STATION, Erie County Field Research Laboratory, Pennsylvania State University, Cemetery Road, North East 16428

EASTERN REGION RESEARCH CENTER, Office of Director—USDA, Philadelphia 19118

PENNSYLVANIA AGRICULTURAL EXPERIMENT STATION, Pennsylvania State University, University Park 16802

Rhode Island

RHODE ISLAND AGRICULTURAL EXPERIMENT STATION, University of Rhode Island, Kingston 02881

South Carolina

EDISTO EXPERIMENT STATION, P.O. Box C 247, Blackville 29817

PEE DEE EXPERIMENT STATION, Clemson University, Box 271, Florence 29501

SANDHILL EXPERIMENT STATION, Box 1771, Columbia 29202

SOUTH CAROLINA AGRICULTURAL EXPERIMENT STATION, Clemson University, Box 3158, St. Andrews, Charleston 29407

U.S. VEGETABLE BREEDING LABORATORY, USDA-ARS Plant Science Research Division, Box 3348, Charleston 29407

South Dakota

SOUTH DAKOTA AGRICULTURAL EXPERIMENT STATION, South Dakota State University, Brookings 57006

Tennessee

AMES PLANTATION, University of Tennessee, Grand Junction 38039

HIGHLAND RIM EXPERIMENT STATION, University of Tennessee, R.R. 6, Springfield 37172

MIDDLE TENNESSEE EXPERIMENT STATION, University of Tennessee, Box 160, Spring HIll 37174

PLATEAU EXPERIMENT STATION, University of Tennessee, Route 9, Grossville 38555

TENNESSEE AGRICULTURAL EXPERIMENT STATION, University of Tennessee, Knoxville 37901

UT-AED AGRICULTURAL RESEARCH LABORATORY, 1299 Bethel Valley Road, Oak Ridge 37830

WEST TENNESSEE EXPERIMENT STATION, University of Tennessee, 605 Airways Boulevard, Jackson 38301

Texas

AGRICULTURAL RESEARCH AND EXTENSION CENTER, Texas A & M University, RFD 3, Lubbock 79401

FRUIT RESEARCH DEMONSTRATION STATION, Texas A & M University, Montague 76251

RIO GRANDE SOIL AND WATER RESEARCH CENTER, Box 267, Weslaco 78596

TEXAS AGRICULTURAL EXPERIMENT STATION, Texas A & M University, College Station 77843

U. S. PECAN FIELD STATION, USDA-ARS Box 579, Brownwood 76801

Utah

BRIGHAM YOUNG UNIVERSITY AGRICULTURAL EXPERIMENT STATION, Provo 84601

FARMINGTON FIELD STATION, Utah State University, 1817 North Main, Farmington 84025

UNIVERSITY OF UTAH, Department of Botany, Salt Lake City 84112

UTAH AGRICULTURAL EXPERIMENT STATION, Utah State University, Logan 84321

UTAH EXPERIMENT STATION, Howell Field Station, 530 West Elberta Drive, Ogden 84404

Vermont

VERMONT AGRICULTURAL EXPERIMENT STATION, University of Vermont, Burlington 05401

Virginia

PIEDMONT RESEARCH LABORATORY, Virginia Polytechnic Institute, Charlottesville 22903

VIRGINIA AGRICULTURAL EXPERIMENT STATION, Virginia Polytechnic Institute, P.O. Box 2160, Norfolk 23501

Washington

COASTAL WASHINGTON RESEARCH AND EXTENSION UNIT, Washington State University, Rt. 1, Box 570, Long Beach 98631

IRRIGATED AGRICULTURE RESEARCH AND EXTENSION CENTER, Washington State University, Prosser 99350

NORTHWESTERN WASHINGTON RESEARCH AND EXTENSION UNIT, Washington State University, 1468 Memorial Highway, Mt. Vernon 98273

PLANT MATERIALS INVESTIGATIONS AGRICULTURAL EXPERIMENT STATION, Washington State University Campus, Pullman 99163

SOUTHWESTERN WASHINGTON RESEARCH UNIT, Washington State University, Vancouver 98665

TREE FRUIT RESEARCH CENTER, Washington State University, 1100 North Western Avenue, Wenatchee 98801

USDA-ARS, Yakima and Mission Streets, Wenatchee 98801

West Virginia

OHIO VALLEY EXPERIMENT STATION, West Virginia University, Rt. 1, Box 113, Point Pleasant 25550

WEST VIRGINIA AGRICULTURAL EXPERIMENT STATION, West Virginia University, Morgantown 26506

WEST VIRGINIA UNIVERSITY EXPERIMENT FARM, State Route 9, Kearneysville 25430

Wisconsin

HANCOCK EXPERIMENTAL FARM, College of Agricultural and Life Sciences, University of Wisconsin, Hancock 54943

PENINSULAR BRANCH EXPERIMENT STATION, University of Wisconsin, Sturgeon Bay 54235

UNIVERSITY OF WISCONSIN EXPERIMENTAL STATION, Rural Rt. 2, Marshfield 54449

UNIVERSITY OF WISCONSIN EXPERIMENTAL FARM, Ashland 54806

UNIVERSITY OF WISCONSIN EXPERIMENTAL FARM, RFD 1, Box 81, Lancaster 53813

Wyoming

CHEYENNE HORTICULTURAL FIELD STATION, USDA-ARS Plant Science Research Division, Box 1087, Cheyenne 82001

WYOMING AGRICULTURAL EXPERIMENT STATION, University of Wyoming, Laramie 82070

Puerto Rico

ADJUNTAS SUBSTATION, University of Puerto Rico, Agricultural Experiment Station, Box 61, Castaner 00631

AGRICULTURAL EXPERIMENT STATION, University of Puerto Rico, Mayaguez Campus, Box H, Rio Piedras 00928

Canada

ALBERTA HORTICULTURAL RESEARCH CENTER, Alberta Department of Agriculture, Brooks, Alberta

A Garden Where Deadly Plants Grow

Deadly plants, far more numerous and dangerous than Nathaniel Hawthorne's fictional "flowers of evil," are being carefully cultivated in a poison-plant garden at Cornell University. The plants are growing to save, rather than take, lives.

Poison plants, according to Public Health Service figures, are the sixth leading cause of poisoning in children under five. Some 15,000 people suffer illnesses from plant poisoning every year; an estimated 750 die every decade, not to mention a much higher death toll for pets and livestock, for which no records are kept.

The poison garden, which charges no admission and is open to the public at all times, was planted by the late Dr. Walter Conrad Muenscher during his 38 years of service at Cornell University. He served on the faculty of the New York State College of Agriculture at Cornell until his retirement in 1954. Professor Muenscher was a pioneer in poison plant identification. His book *Poisonous Plants of the*

United States has long been a standard text. During his long career, he answered some 28,000 letters from all over the world asking for information about weeds and poisonous plants.

Although the poison-plant garden was begun as an instruction aid for veterinary students, and is still used primarily by the Veterinary College, it is visited each year by hundreds of persons, mostly physicians (especially pediatricians), students of phytotoxicology and organized groups such as garden and 4-H clubs. Dr. John M. Kingsbury, who succeeded Dr. Muenscher upon his retirement, is an authority on poison plants and began to rehabilitate the plot in 1954. It was not until 1958, after considerable pruning, weeding and planting, that it was formally dedicated as the Walter C. Muenscher Poisonous Plants Garden.

Over the years, Professor Muenscher gathered specimens from the wild and planted them near the Plant Science Building, but the garden had to be moved from this site in 1962 to make room for additional buildings. At their new location, behind the James Law Auditorium at Cornell's Veterinary College, the plants were given special attention for the first time.

The garden is surrounded now by a low yew hedge in the front and privet hedges on each side. Both these plants are poisonous, as is, of course, the large unpruned yew backing the granite boulder memorial. All of the plants are labeled with their scientific names, their common names and the names of the plant families to which they belong.

The plants are all harmless if not ingested. Their danger lies in their anonymity. Although the approximately 700 poisonous plant species constitute only one percent of all the plants in North America north of Mexico, the poisonous principle has been isolated in only about half of these species. Therefore, identification is important. Few are aware, as is pointed out in Professor Kingsbury's *Poisonous Plants of the United States and Canada,* that mistletoe can deliver the kiss of death if eaten, that the beautiful bleeding heart is poisonous or that meat skewered on oleander branches can kill a person.

In addition to the poison garden, the New York State College of

Agriculture maintains a free plant identification service to identify poisonous plants for residents of all states. Suspected plants should be packaged carefully and mailed to the Extension Specialist, L. H. Bailey Hortorium, Ithaca, New York, along with a letter telling the specimen's locality, habitat and the date collected.

50 Free Garden Festivities

It is good to be able to report these 50 free garden festivities at a time when garden shows are generally becoming so high-priced that they are driving folk away instead of making new converts to gardening. The dates given are the latest available opening day dates for each event in 1983, but check first just to be sure there hasn't been a change, especially if the date given doesn't fall on a weekend. Fun ranges from the exhibitions of "the world's largest pie" at the South Carolina Peach Festival to "the world's largest breakfast table" at the Cereal City Festival in Battle Creek, Michigan, and "the world's largest geranium show" in Hollywood, California.

January 29—Vermont Farm Show, Barre City Auditorium, Barre, Vermont

February 9—Annual Carrot Festival, Holtville, California

February 9—Azalea Show, Lincoln Park Conservatory, Fullerton Avenue and Stockton, Chicago, Illinois

February 23—Annual Beaufort Camellia Show, Beaufort Academy Gymnasium, Lady's Island, Beaufort, South Carolina

March 17—Lake County Fair & Flower Show, Lake County Fairgrounds, 2101 Highway 452, Eustis, Florida

March 22—Highland Maple Sugar Festival, Highland County Headquarters, Monterey, Virginia

March 22—Puyallup Daffodil Festival, Puyallup, Washington

March 22—Spring Flower & Azalea Trail, Tyler Spring Flower & Bergfeld Park, Tyler, Texas

March 22—Texas Dogwood Trails, throughout Palestine, Texas

March 29—Tyler County Dogwood Festival, Woodville, Texas

March 29—Easter Show, Lincoln Park Conservatory, Fullerton Avenue and Stockton, Chicago, Illinois

April 10—Annual Historic Beaufort Tours, Beaufort, South Carolina

April 11—Come See Me Festival, Rock Hill, South Carolina

April 11—Geauga County Maple Festival, Uptown Chardon Square Park, Chardon, Ohio

April 12—Society for Louisiana Irises Show, USL Conference Center, Res Street, Lafayette, Louisiana

April 23—Annual Flower Show "April in Paris," Saint Benedict's Catholic Church, Highway 19 South, Crystal River, Florida

April 24—Wildflower Pilgrimage, W. L. Mills Convention Center, Airport Road, Gatlinburg, Tennessee

May 1—Shenandoah Apple Blossom Festival, Winchester, Virginia

May 1—World Bromeliad Conference, Sheraton-Twin Towers, Major Boulevard, Orlando, Florida

May 2—Garden Fair, Albuquerque Garden Center, 10200 Lomas N.E., Albuquerque, New Mexico

May 2—South Carolina Festival of Roses, Edisto Gardens, Orangeburg, South Carolina

May 3—Wilmington Garden Day, Wilmington, Delaware

May 8—Pella Tulip Festival, Pella, Iowa

May 10—Dwarf Iris Exhibition, Yorktown Shopping Center, Route 56 at Highland Avenue, Lombard, Illinois

May 10—Geranium Show, New Community Building, Plummer Park, 7377 Santa Monica Boulevard, Hollywood, California

May 14—Holland Tulip Time Festival, Holland, Michigan

May 15—Orange City Tulip Festival, Orange City, Iowa

May 23—Spring Flower Show, Albuquerque Garden Center, 10200 Lomas N.E., Albuquerque, New Mexico

May 31—Tall Bearded Iris Exhibition, Yorktown Shopping Center, Route 5 at Highland Avenue, Lombard, Illinois

June 14—Cereal City Festival, Michigan Mall, Michigan Avenue, Battle Creek, Michigan

June 29—Tropical Fruit Festival, Mounts Agricultural Center, 531 North Military Trail, West Palm Beach, Florida

July 2—South Carolina Peach Festival, Gaffney, South Carolina

July 6—National Cherry Festival, Traverse City, Michigan

July 11—Annual International Lily Show, Kingwood Center, 900 Park Avenue, West Mansfield, Ohio

July 19—Festival of Flowers and Flower Day, Park Seed Company, Greenwood, South Carolina

July 26—Horticulture Park Open House, Horticulture Park, West State Street, West Lafayette, Indiana

July 26—Iris Sale and Auction, Hinsdale Community House, Eighth and Madison Streets, Hinsdale, Illinois

August 2—Porter Peach Festival, Porter, Oklahoma

August 6—Home Gardener's Day, Agriculture Hall, University of Delaware, Newark, Delaware

August 8—South Carolina Grape Festival, York, South Carolina

August 10—American Hibiscus Society Exhibition, Burdine, Pompano Fashion Square, Pompano Beach, Florida

August 13—Tanana Valley Alaska State Fair, College Road, Fairbanks, Alaska

August 24—Annual Flower and Garden Show, University of Rhode Island Gardens, Kingston, Rhode Island

August 27—Horticulture Night, North Central Experiment Station, University of Minnesota, Grand Rapids, Minnesota

August 30—Maple Lawn Farms Peachilicious Labor Day Weekend, Maple Lawns Farms, Gatchellville, Pennsylvania

August 30–Sept. 1—Milan Melon Festival, Village Square, Park and Main Streets, Milan, Ohio

September 3—Tomato Festival, Huber Park, Retton Road and Haft Drive, Reynoldsburg, Ohio

Sept. 18—Food and Agriculture Exhibition, Charleston Civic Center, Charleston, West Virginia

October 15—Circleville Pumpkin Show, Circleville, Ohio

Arboretums Where You Can Get Free Advice

Horticultural experts at these famous arboretums, vast gardens of trees, shrubs and plants growing outdoors, will provide help for the home garden. Many of these magnificent gardens are free to visit as well.

Alabama
UNIVERSITY OF ALABAMA ARBORETUM, Tuscaloosa 35486
AUBURN UNIVERSITY ARBORETUM, Auburn 36830

Arizona
BOYCE THOMPSON ARBORETUM, Superior 85273

California
C. M. GOETHE ARBORETUM, 6000 Jay Street, Sacramento 95819
IRVINE ARBORETUM, University of California, Irvine 92664
LOS ANGELES STATE & COUNTY ARBORETUM, 301 N. Baldwin Avenue, Arcadia 91006
STRYBING ARBORETUM, Golden Gate Park, San Francisco 94122

Connecticut
BARTLETT ARBORETUM, 151 Brookdale Road, Stamford 06903
CONNECTICUT ARBORETUM, Connecticut College, New London 06320

District of Columbia
U.S. NATIONAL ARBORETUM, Washington, D.C. 20250

Florida
GIFFORD ARBORETUM, University of Miami, Coral Gables 33134

Hawaii
LYON ARBORETUM, 3860 Manoe Road, Honolulu 96822

Idaho
CHARLES HUSTON SHATTUCK ARBORETUM, University of Idaho, Moscow 83843

Illinois
MORTON ARBORETUM, Route 53, Lisle 60532

Indiana
CHRISTY WOODS ARBORETUM, Ball State Teachers College, Muncie 47302
HAYES REGIONAL ARBORETUM, 801 Elks Road, Richmond 47374

Iowa
LILAC ARBORETUM, McKinley Avenue, Des Moines 50300

Kansas
INDIAN HILL ARBORETUM, Topeka 66601

Kentucky
BERNHEIM FOREST ARBORETUM, Clermont 40110

Louisiana
LOUISIANA ARBORETUM, Baton Rouge 70821

Massachusetts
ARNOLD ARBORETUM, Jamaica Plain 02130

Michigan
MICHIGAN ARBORETUM, Michigan Avenue and Southfield Road, Dearborn 48121
NICOLS ARBORETUM, University of Michigan, Ann Arbor 48107

Minnesota
HORMEL FOUNDATION ARBORETUM, Austin 55912
UNIVERSITY OF MINNESOTA ARBORETUM, Chanhassen 55317

Mississippi
GLOSTER ARBORETUM, Gloster 39638

Nebraska
ARBOR LODGE STATE PARK ARBORETUM, Nebraska City 68410

New Jersey
HANOVER PARK ARBORETUM, Mt. Pleasant Avenue, East Hanover 07936

CORA HARTSHORN ARBORETUM, Forest Drive, Short Hills 07078
WILLOWWOOD ARBORETUM, Rutgers University, Gladstone 07934

New York
BAYARD CUTTING ARBORETUM, Great River 11739
THOMAS C. DESMOND ARBORETUM, Rt. 1, Newburgh 12550
GEORGE LANDIS ARBORETUM, Esperance 12066
NEW YORK BOTANICAL GARDEN, Bronx 10458
PLANTING FIELDS ARBORETUM, Oyster Bay 11771
ROBIN HILL ARBORETUM, Platten Road, Lydonville 14098
THE MEYER ARBORETUM, Cross River 10518

North Carolina
COKER ARBORETUM, University of North Carolina, Chapel Hill 27514

Ohio
DAWES ARBORETUM, Route 5, Newark 43055
HOLDEN ARBORETUM, 9500 Sperry Road, Mentor 44060
STANLEY M. ROWE ARBORETUM, 4500 Muchmore Road, Cincinnati 45243
SECOR PARK ARBORETUM, Rt. 1, Berkey 43504
R. A. STRANAHAM ARBORETUM, University of Toledo, 33 Birkhead Place,
Toledo 43606

Oregon
HOYT ARBORETUM, 4000 SW Fairview Boulevard, Portland 97221
PEAVY ARBORETUM, Oregon State College, Corvallis 97330

Pennsylvania
BARNES FOUNDATION ARBORETUM, 300 Latches Lane, Merion Station
19066
AWBURY ARBORETUM, Washington Lane and Ardleigh Street, Germantown
19152
COOVER ARBORETUM, Route 3, Dillsburg 17019
MORRIS ARBORETUM, University of Pennsylvania, Rt. 422, Chestnut Hill,
Philadelphia 19118
TAYLOR MEMORIAL ARBORETUM, 10 Ridley Drive, Garden City, Chester
19013

Tennessee

SOUTHWESTERN ARBORETUM, Southwestern College of Memphis, Memphis 38117

UNIVERSITY OF TENNESSEE ARBORETUM, 901 Kerr Hollow Road, Oak Ridge 37830

Texas

ARBORETUM FOUNDATION, INC., 4215 University Avenue, Lubbock 79413

Wisconsin

UNIVERSITY OF WISCONSIN ARBORETUM, 1207 Seminole Highway, Madison 53711

Puerto Rico

SAN GERMAN ARBORETUM, Inter-American University, San German, Puerto Rico

Virgin Islands

ST. THOMAS GARDENS AND ARBORETUM (ORCHIDARIUM), Charlotte Amalie, Virgin Islands

Canada

GUELPH ARBORETUM, University of Guelph, Guelph, Ontario, Canada

Nature Magazine

A free sample copy of the colorful bimonthly nature magazine *The Nature Conservancy News* is available as an introduction to the Nature Conservancy, a nonprofit organization dedicated to safeguarding natural areas and the variety of life they shelter. Write: The Nature Conservancy, 1800 N. Kent Street, Arlington, Virginia 22209.

Free Help for Indoor Plants

Conservatories, huge greenhouses where plants and trees are grown under glass, are a potential source of free help for the indoor gardener.

Many arboretums maintain conservatories (see the preceding list) and you should investigate those in your area, but should your efforts fail, here is a short sure-fire list.

DENVER BOTANIC GARDENS, 909 York Street, Denver, Colorado 80206

MIAMI BEACH GARDEN CENTER AND CONSERVATORY, 2000 Garden Center Drive, Miami Beach, Florida 33134

LINCOLN PARK CONSERVATORY, 2400 N. Stockton Drive, Chicago, Illinois 60614

ANNA SCRIPPS WHITCOMB CONSERVATORY, Belle Isle, Detroit, Michigan 48207

COMO PARK CONSERVATORY, 1224 N. Lexington Parkway, St. Paul, Minnesota 55103

MISSOURI BOTANICAL GARDEN, 2315 Tower Grove Avenue, St. Louis, Missouri 63110

BROOKLYN BOTANIC GARDENS, 1000 Washington Avenue, Brooklyn, New York 11225

KROHN CONSERVATORY, Cincinnati Park Board, Cincinnati, Ohio 45201

PHIPPS CONSERVATORY, Schenley Park, Pittsburgh, Pennsylvania 15213

U.S. BOTANIC GARDEN CONSERVATORY, Maryland Avenue, between First and Second Streets S.W., Washington, D.C. 20024

An Ecology Primer

Misuse of land and its effects throughout the world are the themes of this valuable educational illustrated booklet that has been in print almost 30 years now and was recently revised. Send 35¢ for "Conquest of the Land through 7000 Years," sales number 001-000-03446-4, Superintendent of Documents, U.S. Government Printing Office, Washington, D.C. 20402.

Free Government Assistance

As a taxpayer you are entitled to government assistance with any gardening problem, from which pesticide to use to which vegetable varieties do best in your area. State cooperative extension agents are horticultural experts on hand to help you with any gardening question at every state cooperative extension office in the country. You may write to these state agents at the addresses shown below for your state, or consult your phone book for the number of your county cooperative extension agent, who will be glad to talk to you or even pay a visit in reference to your problem. The Agricultural Extension Service is a joint effort of the U.S. Department of Agriculture and your state and county governments. It also sponsors the 4-H program, the nation's largest agricultural and horticultural youth organization, which has branches in every state. Your state cooperative extension office will provide you with information about the 4-H program for your youngsters. It also provides free and low-cost publications written in its offices to help state residents with gardening. There are lists or catalogs of these publications available from each state cooperative extension office that would be worthwhile for even out-of-state residents to request.

ALABAMA COOPERATIVE EXTENSION SERVICE, Auburn University, Auburn Alabama 38630

ALASKA COOPERATIVE EXTENSION SERVICE, University of Alaska, Box 95151, Fairbanks, Alaska 99701

ARIZONA COOPERATIVE EXTENSION SERVICE, University of Arizona, Tucson, Arizona 85721

ARKANSAS COOPERATIVE EXTENSION SERVICE, University of Arkansas, Box 391, Little Rock, Arkansas 72203

CALIFORNIA COOPERATIVE EXTENSION SERVICE, University Hall, University of California, Berkeley, California 94720

COLORADO COOPERATIVE EXTENSION CENTER, Colorado State University, Fort Collins, Colorado 80521

CONNECTICUT COOPERATIVE EXTENSION SERVICE, University of Connecticut, Storrs, Connecticut 06268

DELAWARE COOPERATIVE EXTENSION SERVICE, Agricultural Hall, University of Delaware, Newark, Delaware 19711

FLORIDA COOPERATIVE EXTENSION SERVICE, Building 440, University of Florida, Gainesville, Florida 32601

GEORGIA COOPERATIVE EXTENSION SERVICE, University of Georgia, Athens, Georgia 30601

HAWAII COOPERATIVE EXTENSION SERVICE, Krauss Hall, University of Hawaii, 2500 Dole Street, Honolulu, Hawaii 96822

IDAHO COOPERATIVE EXTENSION SERVICE, Agricultural Science Building, University of Idaho, Moscow, Idaho 83843

ILLINOIS COOPERATIVE EXTENSION SERVICE, 123 Mumford Hall, University of Illinois, Urbana, Illinois 61801

INDIANA COOPERATIVE EXTENSION SERVICE, Agricultural Administration Building, Purdue University, West Lafayette, Indiana 47907

IOWA COOPERATIVE EXTENSION SERVICE, Printing and Publications Building, Iowa State University, Ames, Iowa 50010

KANSAS COOPERATIVE EXTENSION SERVICE, Umberger Hall, Kansas State University, Manhattan, Kansas 66506

KENTUCKY COOPERATIVE EXTENSION SERVICE, Experiment Station Building, University of Kentucky, Lexington, Kentucky 40506

LOUISIANA COOPERATIVE EXTENSION SERVICE, Room 192, Knapp Hall, Louisiana State University, Baton Rouge, Louisiana 70803

MAINE COOPERATIVE EXTENSION SERVICE, PICS Building, University of Maine, Orono, Maine 04473

MARYLAND COOPERATIVE EXTENSION SERVICE, University of Maryland, College Park, Maryland 20742

MASSACHUSETTS COOPERATIVE EXTENSION SERVICE, Stockbridge Hall, University of Massachusetts, Amherst, Massachusetts 01002

MICHIGAN COOPERATIVE EXTENSION SERVICE, Box 231, Michigan State University, East Lansing, Michigan 48823

MINNESOTA COOPERATIVE EXTENSION SERVICE, Coffey Hall, University of Minnesota, St. Paul, Minnesota 55101

MISSISSIPPI COOPERATIVE EXTENSION SERVICE, Mississippi State University, State College, Mississippi 39762

MISSOURI COOPERATIVE EXTENSION SERVICE, Whitten Hall, University of Missouri, Columbia, Missouri 65201

MONTANA COOPERATIVE EXTENSION SERVICE, Montana State University, Bozeman, Montana 59715

NEBRASKA COOPERATIVE EXTENSION SERVICE, College of Agriculture, University of Nebraska, Lincoln, Nebraska 68503

NEVADA COOPERATIVE EXTENSION SERVICE, University of Nevada, Reno, Nevada 89507

NEW HAMPSHIRE COOPERATIVE EXTENSION SERVICE, Hewitt Hall, University of New Hampshire, Durham, New Hampshire 03824

NEW JERSEY COOPERATIVE EXTENSION SERVICE, College of Agriculture, Rutgers University, New Brunswick, New Jersey 08903

NEW MEXICO COOPERATIVE EXTENSION SERVICE, Department of Agricultural Information, New Mexico State University, Las Cruces, New Mexico 88001

NEW YORK COOPERATIVE EXTENSION SERVICE, 7 Research Park, Cornell University, Ithaca, New York 14850

NORTH CAROLINA COOPERATIVE EXTENSION SERVICE, Department of Agricultural Information, Box 5037, North Carolina State University, Raleigh, North Carolina 27607

NORTH DAKOTA COOPERATIVE EXTENSION SERVICE, North Dakota State University, Fargo, North Dakota 58102

OHIO COOPERATIVE EXTENSION SERVICE, Ohio State University, 2120 Fyffe Road, Columbus, Ohio 43210

OKLAHOMA COOPERATIVE EXTENSION SERVICE, Oklahoma State University, Stillwater, Oklahoma 74074

OREGON COOPERATIVE EXTENSION SERVICE, Oregon State University, Corvallis, Oregon 97331

PENNSYLVANIA COOPERATIVE EXTENSION SERVICE, 230 Agricultural Administration Building, Pennsylvania State University, University Park, Pennsylvania 16802

RHODE ISLAND COOPERATIVE EXTENSION SERVICE, 16 Woodward Hall, University of Rhode Island, Kingston, Rhode Island 02881

SOUTH CAROLINA COOPERATIVE EXTENSION SERVICE, Clemson University, Clemson, South Carolina 29631

SOUTH DAKOTA COOPERATIVE EXTENSION SERVICE, Extension Building, South Dakota State University, Brookings, South Dakota 57006

TENNESSEE COOPERATIVE EXTENSION SERVICE, Box 1071, University of Tennessee, Knoxville, Tennessee 37901

TEXAS COOPERATIVE EXTENSION SERVICE, Texas A & M University, College Station, Texas 77843

UTAH COOPERATIVE EXTENSION SERVICE, Agricultural Science Building, Utah State University, Logan, Utah 84321

VERMONT COOPERATIVE EXTENSION SERVICE, Morrill Hall, University of Vermont, Burlington, Vermont 05401

VIRGINIA COOPERATIVE EXTENSION SERVICE, Virginia Polytechnic Institute, Blacksburg, Virginia 24061

WASHINGTON COOPERATIVE EXTENSION SERVICE, Publications Building, Washington State University, Pullman, Washington 99163

WEST VIRGINIA COOPERATIVE EXTENSION SERVICE, Patterson Drive, West
  Virginia University, Morgantown, West Virginia 26506
WISCONSIN COOPERATIVE EXTENSION SERVICE, 1535 Observatory Drive,
  University of Wisconsin, Madison, Wisconsin 53706
WYOMING COOPERATIVE EXTENSION SERVICE, Box 3354, College of Agri-
  culture, University of Wyoming, Laramie, Wyoming 82071
DISTRICT OF COLUMBIA COOPERATIVE EXTENSION SERVICE, University of
  the District of Columbia, H Street N.W., Washington, D.C. 20005
PUERTO RICO COOPERATIVE EXTENSION SERVICE, University of Puerto
  Rico, Mayaguez Campus, P.O. Box AR, Rio Piedras, Puerto Rico
  00928

Help from Horticultural Societies and Garden Clubs

Another good source for free help with gardening questions is your
state or local horticultural society, which often has an extensive library and excellent gardens with expert staffs. Local garden clubs,
while not nearly so well-endowed, should be able to answer most
questions or at least direct you to a source. Both would be excellent
organizations to join.

ARKANSAS STATE HORTICULTURAL SOCIETY, University of Arkansas, Fay-
  etteville, Arkansas 72701
CALIFORNIA HORTICULTURAL SOCIETY, % California Academy of Sciences,
  Golden Gate Park, San Francisco, California 94118
SOUTHERN CALIFORNIA HORTICULTURAL SOCIETY, P.O. Box 587, Palisade,
  California 81526
CONNECTICUT HORTICULTURAL SOCIETY, 199 Griswold Road, Wethers-
  field, Connecticut 06109
PENINSULA HORTICULTURAL SOCIETY, University of Delaware, Newark,
  Delaware 19711
FLORIDA STATE HORTICULTURAL SOCIETY, P.O. Box 552, Lake Alfred,
  Florida 33850
HORTICULTURE STUDY SOCIETY OF FLORIDA, 3280 S. Miami Avenue,
  Miami, Florida 33129
ALBANY HORTICULTURAL SOCIETY, 1605 Orchard Drive, Albany, Georgia
  31705

GEORGIA HORTICULTURAL SOCIETY, INC., 116 Sandra Avenue, Warner Robins, Georgia 31093

CHICAGO HORTICULTURAL SOCIETY, Room 402, 116 S. Michigan Avenue, Chicago, Illinois 60603

INDIANA HORTICULTURAL SOCIETY, Department of Horticulture, Purdue University, Lafayette, Indiana 47907

IOWA STATE HORTICULTURAL SOCIETY, State House, Des Moines, Iowa 50319

KANSAS STATE HORTICULTURAL SOCIETY, Waters Hall, Manhattan, Kansas 66502

KENTUCKY STATE HORTICULTURAL SOCIETY, West Kentucky Extension Substation, Princeton, Kentucky 42445

MEN'S GARDEN CLUB OF AMERICA, 5560 Merle Hay Road, Des Moines, Iowa 50323

LOUISIANA HORTICULTURE SOCIETY, Lafayette, Louisiana 70501

HORTICULTURAL SOCIETY OF MARYLAND, 114 W. Melrose Avenue, Baltimore, Maryland 21210

MARYLAND STATE HORTICULTURAL SOCIETY, University of Maryland, College Park, Maryland 20740

MASSACHUSETTS HORTICULTURAL SOCIETY, 300 Massachusetts Avenue, Boston, Massachusetts 02115

WORCESTER COUNTY HORTICULTURAL SOCIETY, 30 Elm Street, Worcester, Massachusetts 01608

MICHIGAN HORTICULTURAL SOCIETY, The White House, Belle Isle, Detroit, Michigan 48207

MICHIGAN STATE HORTICULTURAL SOCIETY, Michigan State University, East Lansing, Michigan 48823

WOMEN'S NATIONAL FLOWER AND GARDEN ASSOCIATION, 8200 Jefferson Avenue, Detroit, Michigan 48214

MINNESOTA STATE HORTICULTURAL SOCIETY, St. Paul Campus, University of Minnesota, St. Paul, Minnesota 55101

MISSOURI STATE HORTICULTURAL SOCIETY, P.O. Box 417, Columbia, Missouri 65201

NATIONAL COUNCIL OF STATE GARDEN CLUBS, 4401 Magnolia Avenue, St. Louis, Missouri 63110

NEBRASKA HORTICULTURAL SOCIETY, 1739 S. 49th Street, Lincoln, Nebraska 68506

NEW HAMPSHIRE HORTICULTURAL SOCIETY, State Office Annex, Concord, New Hampshire 03300

GARDEN STATE HORTICULTURAL ASSOCIATION, Blake Hall, College of Agriculture & Environmental Science, New Brunswick, New Jersey 08903

NEW JERSEY STATE HORTICULTURAL SOCIETY, Rutgers State University, Horticulture and Forestry Department, New Brunswick, New Jersey 08903

GARDEN CLUB OF AMERICA, 598 Madison Avenue, New York, New York 10022

HORTICULTURAL SOCIETY OF NEW YORK, 128 W. 58th Street, New York, New York 10009

NEW YORK STATE HORTICULTURAL SOCIETY, 145 Beresford Road, Rochester, New York 14610

NORTH DAKOTA STATE HORTICULTURAL SOCIETY, State University Station, Fargo, North Dakota 58102

OHIO STATE HORTICULTURAL SOCIETY, 151 Chaucer Court, Worthington, Ohio 43085

BLUE MOUNTAIN HORTICULTURAL SOCIETY, Route 2, P.O. Box 348, Milton-Freewater, Oregon 97862

OREGON HORTICULTURAL SOCIETY, 236 Cordley Hall, Oregon State University, Corvallis, Oregon 97331

PENNSYLVANIA HORTICULTURAL SOCIETY, INC., Independence National Historical Park, 325 Walnut Street, Philadelphia, Pennsylvania 19106

STATE HORTICULTURAL ASSOCIATION OF PENNSYLVANIA, Loganville, Pennsylvania 17403

SOUTH DAKOTA STATE HORTICULTURAL SOCIETY, 414 Tenth Street, Brookings, South Dakota 57006

HORTICULTURAL SOCIETY OF DAVIDSON COUNTY, Sears, Roebuck & Company, 639 Lafayette Street, Nashville, Tennessee 37203

TENNESSEE STATE HORTICULTURAL SOCIETY, University of Tennessee, P.O. Box 107, Weslaco, Tennessee 78596

UTAH STATE HORTICULTURAL SOCIETY, 1750 S. Redwood Road, Salt Lake City, Utah 84104

VERMONT STATE HORTICULTURAL SOCIETY, Department of Plant and Soil Science, University of Vermont, Burlington, Vermont 05401

AMERICAN HORTICULTURAL SOCIETY, Mount Vernon, Virginia 22121

GARDEN CLUB OF VIRGINIA, 37 Chatham Square, Richmond, Virginia 23236

HAMPTON ROADS HORTICULTURAL SOCIETY, Box 251-A, Maxwell Lane, Newport News, Virginia 23606

VIRGINIA STATE HORTICULTURAL SOCIETY, P.O. Box 718, Staunton, Virginia 24401

WEST VIRGINIA STATE HORTICULTURAL SOCIETY, P.O. Box 592, Charlestown, West Virginia 25414

Special Assistance from Plant Societies

These 67 plant societies will send you free information about their organizations, and for a well-spent few dollars a year you can become a member of most of them. For your nominal yearly dues you'll receive monthly bulletins about your specialty and share in up-to-the-minute developments, putting you far ahead of most gardeners in your area. Choose your specialty and write for details.

AFRICAN VIOLET SOCIETY OF AMERICA, P.O. Box 1326, Knoxville, Tennessee 37901

AMERICAN BEGONIA SOCIETY, INC., 369 Ridge Vista Avenue, San Jose, California 95127

THE AMERICAN BONSAI SOCIETY, 229 North Shore Drive, Lake Waukomis, Parksville, Missouri 64151

AMERICAN BOXWOOD SOCIETY, P.O. Box 85, Boyce, Virginia 22620

AMERICAN CAMELLIA SOCIETY, P.O. Box 212, Fort Valley, Georgia 31030

AMERICAN DAFFODIL SOCIETY, INC., 89 Chichester Road, New Canaan, Connecticut 06840

AMERICAN DAHLIA SOCIETY, 92-21 W. Delaware Drive, Mystic Islands, Tuckerton, New Jersey 07087

AMERICAN FERN SOCIETY, Department of Botany, University of Tennessee, Knoxville, Tennessee 37916

AMERICAN FUCHSIA SOCIETY, Hall of Flowers, Ninth Avenue and Lincoln Way, San Francisco, California 94122

AMERICAN GESNERIAD SOCIETY, 11983 Darlington Avenue, Los Angeles, California 90049

AMERICAN GLOXINIA AND GESNERIAD SOCIETY INC., Department AMS, Eastford, Connecticut 06242

AMERICAN GOURD SOCIETY, R.R. 1, P.O. Box 274, Mt. Gilead, Ohio 43338

AMERICAN HEMEROCALLIS SOCIETY, P.O. Box 586, Woodstock, Illinois 60098

AMERICAN HIBISCUS SOCIETY, P.O. Box 98, Eagle Lake, Florida 33839

AMERICAN HOSTA SOCIETY, 4392 W. 20th Street Road, Oshkosh, Wisconsin 54901

AMERICAN IRIS SOCIETY, 2315 Tower Grove Avenue, St. Louis, Missouri 63110

AMERICAN IVY SOCIETY, 128 West 58th Street, New York, New York 10019

AMERICAN MAGNOLIA SOCIETY, 2150 Woodward Avenue, Broomfield Hills, Michigan 48013

AMERICAN ORCHID SOCIETY, Botanical Museum, Harvard University, Cambridge, Massachusetts 02138

AMERICAN PENSTEMON SOCIETY, P.O. Box 64, Somersworth, New Hampshire 03878

AMERICAN PEONY SOCIETY, 107½ W. Main Street, Van Wert, Ohio 45981

AMERICAN PLANT LIFE SOCIETY AND AMERICAN AMARYLLIS SOCIETY, P.O. Box 150, La Jolla, California 92037

AMERICAN PRIMROSE SOCIETY, 14015 84th Avenue N.E., Bothell, Washington 98011

AMERICAN RHODODENDRON SOCIETY, 24450 S.W. Grahams Ferry Road, Sherwood, Oregon 97140

AMERICAN ROCK GARDEN SOCIETY, P.O. Box 26, Closter, New Jersey 07624

AMERICAN ROSE SOCIETY, P.O. Box 30000, Shreveport, Louisiana 71130

ARIL SOCIETY, INTERNATIONAL, 7802 Kyle Street, Sunland, California 91040

BONSAI CLUBS INTERNATIONAL, 2354 Lida Drive, Mountain View, California 94040

BONSAI SOCIETY OF GREATER NEW YORK, P.O. Box E, Bronx, New York 10466

BONSAI SOCIETY OF TEXAS, P.O. Box 11054, Dallas, Texas 75223

BROMELIAD SOCIETY, 1811 Edgecliffe Drive, Los Angeles, California 90026

CACTUS AND SUCCULENT SOCIETY OF AMERICA, P.O. Box 167, Reseda, California 91335

CALIFORNIA BONSAI SOCIETY, INC., P.O. Box 78211, Los Angeles, California 90016

CALIFORNIA NATIVE PLANT SOCIETY, Suite 317, 2490 Channing Way, Berkeley, California 94705

CANADIAN ROSE SOCIETY, 31 Learmont Drive, Weston, Ontario, Canada

CYMBIDIUM SOCIETY OF AMERICA, INC., P.O. Box 4202, Downey, California 90242

DWARF FRUIT TREES ASSOCIATION, Department of Horticulture, Michigan State University, East Lansing, Michigan 48823

DELPHINIUM SOCIETY, 7540 Ridgeway Road, Minneapolis, Minnesota 55426

DWARF IRIS SOCIETY, P.O. Box 13, Middlebury, Indiana 46540

ELM RESEARCH INSTITUTE, HARRISVILLE, NEW HAMPSHIRE 03450

EPIPHYLLUM SOCIETY, 218 E. Greystone Avenue, Monrovia, Georgia 91016

GREATER NEW YORK ORCHID SOCIETY, 116-31 Parkway Drive, Elmont, New York 11003

HERB SOCIETY OF AMERICA, 300 Massachusetts Avenue, Boston, Massachusetts 02115

HOLLY SOCIETY OF AMERICA, INC., P.O. Box 8445, Baltimore, Maryland 21234

INDOOR LIGHT GARDENING SOCIETY OF AMERICA, 4 Wildwood Road, Greenville, South Carolina 29607

INTERNATIONAL LILAC SOCIETY, Box 66, Oakdale, New York 11769

INTERNATIONAL GERANIUM SOCIETY, 1413 Shoreline Drive, Santa Barbara, California 93105

LOS ANGELES INTERNATIONAL FERN SOCIETY, 13715 Cordary Avenue, Hawthorne, California 90250

MEDIAN IRIS SOCIETY, 10 South Franklin Circle, Littleton, Colorado 80121

NATIONAL CHRYSANTHEMUM SOCIETY, INC., 8504 La Verne Drive, Adelphi, Maryland 20763

NATIONAL FUCHSIA SOCIETY, 10954 East Flory Street, Whittier, California 90606

NATIONAL OLEANDER SOCIETY, 22 S. Shore Drive, Galveston, Texas 77550

NATIONAL TULIP SOCIETY, 250 West 57th Street, New York, New York 10019

NEW ENGLAND WILD FLOWER SOCIETY, INC., Hemenway Road, Framingham, Massachusetts 10701

NORTH AMERICAN FRUIT EXPLORERS, 210 S.E. 108th Avenue, Portland, Oregon 97216

NORTH AMERICAN GLADIOLUS COUNCIL, 234 South Street, South Elgin, Illinois 60177

NORTH AMERICAN LILY SOCIETY, INC., North Ferrisburg, Vermont 05473

NORTHERN NUT GROWERS ASSOCIATION, INC., 4518 Holston Hills Road, Knoxville, Tennessee 37914

PALM SOCIETY, 7229 S.W. 54th Avenue, Miami, Florida 33143

REBLOOMING IRIS SOCIETY, 903 Tyler Avenue, Radford, Virginia 24141

SAINTPAULIA INTERNATIONAL, P.O. Box 10604, Knoxville, Tennessee 37919

SOCIETY FOR JAPANESE IRISES, 17225 McKenzie Highway, Route 2, Springfield, Oregon 97477

SOCIETY FOR SIBERIAN IRISES, South Harpswell, Maine 04079

SOCIETY FOR LOUISIANA IRISES, P.O. Box 175, University of Southwestern Louisiana, Lafayette, Louisiana 70501

SPURIA IRIS SOCIETY, Route 2, Box 35, Purcell, Oklahoma 73080

WILDFLOWER PRESERVATION SOCIETY, The New York Botanical Gardens, Bronx, New York 10458

Free Conservation Help

Conservation societies answer any questions you have about the ecology and will often send free information kits or sample copies of their organization's magazine to interested groups or individuals. These national organizations will certainly help raise your conservation consciousness and might assist you with a conservation-related problem when you have been stymied everywhere else. Remember, too, that the U.S. government is committed to conservation and that federal and state organizations like the Soil Conservation Service of the USDA will give technical assistance to individuals.

THE AMERICAN FORESTRY ASSOCIATION, 1919 17th Street, Washington, D.C. 20006

THE IZAAK WALTON LEAGUE OF AMERICA, 1326 Waukegan Road, Glenview, Illinois 60025

COUNCIL ON ENVIRONMENTAL QUALITY, 722 Jackson Place N.W., Washington, D.C. 20006

FRIENDS OF THE EARTH, 30 East 42nd Street, New York, New York 10017

NATIONAL AUDUBON SOCIETY, 1130 Fifth Avenue, New York, New York 10028

NATIONAL COUNCIL OF CONSERVATION DISTRICTS, Box 855, League City, Texas 77573

NATIONAL PARKS AND CONSERVATION ASSOCIATION, 1701 18th Street N.W., Washington, D.C. 20009

SIERRA CLUB, 1050 Mills Tower, San Francisco, California 94104

THE NATIONAL WILDLIFE FEDERATION, 1412 16th Street N.W., Washington, D.C. 20036

THE NATURE CONSERVANCY, Suite 800, 1800 North Kent Street, Arlington, Virginia 22209

THE WILDERNESS SOCIETY, 729 15th Street N.W., Washington, D.C. 20005

Magazines for Up-to-Date Data

You can consult the gardening magazines listed here in any reasonably well-stocked public library, or you might want to subscribe to one. Some offer free sample copies or trial subscription offers and others offer premiums with subscriptions. The trade journals mentioned are for those with special problems or for anyone who leans toward embarking on a career in some special area of gardening. This is a fairly representative list, but it should be remembered that there are many more periodicals featuring garden information—the Sunday gardening pages of *The New York Times* and other newspapers are excellent sources. Check the *Reader's Guide to Periodical Literature* in your library for articles on plants as well. Then, too, there are scores of specialized periodicals published by plant societies devoted to a particular plant, such as *American Camellia Quarterly,* or the *American Fuchsia Society Bulletin.* See our list of Plant Societies for addresses of these.

General Magazines

American Horticulturist, Mt. Vernon, Virginia 22121

The Avant Gardener, P.O. Box 489, New York, New York 10028

Flower and Garden, 4251 Pennsylvania, Kansas City, Missouri 64111

Horticulture, 300 Massachusetts Avenue, Boston, Massachusetts 02115

Organic Gardening, Emmaus, Pennsylvania 18049

Sunset Magazine, Menlo Park, California 92045

Trade Journals

American Nurseryman, 343 South Dearborn Street, Chicago, Illinois 60604

Florist and Nursery Exchange, 9 South Clinton Street, Chicago, Illinois 60606

Lawn/Garden/Outdoor Living, 1014 Wyandotte Street, Kansas City, Missouri 64105

Grounds Maintenance, 1014 Wyandotte Street, Kansas City, Missouri 64105

Landscape Industry, 910 Elm Grove Road, Elm Grove, Wisconsin 53112

Southern Florist And Nurseryman, P.O. Box 1868, 120 St. Louis Avenue, Fort Worth, Texas 76101

Trees Magazine, 7621 Lewis Road, Olmsted Falls, Ohio 44138

Lawn and Garden Merchandising, 481 University Avenue, Toronto 2, Ontario, Canada

Home and Garden Supply Merchandiser, P.O. Box 67, Minneapolis, Minnesota 55440

Nursery Business, 850 Elm Grove Road, Elm Grove, Wisconsin 53122

Pacific Coast Nurserymen, 832 South Baldwin Avenue, Arcadia, California 91006

You Be the Expert: Free Gardening Libraries You Can Use

Consult these magnificent libraries often and assiduously enough and *you* might become the expert on what has been your problem. Most of the libraries listed here are open to the public and all can be persuaded to let you use their resources if you are persuasive and/or persistent enough. Some of these libraries specialize in areas such as landscape design, but all areas of horticulture are amply covered in each. All are exemplars of botanical libraries with extensive holdings in the way of books, pamphlets, magazines, maps, photographs and botanical art. You'll come across unexpected delights, such as one of the world's largest collection of nursery catalogs at the Massachusetts Horticultural Society Library, or the 50,000-card index of flowering plant illustrations at the Eleanor Squire Library in Cleveland. Some of these horticultural libraries are strictly for reference work and others lend books, those that do often having interlibrary loan programs that will enable your local library to procure a hard-to-find book you need. Be sure to use any of these libraries in your area and make it a point to visit any you might be near in your travels. But write or call first to be sure of business hours.

CALIFORNIA ACADEMY OF SCIENCES LIBRARY, Golden Gate Park, San Francisco, California 94118

LOS ANGELES STATE AND COUNTY ARBORETUM PLANT SCIENCE LIBRARY, 301 North Baldwin Avenue, Arcadia, California 91006

DENVER BOTANIC GARDENS, Helen K. Fowler Library, 10005 York Street, Denver, Colorado 80206

DUMBARTON OAKS GARDEN LIBRARY, 1703 32nd Street N.W., Washington, D.C. 20007

SMITHSONIAN INSTITUTION LIBRARIES, Natural History Building, Washington, D.C. 20560

U.S. NATIONAL ARBORETUM LIBRARY, WASHINGTON, D.C. 20002

FAIRCHILD TROPICAL GARDENS, Montgomery Library, 10901 Old Cutler Road, Miami, Florida 33156

UNIVERSITY OF FLORIDA, Hume Library, Gainesville, Florida 32611

CALLAWAY GARDENS LIBRARY, Pine Mountain, Georgia 31822

CHICAGO HORTICULTURAL SOCIETY LIBRARY, Botanic Garden, P.O. Box 90, Glencoe, Illinois 60022

FIELD MUSEUM OF NATURAL HISTORY LIBRARY, Roosevelt Road and Lake Shore Drive, Chicago, Illinois 60605

MORTON ARBORETUM, Sterling Morton Library, Lisle, Illinois 60532

UNIVERSITY OF KENTUCKY AGRICULTURE LIBRARY, Agricultural Science Center North, Lexington, Kentucky 40506

AMERICAN ROSE SOCIETY LENDING LIBRARY, P.O. Box 30,000, Shreveport, Louisiana 71130

ARNOLD ARBORETUM LIBRARY, Harvard University, 22 Divinity Avenue, Cambridge, Massachusetts 02138

GRAY HERBARIUM LIBRARY, Harvard University, 22 Divinity Avenue, Cambridge, Massachusetts 02138

MASSACHUSETTS HORTICULTURAL SOCIETY LIBRARY, 300 Massachusetts Avenue, Boston, Massachusetts 02115

OAKES AMES ORCHID LIBRARY, Harvard University, 22 Divinity Avenue, Room 109, Cambridge, Massachusetts 02138

OLD STURBRIDGE VILLAGE RESEARCH LIBRARY, Sturbridge, Massachusetts 01566

UNIVERSITY OF MASSACHUSETTS, Amherst Morrill Library, Amherst, Massachusetts 01002

WORCESTER COUNTY HORTICULTURAL SOCIETY LIBRARY, 30 Elm Street, Worcester, Massachusetts 01608

MICHIGAN HORTICULTURAL SOCIETY LIBRARY, The White House, Belle Isle, Detroit, Michigan 48207

UNIVERSITY OF MINNESOTA LANDSCAPE ARBORETUM, Andersen Horticultural Library, Route 1, Box 132-1, Chaska, Minnesota 55318

UNIVERSITY OF MINNESOTA, St. Paul Campus Library, St. Paul, Minnesota 55101

NATIONAL COUNCIL OF STATE GARDEN CLUBS LIBRARY, 4401 Magnolia Avenue, St. Louis, Missouri 63108

UNIVERSITY OF NEBRASKA, C. Y. Thompson Library, Lincoln, Nebraska 68503

UNIVERSITY OF NEW HAMPSHIRE, Biological Sciences Library, Kendall Hall, Durham, New Hampshire 03824

RUTGERS UNIVERSITY LIBRARY, Cook College, Box 231, New Brunswick, New Jersey 08903

BROOKLYN BOTANIC GARDEN LIBRARY, 1000 Washington Avenue, Brooklyn, New York 11225

CORNELL UNIVERSITY, Albert R. Mann Library, Ithaca, New York 14850

MONROE COUNTY PARK DEPARTMENT, Herbarium Library, County Park Office, 375 Westfall Road, Rochester, New York 14620

NEW YORK BOTANICAL GARDEN LIBRARY, Bronx, New York 10458

NEW YORK STATE AGRICULTURAL EXPERIMENT STATION LIBRARY, Geneva, New York 14456

FRED W. GREEN MEMORIAL GARDEN CENTER LIBRARY, 123 McKinley Avenue, Youngstown, Ohio 44509

KINGWOOD CENTER LIBRARY, Box 966, Mansfield, Ohio 44901

OHIO AGRICULTURAL RESEARCH AND DEVELOPMENT CENTER LIBRARY, Wooster, Ohio 44691

THE GARDEN CENTER OF GREATER CLEVELAND, Eleanor Squire Library, 11030 East Boulevard, Cleveland, Ohio 44106

THE HOLDEN ARBORETUM LIBRARY, 9500 Sperry Road, Kirtland P.O., Mentor, Ohio 44066

KERR LIBRARY, Oregon State University, Corvallis, Oregon 97331

HUNT BOTANICAL LIBRARY, Carnegie-Mellon University, Pittsburgh, Pennsylvania 15213

LONGWOOD GARDENS LIBRARY, Kennett Square, Pennsylvania 19348

TEMPLE UNIVERSITY LIBRARY, Ambler Campus, Ambler, Pennsylvania 19002

MORRIS ARBORETUM LIBRARY, University of Pennsylvania, 9414 Meadowbrook Avenue, Philadelphia, Pennsylvania 19118

PENNSYLVANIA STATE UNIVERSITY, Agricultural and Biological Sciences Library, University Park, Pennsylvania 16802

THE PENNSYLVANIA HORTICULTURAL SOCIETY LIBRARY, 325 Walnut Street, Philadelphia, Pennsylvania 19106

SOUTH DAKOTA STATE UNIVERSITY, Lincoln Memorial Library, Brookings, South Dakota 57006

TENNESSEE BOTANICAL GARDENS LIBRARY, Cheek Road, Nashville, Tennessee 37205

TEXAS A & I UNIVERSITY, Citrus Center Library, P.O. Box 2000, Weslaco, Texas 78596

THE AMERICAN HORTICULTURAL SOCIETY, Harold B. Tukey Memorial Library, Mount Vernon, Virginia 22121

UNIVERSITY OF WASHINGTON ARBORETUM LIBRARY, Seattle, Washington 98105

Free Horticultural College Catalogs (and Advice)

Should you be thinking of a career in horticulture, all of the colleges listed below offer bachelor's degrees (four years) in the subject, many of them offering master's degrees and doctorates as well. You would do well to select several schools and send for their free catalogs, comparing their specialties, staff and course offerings, among other factors, before making a choice. This list is also valuable as a source of experts in your area who can answer your gardening questions or refer you to the proper authorities. Remember, too, that there are hundreds more colleges and junior colleges that offer two-year degrees in horticulture, or offer no specific degree in the subject but do offer horticulture courses.

Alabama

ALABAMA A & M UNIVERSITY, Department of Natural Resource and Environmental Studies, Normal 35762

AUBURN UNIVERSITY, Department of Horticulture, Auburn 36830

Alaska
UNIVERSITY OF ALASKA COLLEGE, Fairbanks

Arizona
ARIZONA STATE UNIVERSITY, Department of Horticulture, Tempe 85281
UNIVERISTY OF ARIZONA, Department of Horticulture and Landscape Architecture, Tucson 85721

Arkansas
ARKANSAS STATE UNIVERSITY, Department of Horticulture, State University 72467
UNIVERSITY OF ARKANSAS, Department of Horticulture, Fayetteville 72701

California
CALIFORNIA POLYTECHNIC STATE UNIVERSITY, Department of Horticulture, San Luis Obispo 93407
CALIFORNIA STATE POLYTECHNIC UNIVERSITY, Ornamental Horticulture Department, Pomona 91768
CALIFORNIA STATE UNIVERSITY, Department of Plant Science, Fresno 93740
CALIFORNIA STATE UNIVERSITY–CHICO, Department of Plant and Soil Sciences, Chico 95929
UNIVERSITY OF CALIFORNIA, Environmental Horticulture Department, Davis 95616

Colorado
COLORADO STATE UNIVERSITY, Department of Horticulture, Fort Collins 80523

Connecticut
UNIVERSITY OF CONNECTICUT, Plant Science Department, College of Agriculture and Natural Resources, Storrs 06268

Delaware
UNIVERSITY OF DELAWARE, Plant Science Department, College of Agricultural Sciences, Newark 19711

Florida

FLORIDA SOUTHERN COLLEGE, Citrus Institute, Lakeland 33802

UNIVERSITY OF FLORIDA, Department of Ornamental Horticulture, 105 Rolff Hall, Gainesville 32611

Georgia

UNIVERSITY OF GEORGIA, Department of Horticulture, Athens 30602

Hawaii

UNIVERISTY OF HAWAII, Department of Horticulture, Honolulu 96822

Iowa

IOWA STATE UNIVERSITY OF SCIENCE AND TECHNOLOGY, Department of Horticulture, Ames 50011

Illinois

ILLINOIS STATE UNIVERSITY, Department of Agriculture, Normal 61761

SOUTHERN ILLINOIS UNIVERSITY, Department of Plant and Soil Science, Carbondale 62901

UNIVERSITY OF ILLINOIS, Department of Horticulture, Urbana 61801

Indiana

PURDUE UNIVERSITY, Department of Horticulture, Lafayette 47907

Kansas

KANSAS STATE UNIVERSITY, Department of Horticulture, Manhattan 66506

Kentucky

EASTERN KENTUCKY UNIVERSITY, Department of Horticulture, Richmond 40475

MURRAY STATE UNIVERSITY, Horticulture Section, Department of Agriculture, Murray 42071

UNIVERSITY OF KENTUCKY, Department of Horticulture, Lexington 40506

Louisiana

LOUISIANA STATE UNIVERSITY AND A & M UNIVERSITY, Department of Horticulture, Baton Rouge 70803

LOUISIANA TECHNICAL UNIVERSITY, Department of Horticulture, Ruston 71270

SOUTHEASTERN LOUISIANA UNIVERSITY, Department of Agriculture, Hammond 70402

UNIVERSITY OF SOUTHWESTERN LOUISIANA, Department of Horticulture, Lafayette 70501

Maine

UNIVERSITY OF MAINE, Department of Plant and Soil Sciences, Orono 04473

Maryland

UNIVERSITY OF MARYLAND, Department of Horticulture, College Park 20742

Massachusetts

UNIVERSITY OF MASSACHUSETTS, Department of Plant and Soil Sciences, Amherst 48823

Michigan

MICHIGAN STATE UNIVERSITY, Institute of Agricultural Technology, Department of Horticulture, East Lansing 48823

Minnesota

UNIVERSITY OF MINNESOTA, Department of Horticultural Science, St. Paul 55108

Mississippi

MISSISSIPPI STATE UNIVERSITY, Department of Horticulture, State College 39762

Missouri

LINCOLN UNIVERSITY, Department of Agriculture, Jefferson City 65101

NORTHWEST MISSOURI STATE UNIVERSITY, Department of Horticulture, Maryville 64468

SOUTHWEST MISSOURI STATE UNIVERSITY, Department of Horticulture, Springfield 65802

UNIVERSITY OF MISSOURI, Department of Horticulture, Columbia 65201

Montana
MONTANA STATE UNIVERSITY, Department of Horticulture, Bozeman 59715

Nebraska
UNIVERSITY OF NEBRASKA, Department of Horticulture, Lincoln 68503

Nevada
UNIVERSITY OF NEVADA, College of Agriculture, Ninth and Valley Road, Reno 89507

New Hampshire
UNIVERSITY OF NEW HAMPSHIRE, Department of Plant Science, Durham 03824

New Jersey
RUTGERS—THE STATE UNIVERSITY, Department of Horticulture, New Brunswick 08903

New Mexico
NEW MEXICO STATE UNIVERSITY, Department of Horticulture, Las Cruces 88003

New York
CORNELL UNIVERSITY, Department of Floriculture and Ornamental Horticulture, Ithaca 14850

North Carolina
NORTH CAROLINA AGRICULTURAL AND TECHNICAL UNIVERSITY, Department of Horticulture, Greensboro 27411

North Dakota
NORTH DAKOTA STATE UNIVERSITY, Department of Horticulture, Fargo 58102

Ohio
OHIO STATE UNIVERSITY, Department of Horticulture, Columbus 43210

Oklahoma
OKLAHOMA STATE UNIVERSITY, Department of Horticulture, Stillwater 74074

Oregon
OREGON STATE UNIVERSITY, Department of Horticulture, Corvallis 97331

Pennsylvania
DELAWARE VALLEY COLLEGE OF SCIENCE AND AGRICULTURE, Department of Horticulture, Doylestown 18901

PENNSYLVANIA STATE UNIVERSITY, Department of Horticulture, 103 Tyson Building, University Park, 16802

Rhode Island
UNIVERSITY OF RHODE ISLAND, Plant and Soil Science Department, Woodward Hall, Kingston 02881

South Carolina
CLEMSON UNIVERSITY, Department of Horticulture, Clemson 29631

South Dakota
SOUTH DAKOTA STATE UNIVERSITY, Department of Horticulture-Forestry, Brookings 57006

Tennessee
MIDDLE TENNESSEE STATE UNIVERSITY, Department of Horticulture, Nashville 37202

TENNESSEE STATE UNIVERSITY, Department of Horticulture, Cookeville 38501

TENNESSEE TECHNOLOGICAL UNIVERSITY, Department of Ornamental Horticulture, Knoxville 37916

Texas
SAM HOUSTON STATE UNIVERSITY, Department of Horticulture, Huntsville 77340

Texas A & I University, Department of Horticulture, Kingsville 87363
Texas State Technical Institute, Department of Plant and Soil Science, Waco 76705
Texas Tech University, Department of Horticulture, Lubbock 79407

Utah
Brigham Young University, Provo 84602

Vermont
University of Vermont, Burlington 05402

Virginia
Virginia Polytechnic Institute, Blacksburg 24061
Virginia State College, Petersburg 23804

Washington
Washington State University, Pullman 99164

West Virginia
University of West Virginia, Morgantown 26506

Wisconsin
University of Wisconsin, Madison 53706

Wyoming
University of Wyoming, Plant Pathology and Horticulture Section, Laramie 82071

Puerto Rico
University of Puerto Rico, Department of Horticulture, College Station, Mayaguez, Puerto Rico 00708

Gardening for Kids

This excellent book instructs how to interest youngsters in gardening and includes a lot of practical information valuable to experienced gardeners. Send 50¢ for "A Child's Garden—A Guide for Parents and

Teachers" from the Ortho Division, Chevron Chemical Company, 200 Bush Street, San Francisco, California 94120.

Free Book Catalogs

These book dealers will furnish you with catalogs of their gardening books at no cost or for a nominal charge. You'll come across specialized books you never thought existed, whether they be from "Heather Lee's" catalog of out-of-print garden books, or Elizabeth Woodburn's huge stock, or the tropical climate gardening books that are Horticultural Books' specialty. Specify that you want the gardening book catalog, or indicate exactly the gardening area in which you are interested.

THE BOOK CHEST, 19 Oxford Place, Rockville Center, New York 11570

WARREN F. BRODERICK, RARE BOOKS, 695 4th Avenue, Lansingburgh, New York 12182

G. A. BIBBY, 714 Pleasant Street, Roseville, California 95678

EDWARD C. FALES, Box 56, Salisbury, New Hampshire 03268

H. L. FERGUSON, Box 5129, Ocean Park Station, Santa Monica, California 90405

GARDEN WAY RESEARCH, Charlotte, Vermont 05445

MARIAN L. GORE, Box 433, San Gabriel, California 91775

K. GREGORY, 221 East 71st Street, New York, New York 10021

"HEATHER LEE," 4 Hillcrest Avenue, Chertsey, Surrey, England

LEW HEYMANN BOOKS, Box 6448, Carmel-by-the-Sea, California 93921

HHH HORTICULTURAL, 68 Brooktree Road, Hightstown, New Jersey 08520

HILLTOP HOUSE, 1 The Loch, Roslyn, New York 11576

HORTICULTURAL BOOKS, INC., 219 Martin Avenue, Stuart, Florida 33494

JOHN JOHNSON, R.F.D. 2, North Bennington, Vermont 05257

NADA KRAMER, 927 15th Street N.W., Washington, D.C. 20005

ERIC LUNDBERG, Ashton, Maryland 20702

MOTHER'S BOOKSHELF, Box 70, Hendersonville, North Carolina 28739

POMONO BOOK EXCHANGE, 33 Beaucourt Road, Toronto 18, Canada

SANTA PAULA BOOKS, Box 384, Santa Paula, California 93060

S. J. SINGER COMPANY, 1133 Broadway, New York, New York 10010

ELIZABETH WOODBURN, Booknoll Farm, Hopewell, New Jersey 08525

ZIMMER'S INC., 1244 Santa Fe Drive, Denver, Colorado 80223

$45 Worth of Free Books

Join the American Garden Guild, Garden City, New York 11530, and you can get up to $45 worth of gardening books for $1 with your membership, under which you must buy four more books at discounts of up to 30 percent on original publishers' editions. A great way to stock your gardening library. Write for details.

Know How Much You're Buying Metrically

Metric Packaging	Approximate Comparison
1 gram	$\frac{1}{32}$ oz.
2 grams	$\frac{1}{16}$ oz.
4 grams	$\frac{1}{8}$ oz.
8 grams	$\frac{1}{4}$ oz.
15 grams	$\frac{1}{2}$ oz.
30 grams	1 oz.
125 grams	$\frac{1}{4}$ lb.
250 grams	$\frac{1}{2}$ lb.
500 grams	1.1 lb.
1 kilo	2.2 lbs.

Added Bonus—Specific Plant and Seed Sources

Just as this book goes to press comes news of a new free book that may alone be worth the price of this volume to the dedicated gardener. The Mailorder Association of Nurserymen has recently published a booklet listing alphabetically over 300 different kinds of plants, seeds and gardening-related items, along with the names and addresses of nurserymen that carry them. This up-to-date index tells you where to order everything from abelia to zucchini, including many hard-to-find varieties. For your free copy send a #10 self-addressed envelope stamped with 40¢ in postage to Mailorder Association of Nurserymen, Dept. MFG, 210 Cartwright Boulevard, Massapequa Park, New York 11762.

The Worms at the Heart of the Rose: Save Money by Rooting Out the Gardening Gypsters

• A Texas housewife purchases five large evergreen trees ("left over from a big landscaping job") from a door-to-door salesman. Her husband agrees that $200 was a good price—until he opens the burlap and discovers that the trees, stolen from a state park, have been cut off at the roots and wrapped in leaves and rocks. The evergreens soon become everbrowns.

• A New York woman tells itinerant "landscape gardeners" to go ahead and spread humus on her lawn—she's been told they would charge only 75 cents a basket. Later they present her with a bill for $150, pointing to 200 empty baskets.

• A New Jersey homeowner waits impatiently for the pink dogwood tree he was promised as a "free bonus" when he placed a $25 order the preceding winter with a mail-order nursery. Actually, the unlabeled photograph depicted in their catalog showed a tree 20 years old. The tree he finally receives arrives in a letter-size envelope.

• A Chicago landscaping outfit charges customers up to $100 to "treat" 400 square feet of lawn with their "combination fertilizer, peat moss, and weed killer." Petitioning for an injunction against the concern, the Illinois Attorney General charges that their product is a "combination of straw, sawdust, wood shavings, and negligible traces of horse manure" that is actually destructive to the grass it's meant to nourish.

The above represent only a fraction of the flimflams that flower each spring, the worms that begin to feed at the heart of the rose once the growing season begins. For as the crocuses rise, so also do the drummers for strawberry plants that produce berries "as big as hen's eggs"; the hucksters who sell "blacklight lanterns" which the national Better Business Bureau claims attract more insects than they repel; the purveyors of the male ailanthus or stink tree, whose flowers are so putrid that it is banned in certain areas; and even those post-office-box swindlers who offer virtual Gardens of Eden for nothing in full-page newspaper ads, cash the checks of the gullible, and move out of state long before the promised delivery date. Although the great majority of nurserymen are honest and will fully guarantee their stock, homeowners lose millions each year to unscrupulous dealers who spend their time propagating ploys to dupe the gardener.

The climbing strawberry is probably the latest and most ubiquitous of useless plants offered by dishonest nurserymen. Homeowners buy this novelty dreaming of garden walls perennially festooned with bright red berries. In fact, the climbing strawberry really is a "dream plant," as its advertisers claim. I have it on expert authority that, with the exception of a French variety rarely seen in this country, there is no such thing. Strawberry plants refuse to climb. What the hucksters do is sell a vigorous variety and provide "easy instructions" suggesting that you trellis the runner plants, which would normally root in the soil. What results is an undernourished family of runner plants feeding off the roots of one mother plant—a very inefficient arrangement, considering that runner plants normally develop their own root systems and are able to provide for themselves. Nor can the trellised strawberry plant be adequately protected against the winter even if removed from its support and laid on the ground. Yet some dealers sell these "startling new advances" for as much as $12 a dozen, despite the fact that perfectly good strawberry plants can be purchased for as little as $2 a dozen.

Sleeping Beauty might still be sleeping if Prince Charming had had to hack his way through the multiflora rose bushes advertised everywhere by unscrupulous nurserymen. Multiflora and zoysia grass are among the many garden items that are often advertised mis-leadingly, although they serve a purpose if used in the right situations. Multiflora is excellent for a large piece of property, but it grows so fast that it can be disastrous on small home grounds, unless it is severely and constantly pruned. Zoysia grass, on the other hand, should not be planted where fast growth and constant color are required. Although the grass makes an excellent, sturdy lawn, it takes years to grown into dense turf unless some 40 to 60 plugs are planted to a square foot; and it also turns brown from early in the fall until midspring. Similarly, the "everbearing" strawberry is not really everbearing; it bears lightly in June and then lightly again from August or September through the first frost. Professor J. P. Tomkins of Cornell University advises that "most growers would do better with a good June-bearing variety, to produce their fruit over a two-week period and store it in a freezer for the remainder of the growing season." Other pomologists have recommended the everbearer, but at best it has not yet been perfected. The same would apply to five-in-one fruit trees, which might be a good idea where there is room for only one variety, but which are difficult to keep well balanced.

It's a rule of green thumbs that bargain-basement prices mean bargain-basement plants—culls, half-matured seedlings, worthless species, or diseased plants. Here, as elsewhere, you generally get what you pay for. Remember that nursery stock is graded in accordance with the American Standard of Nursery Stock as sponsored by the American Association of Nurserymen, Inc. Roses, for instance, are graded by number: No. 1, No. 1½, No. 2, culls and rejects, etc. Be sure to find out the grade of the plant you're buying.

Most plant laws protecting America's home gardeners are ineffective; the buyer must beware. In the case of grass seed, one often sees five-pound bags offered for a dollar or less. These are usually quick-growing "hay" grasses, which last only a year; large-husked seeds are used to bulk up mixtures containing low percentages of perennial bluegrass and fescue. Various laws do prescribe that there be an analysis of grasses on the seed bag, but this invariably appears on the back and is often in such small type and so elaborately worded that only the eagle-eyed agronomist can decipher it. A pound or less of smaller, more expensive seed will sow a larger area than five pounds of cheap grass seed, and it will both save you money and produce a much higher quality of grass. An ounce of Merion bluegrass, for example, contains 135,000 seeds, whereas an ounce of inferior alta tall fescue contains only 14,000 seeds. It is a good idea to remember that the smaller the seed, the better the bargain, no matter what the advertisement claims. Plant larger types only for special purposes. Avoid "shotgun" mixtures as well; seed mixtures should contain at least 55 to 58 percent bluegrass, or 45 to 65 percent red fescue for shady lawns, and there should be no more than ten percent of a temporary or annual seed present. One way to figure the relative efficiency of packaged grass seed is to multiply the percentage of pure seed by the percentage of germination, both of which are marked on each package label; the package yielding the highest figure will produce the most new grass.

Peat moss and fertilizer cause home gardeners as much trouble as grass seed. Peat moss will not, as is often claimed, make the soil more fertile; in fact, large quantities can deplete the soil if nitrogen isn't added. Peat moss is valuable because it improves the water retention and workability of the soil. However, it shouldn't be added to a soil high in organic content or where there is a shallow water table. In addition to knowing what kind you are buying, and for what purpose, you should realize that peat moss, which is usually sold by weight, ranges anywhere from 5 to 80 percent in moisture or even weed-seed content; the only safeguard is to buy from a dealer you can trust.

The same applies to fertilizers. It is surprising how many experienced gardeners don't know that a complete fertilizer marked 1-1-1 on the bag (the ratio of the primary nutrients nitrogen, phosphorus, and potassium) contains only one-tenth of the nutrients in a fertilizer marked 10-10-10. The gardener who rushes out to buy ten $1 bags of 1-1-1 when it goes on "sale" would get twice his money's worth if he bought two $5 bags of 10-10-10. Fertilizer bags should also list the nitrogen-phosphorous-potassium ratio appropriate for the plant it's to be used for, and acid-type fertilizers should be labeled as such. It's a good idea to read up on the fertilizers needed for your plants before buying—you'll save money this way. By all means avoid unmarked bags of "humus," or truckloads full. This often turns out to be ground tea leaves mixed with sand, or something colored with crankcase oil to look like humus. Never buy fertilizer from trucks traveling house-to-house, even if the operators tell you they have a supply left over from a big job. Several years ago, thousands of trees and lawns on Long Island were sprayed with an expensive "liquid potash" fertilizer peddled from a truck. The stuff turned out to be water colored with whitewash. Above all, don't give down payments to itinerant landscapers for any job; they often take the money and never return.

"Why wait" plants, all ready to bear or flower, are another standard sophism in the shady nurseryman's greedbag. "Ready to Bear!" their ads proclaim in boldface type, but at the most inconspicuous spot in the ad there is inevitably the italicized phrase *perhaps next year*, or sometimes *the year after planting*. And "why wait" plants are a risk to the buyer even if they do bear quickly; the transplanting of large established trees and shrubs is a hazardous practice at best. The same risk holds true for many items, such as asparagus roots, which are best planted when one year old, and roses, which are most likely to last if they are two years old when set out. The buyer must beware, too, of bareroot evergreens; unlabeled "specials"; one plant of a kind where two are required for pollination; and plants grown in warmer climates or offered for sale in the wrong season. Many growers also fail to advertise that the soil for certain plants, such as azaleas and blueberries, must be acid, and that it takes a lot of work to make soil acid if it's naturally alkaline.

Advertising omissions can be just as deceitful as exaggerated claims. No plant should be ordered unless its full botanical name is given, so that its characteristics can be checked in a standard reference work. The nationally advertised "amazing climbing peach vine," for example, is not a peach species at all, but a hard, gourdlike fruit edible only when it is canned as a preserve. Fantastic ads assuring you that you can make a fortune by growing such crops as ginseng or mushrooms, or by hybridizing and patenting flowers, are also aimed at the gullible. Most crops are difficult and expensive to grow, especially on a small scale, and once you grow them it is quite difficult to market them. And the patented flowers that have made someone a fortune in the past ten years can be counted on the knuckles of one finger. The cost for patenting a rose, incidentally, is over $500; and the chances of creating a rose worth marketing have been estimated at about 10,000 to one. Jackson & Perkins, for instance, raises more than 100,000 embryo plants each year at a cost of more than $300,000 just to obtain the handful of new plants that reach the market.

Needless to say, buyers shouldn't consider purchasing garden contraptions like the "Electra-Charge Insect Destroyer," or small pressure sprayers whose ads claim they can shoot a spray up to 75 feet, without testing such products first. The novelties and bargains advertised in many nursery catalogs are often fit only for Dr. Rappaccini's garden. Most novelties have some glaring defect that is never mentioned, and it's generally best to put off buying that golden money tree, if only to wait for a reasonable price. As for "bargains," they're usually anything but. Bulbs of all kinds probably lead the list here. Hundreds are commonly offered at the "astronomically low price of $1.98." These are often the size of almonds and will not bloom for many years, if at all. Some tulip bulbs are measured by circumference rather than diameter to give a greater impression of size.

There is much to beware of in the shadier nursery catalogs. There are lies of omission, lies of tricky language—"beautiful bonus plants" that are in reality finger-high cuttings. There are lies of commission—when years are added on to the natural age of a plant, when collected wildlings are sold for patented varieties. And many lurid color catalogs and circulars prove that the camera does indeed lie. Before ordering from them the buyer should consult a good gardening encyclopedia, or deal with an established nurseryman who grades his stock and offers a written full-replacement guarantee. Save and use that guarantee if necessary, no matter how much trouble this requires. Without weeding, the worms will thrive at the heart of the rose, the flowers of flimflam will flourish. Given an inch, the gardening gypsters will take your yard.